THE CHARLTO
STANDARD C~

CANADIAN
COLONIAL TOKENS

4TH EDITION

BY
W. K. CROSS

The Charlton Press

TORONTO, CANADA • PALM HARBOR, FLORIDA

Canadian Cataloguing in Publication Data
Main entry under title:
The Charlton standard catalogue of Canadian
    colonial tokens
1st ed. (1988) -
Biennial.
ISSN 0835-748X
ISBN 0-88968-234-8   (4th ed.)
1. Tokens - Canada - Catalogs. I. Charlton Press/
CJ4911.C42   737'.3'0971   C89-031462-4

**Printed in Canada
in the Province of Ontario**

The Charlton Press

**Editorial Office
2040 Yonge Street, Suite 208
Toronto, Canada. M4S 1Z9
Telephone (416) 488-1418 Fax: (416) 488-4656
Telephone (800) 442-6042 Fax: (800) 442-1542**

EDITORIAL AND PRODUCTION

Editor   W. K. Cross

Assistant Editor   Randy Weir

Editorial Assistant   Cindy Raycroft

Graphic Technician   Alan Ho

ACKNOWLEDGEMENTS FOR THE FOURTH EDITION

The Publisher would like to thank the following individuals for their assistance in making this edition possible. Without their help, the necessary improvements would not have been made.

Len Buth	Wayne L. Jacobs
Douglas M. Carlson	William Kamb
Jim Charlton	Melvin H. Kyle
Brian Cornwell	Serge Larameé
Rick Craig	Andrew McKaig
Chris Faulkner	Gord Nichols
Mike Findlay	George H. Thomson
Ian Haire	Kevin Van Koughnett
Tim Henderson	Randy Weir

We would like to thank the following organizations:

Bank of Canada National Currency Collection for the illustrations of the rare and unique tokens from their collections. Also for the photographs of the Blacksmith Tokens of Canada.

American Numismatic Association for the line drawings of the Bouquet Sous which were "reprinted through the courtesy of *The Numismatist*, the official publication of the American Numismatic Association, 818 North Cascade Avenue, Colorado Springs, Colorado 80903."

TABLE OF CONTENTS

NEWFOUNDLAND TOKENS

PRIVATE TOKENS

ANONYMOUS TOKENS

PRINCE EDWARD ISLAND TOKENS

SEMI-REGAL TOKENS

PRIVATE TOKENS

ANONYMOUS TOKENS

NOVA SCOTIA TOKENS

SEMI-REGAL TOKENS

PRIVATE TOKENS

ANONYMOUS TOKENS

NEW BRUNSWICK TOKENS

SEMI-REGAL TOKENS

PRIVATE TOKENS

ANONYMOUS TOKENS

LOWER CANADA TOKENS

SEMI-REGAL TOKENS

PROVINCE OF CANADA TOKENS

SEMI-REGAL TOKENS

ANONYMOUS AND MISCELLANEOUS TOKENS

VEXATOR CANADIENSIS TOKENS

BLACKSMITH TOKENS

INTRODUCTION

Nearly twelve years have passed since the release of the first edition of *Canadian Colonial Tokens*. During this time, considerable research has been carried out by many individuals to improve our knowledge of this subject. The catalogue has been corrected and proofed, and some sections have been rewritten and/or reorganized to assist the collector in accurate token identification and pricing.

While the fourth edition is an improvement over previous versions, it is not perfect. Colonial Tokens, with all their variations, are a complex section of numismatics. While we have attempted to be as thorough as possible, it is difficult to verify all the different bits and pieces that compile this era of Canadian numismatics.

Any assistance from readers concerning new information, errors or omissions we have made, or suggestions for improvement of the fifth edition would be greatly appreciated.

SCOPE OF THIS CATALOGUE

This book has been specifically designed to cover that period of Canadian numismatic history from 1794 to 1867. During this particular time the shortage of official coinage seemed more the rule of the day than occasional exception.

Throughout this time the foreign policy of Great Britain was simply one of rigid control. Her attitude was that the colonies were to produce the raw materials needed by the homeland and during times of civil unrest at home to allow the entry of immigrants into the colonies.

The economies of the colonies were also expected to pay for any imported goods in what the mother country considered legal tender coins. This caused British North America, like all British colonies, to be constantly short of change.

This need for change became quite acute considering the growth in the local colonial economies. Consequently the colonists resorted to their own ingenuity and made use of whatever metal pieces they could find, all this in spite of Great Britain's foreign policy. Needless to say there was a proliferation of these local tokens from many sources, including some counterfeits of same. These tokens varied greatly in the quality of their workmanship and trueness in weight. They have been the subject of much numismatic study and research for over 100 years.

This issue of *The Charlton Standard Catalogue of Canadian Colonial Tokens* lists those coins that were used or issued expressly for the purpose of general circulation in order to alleviate the constant shortage of change that plagued British North America.

Private business cards, trade and transportation tokens, while listed by such numismatic writers as Breton and Courteau, are generally outside the scope of this catalogue as is the various coinage used during the period of the French Regime.

THE LISTING OF COLONIAL TOKENS

The Colonial Tokens of Canada are catalogued from East to West with the last two chapters dealing with listing the Blacksmith and Anonymous Tokens. For the beginner, one of the main stumbling blocks is token identification. Since a high percentage of tokens do not carry the colony, province or other identifying designs or legends an attribution scheme is required. Thus we have divided the tokens of the colonies into three major categories: Semi-Regal, Private and Anonymous.

SEMI-REGAL TOKENS: This category is devoted to tokens issued or authorized by a colonial government authority. An example is the Thistle token of Nova Scotia. We have also listed the Bank Tokens of Lower Canada in this category since they were issued with the authorization of the colonial government.

PRIVATE TOKENS: The private tokens of an individual or business are identified next. These tokens may or may not carry the name of the individual or business. If they do not then their attribution by other numismatic researchers has been established beyond doubt. They are now readily accepted as being from a known issuer.

ANONYMOUS TOKENS: The last category does not carry any issuer identification, nor has it been attributed to any known issuer. That is, no known record has yet been found to indicate who actually did import these tokens into that colony. A great number of these tokens have been found in Canadian hoards and therefore are considered important in the early commerce of what is now known as Canada.

In summary, all tokens are first classified by colonial government, East before West. Each of those general classifications is subdivided according to whether the issue was of a Semi-Regal, Private or Anonymous nature. Within each of these classifications a final, specific listing of tokens appears according to the catalogue numbering system which follows.

CATALOGUE NUMBERING SYSTEM

Canadian tokens in the Charlton Standard Catalogue of Canadian Colonial Tokens have been numbered according to the following rules:

1. **SEMI-REGAL TOKENS:** Listed by date and denomination order.

2. **PRIVATE TOKENS:** Listed by Breton Number.

3. **ANONYMOUS TOKENS:** Listed by Breton Number.

Listings by Breton numbers within each of the above three groups were not strictly followed if a type or family grouping of tokens made a logical following more consistent. The latter format was developed to allow the beginner a logical entry into the field of token numismatics.

All token catalogue numbers consist of up to four parts, each signifying a particular characteristic of that token. The general structure of the numbering scheme is as follows:

PROVINCE OR TYPE Ten different two-letter classifications are possible. Seven of these are used to indicate where the token originated or circulated. The remaining three, WE (Wellington Tokens), BL (Blacksmith Tokens) and AM (Anonymous and Miscellaneous Tokens) indicate type.

TOKEN NUMBER A single digit number follows the Province or Type classification and indicates the placement of the token within that group.

MAJOR VARIETY The single letter following the Token Number classifies major varieties of that token. In all cases, a new die was used in the production of that token. The letters "I" and "O" were omitted from the alpha sequence.

MINOR VARIETY The number following the Major Variety code signifies a minor variation within that variety. In most cases the die of the major variety had been reworked. However, exceptions in classifying the minor varieties and new dies are considered insignificant when the changes are difficult to distinguish. Examples are the portraits of George IV on the Nova Scotia Thistle Halfpenny and Penny tokens.

VARIATIONS Recut, retouched and deteriorated dies are not assigned numbers. However, the more important minor varieties have been listed under the category of Variations. Allowances have been made for expansion of this category in future editions of this catalogue.

TOKEN CHARACTERISTICS SUMMARY

PROVINCE OR LETTER	TOKEN NUMBER	MAJOR VARIETY LETTER	MINOR VARIETY NUMBER
NF- Newfoundland	Issuer	Major design	Minor die
PE- Prince Edward	Series	alterations	alterations
Island	Denomination	Date change	to a major
NS- Nova Scotia		Legend change	variety such
NB- New Brunswick			as retouching,
LC- Lower Canada			polishing,
UC- Upper Canada			recutting,etc.
PC- Province of Canada			Composition,
WE- Wellington Tokens			weight,
BL- Blacksmith Tokens			die axis,
AM- Anonymous and			edge.
Miscellaneous Tokens			

An example of this catalogue numbering system is UC-9A3

UC signifies Upper Canada; **9** is the ninth token in the Upper Canada Series; **A** is the first major variety; **3** is the third minor variety.

CROSS REFERENCE NUMBERS

All tokens have been cross-referenced to other classification numbers as listed by Breton (Br), Courteau (Co), Wood (Wo), Willey (W), Lees (Lees) and McLachlan (Mc).

Courteau numbers are appended with a letter(s) component referring to his monographs as listed by Willey:

    B. Canadian Bouquet Sous, 1908
    BM. Copper Tokens of the Bank of Montreal, 1919
    H. Canadian Bust and Harp Series, 1907
    NB. Coins and Tokens of New Brunswick, 1923
    NF. Coins and Tokens of Newfoundland, 1930
    NL. Non-Local Tokens of Canada, 1924
    NS. Coins and Tokens of Nova Scotia, 1910
    PEI. Coins and Tokens of Prince Edward Island, 1922
    T. Canadian Bust and Commerce (Tiffin) Tokens, 1934
    UC. St. George Copper Tokens of Upper Canada, 1934
    W. Wellington Tokens Relating to Canada, 1914

TOKEN GRADING

Token grading is unlike grading Canadian decimal coins in that a knowledge of the many token manufacturers is important to fairly assess an item's condition. Different manufacturers of the colonial period were known to produce widely different qualities of tokens. This depended on their:

(a) degree of technical expertise;
(b) access to capital and thus decent minting equipment; and
(c) actual desire to produce a quality product.

Two examples, while extreme, help to demonstrate the range of quality produced. On the one hand, the Royal Mint in London had the technical expertise, equipment and desire to turn out quality items. On the other hand the Blacksmith token mints lacked that desire for quality and this can be seen by the examples of their work available today. While these Blacksmith tokens are obviously inferior looking items relative to Royal Mint products their grade or condition is not judged solely by the presence or absence of detail now remaining. That missing detail may never have been there right from the very moment the token was first struck. This knowledge of a manufacturer's workmanship then adds a totally new dimension to grading from that experienced by coin graders. The implication then, when grading tokens, is that grades assigned are intended to mean "for issue." Thus a Royal Mint token and a Blacksmith which are both graded as Fine will undoubtedly display vastly different amounts of absolute design detail remaining to a casual observer. In fact both will have equal detail loss from that which was there at the time the token was originally struck.

The mints which follow are ordered in terms of the quality of product they were renowned for generating. The best quality of production is listed first with the worst last:

Royal Mint	Wright & Bale
Boulton & Watt	Belleville Mint
Ralph Heaton & Co.	Jean Marie Arnault
Thomas Halliday	Various Blacksmith Mints
William Mossop	

The Royal Mint, for example, produced the coinage of the Bank of Upper Canada in 1850. This was a high quality coinage which can be graded similarly to the decimal coins which appeared from 1858 on. On the other hand, the tokens of Jean Marie Arnault probably came from the presses in only Extremely Fine condition.

Another factor affecting token appearance was the inability of the Native Mints to properly store their dies. Improperly stored dies rusted, resulting in relief spots on the finished token. The pimple effect this created cannot be considered damage to a token and must be viewed as part of the "as struck condition."

The following list indicates which items were manufactured by which mints and therefore serves as a handy guide in terms of the general quality of workmanship to be expected when determining a suitable grade:

MINTS	COINAGE
The Royal Mint	Bank of Upper Canada
	Coinage of 1850 and part of 1852
Ralph Heaton & Co.	Bank of Upper Canada
	Coinage of 1852, 1854 and 1857
	Quebec Bank Coinage of 1852
	New Brunswick Coinage 1854
Boulton & Watt	Rutherford Tokens of 1846
	Habitant Coinage of 1837 Lower Canada
	Bank of Montreal 1842-1844
	New Brunswick Halfpennies and Pennies of 1843
Thomas Halliday	Genuine British Copper Tokens of Nova Scotia
	Ships Colonies & Commerce Tokens PEI

Wright & Bale	Ships Colonies & Commerce Tokens of Lower Canada
Belleville Mint	Bouquet Sous
Jean-Marie Arnault	Bouquet Sous

MINTS AND MANUFACTURERS

For the most part the Colonial coinages of Canada were struck by private mints. Only a very few tokens were struck at official mints.

FOREIGN MINTS AND MANUFACTURERS

The Royal Mint, London, England.
Boulton & Watt, Soho Mint, Birmingham, England.
Ralph Heaton & Co., Birmingham Mint, Birmingham, England.
Thomas Halliday, Birmingham, England.
Wright & Bale, New York, N.Y., U.S.A.
Belleville Mint, Belleville, N.J., U.S.A.
Daniel and Benjamin True, Troy, N.Y., U.S.A.
Sir Edward Thomason, Birmingham, England.
William Mossop, Dublin, Ireland.
William Stephen Mossop, Dublin, Ireland.
John Sheriff, Liverpool, England.

NATIVE MINTS AND MANUFACTURERS

Jean-Marie Arnault, Montreal.
Blacksmith Mints, Upper and Lower Canada.

In 1848 the Soho mint of Boulton & Watt was sold by auction with the equipment going to Ralph Heaton & Co. and most of the dies to W.J. Taylor. Taylor's purchases included the dies of:

The New Brunswick Coinage of 1843.
The 1837 "Habitant" Coinage of Lower Canada.
The Bank of Montreal "Front View" Tokens.
The Copper Company of Upper Canada.

DESIGNERS AND ENGRAVERS

Not all engravers were employed at the mints. Engravers such as the Wyon family and Halliday had their own place of business. Issuers and mints often contracted them for token design and dies. The following is a practical listing of the designers and engravers with the tokens they designed.

FOREIGN DESIGNERS AND ENGRAVERS

THOMAS HALLIDAY
Wellington Battle Halfpennies and Pennies
Ships, Colonies and Commerce Tokens
Trade and Navigation Tokens
Wellington Tokens
Waterloo Halfpenny Token
Victoria Nobis Est Halfpenny Token
Genuine British Copper Tokens
John A. Barry Tokens
Hosterman and Etter Tokens
Anonymous Halfpennies and Pennies of 1812 and 1813
(Imitations Imported by Joseph Tiffin)

NOEL-ALEXANDRE PONTHON (BOULTON & WATT)
Copper Company of Upper Canada
JOHN SHERIFF
Sloop Halfpennies of Upper Canada
Starr and Shannon Tokens
THOMAS WELLS INGRAM (BOULTON & WATT)
Lesslie Tokens
WILLIAM MOSSOP
WILLIAM STEPHEN MOSSOP
Nova Scotia Halfpenny For the Convenience of Trade
ISAAC PARKES
Marquis Wellington Tokens
PETER WYON
THOMAS WYON THE ELDER
Carritt and Alport Halfpenny Tokens
Anonymous Irish Penny of 1805
LEONARD CHARLES WYON
New Brunswick Halfpenny and Penny Tokens of 1854
Nova Scotia Mayflower Tokens of 1856
JOHN GIBBS (BELLEVILLE MINT)
Bouquet Sous Tokens
Banque du Peuple Sous Tokens
JOHN PINCHES
Bank of Upper Canada Tokens

NATIVE DESIGNERS AND ENGRAVERS

JEAN-MARIE ARNAULT
Molson Halfpenny Tokens
Rebellion Sou Tokens
Bouquet Sou Tokens
JOHN S. THOMPSON
Reverse design for the Mayflower Coinage of Nova Scotia
JACQUES VIGER
Reverse design for the Bank of Montreal Tokens
MICHAEL WALLACE
Reverse design for the Nova Scotia Thistle Tokens

AGENTS

The British Act of 1803 preventing the counterfeiting of foreign coins, and the legislation of 1812-1817 with the acts relating to coins, tokens etc., resulted in the Mints of England in some cases even refusing to offer an estimate on coinage without proper official authorization. M.R. Boulton of Boulton & Watt in a letter to Albert Furniss stated that "I have always considered it expedient to have the sanction of the Provincial Authorities, of the Government at home, for my security in undertaking such a coinage as the one you propose...."

This reluctance on the part of the minters left the door open to independent agents to negotiate directly with the mints on behalf of the Colonial Issuers for coinage.

FOREIGN AGENTS

Joshua Scholefield, Birmingham, Engand.
John Langdon, Bank of Liverpool, England.
Messrs. Tarratt and Co., England.
Thomas Jones Wilkinson, Birmingham, England.
Captain Dudne, England.
John Walker & Co., Birmingham, England.
Cotterill, Hill & Co., Walsall, England.
Rowe, Kentish & Co., London, England.

NATIVE AGENTS

Albert Furniss, Montreal, Lower Canada.

FRATERNAL AFFILIATION

For many years coin clubs have been formed across Canada with new clubs being organized all the time. Token collecting is attracting the interest of hundreds of collectors. Excitement in this aspect of numismatics has now reached unprecedented heights.

The educational value of collecting tokens is being stressed at both the local and national levels. Coin shows, special meetings, seminars, slide presentations, films and lending libraries help add to the recent enthusiasm in Canadian token collecting.

The following Canadian organizations are recommended to anyone interested in learning more about the history of these tokens:

The Canadian Numismatic Association
Post Office Box 226
Barrie, Ontario, Canada. L4M 4T2

The American Numismatic Association
818 North Cascade Avenue,
Colorado Springs, Colorado, U.S.A. 80903-3279

Canadian Association of Token Collectors
Harry N. James, President
Box 22022
Elmwood Square P.O.
204 First Avenue
St. Thomas, Ontario, Canada.
N5R 6A1

DATA OR SPECIFICATION TABLES FOR TOKENS

Each major variety of a specific token number has specification data to the left of the token illustration. This information includes:

COMPOSITION

The metallic composition of each token is listed as copper, brass, pewter, silver or gold. The exact chemical composition is considered of little value since the analysis of a single token offers no guarantee that the metallic composition of the next token of that same series would be identical. The copper alloy of each batch of tokens struck can vary. This is especially true for tokens of native manufacture where the colour of certain items moves from a normal copper colour to a brassy yellow. This clearly indicates that the alloy was not consistent throughout the production of the flans.

The identification of a token as being of copper, bronze or brass content can be difficult even for experienced collectors. One example is that of a copper token having been cleaned with modern cleaning compounds and taking on the yellow colour of brass.

Copper: Elemental copper. Pure not an alloy. Red copper colour.
Bronze: An alloy of 95% copper, 4% tin, 1% zinc. Chocolate copper colour.
Brass: An alloy of 75% copper, 25% zinc. Yellow brass colour.
Ancient Bronze: An alloy of copper and tin. Yellow brass colour

Thus by varying the amounts of zinc or tin added to a copper base the colour of the finished token can be altered. The above data also illustrates the irrelevance of knowing the exact chemical composition. However, knowing the correct chemical composition could link Native or Foreign manufactured tokens to one minter.

It should be noted that silver and gold tokens were issued only for presentation purposes.

WEIGHT

The weight of each token is specified as a range and expressed in grams. Copper or bronze token production did not require the same close tolerance as that of silver or gold. As a result weights may vary between examples of the same type. Also, the greed of the minters and issuers together with the ease of public acceptance in Colonial times is inversely proportional to weight. If the number of tokens per pound of copper or alloy increased so did the profit.

Early weights were expressed as the number of pieces per pound avoirdupois. The colonial issues of Canada were based on the English halfpenny and penny.

NUMBER OF PIECES PER POUND

Dates	English Halfpenny	Weight in Grains	English Penny	Weight in Grains
1717-1775	46	152.17	-	-
1797-1799	36	194.44	16	437.50
1806-1860	48	145.83	24	291.67
1860-1967	80	87.50	48	145.83

CONVERSION TABLE

1 Pound Avoirdupois = 16 ounces
1 Pound (av.) = 7000 grains
1 Pound (av.) = 454.6 grams
1 Grain = 0.0646 grams

Semi-Regal Colonial Bank Tokens were intended to be issued at five-sixths the weight of British copper equating Sterling to Halifax currency. However, most were issued at full weight.

DIAMETER

The diameter of each token is expressed in millimetres. Collected data indicates that token diameter must also be stated as a range since there are variations in diameter between tokens of the same type.

DIE AXIS

The position of the reverse design in relation to the obverse design is indicated by using small arrows to show the direction the reverse design is pointing.

Medal or upright axis: ↑↑, (ie. obverse, reverse same direction)

Coinage or upset axis: ↑↓, (ie. obverse, reverse opposite directions)

Other die axis combinations exist. One example is a 90 degree rotation of the reverse die from either the normal Medal or Coinage axis. This variation in die axis is usually only found in tokens of native manufacture.

EDGE

Three separate edge designs have been employed on Canadian Colonial tokens.

Plain: Without design.

Reeded: Straight up and down edge grooves with either flat or V - shaped bottom. Diagonal edge grooves may also appear.

Engrailed: A chain or twisted rope design impressed into the edge of the coin during striking. This design will have variations depending on the direction of the design, southwest to northeast or northwest to southeast.

REFERENCE WORKS FOR CANADIAN COLONIAL TOKENS

The following list of reference works is suggested for further research and study by the collector.

Atkins, J.:	The Coins and Tokens of the Possessions and Colonies of the British Empire, 1889.
Baker, Warren:	Some Overstruck Specimens of Br. 1008 and Other Notes on the Blacksmith Series. CNJ Sept. 1985
Batty, T.D.:	Descriptive Catalogue of the Copper Coinage of Great Britain, Ireland, British Isles, and Colonies, 1900. Four Volumes.
Bowman, Fred:	The Bouquet Sou Tokens of Canada, Num. July-Nov. 1955, CNJ Jan.-Feb. 1960. The "Bon Pour Deux Sous" Token of Canada, Num. Oct. 1948. The Case of the Bouquet Sou Breton 712, CNJ Apr. 1957. Cdn. Borderline Tokens, CNJ, Vol.11 No 9. Sept.1966
Breton, P.N.:	Illustrated History of Coins and Tokens Relating to Canada, 1894. Popular Illustrated Guide to Canadian Coins and Medals, 1912.
Buth, L.:	A New Variety of Canadian "Ships Colonies amd Commerce" Token, Canadian Numismatics, 1999.
Carroll, Major S.S.:	More Varieties of the Rutherford Tokens, CNJ July 1955.
Chalmers, R.:	History of Currency in the British Colonies, 1893.
Christmas, Rev.H.:	Copper Coinage of the British Colonies in America, Numismatic Society of London 1862.
Courteau, Dr.E.G.:	The Canadian Bouquet Sous, 1908. (1) The Canadian 1820 Bust and Harp Tokens, Num. May-June 1907. (2) The Canadian Bust and Commerce Tokens, Num. Feb. 1934. (2) The Coins and Tokens of New Brunswick, Num. Aug. 1923. (2) The Coins and Tokens of Newfoundland, Num. Feb. 1930. (2) The Coins and Tokens of Nova Scotia, 1910. Addendum to the Coins and Tokens of Nova Scotia, Num. Feb. 1922. (1) The Coins and Tokens of Prince Edward Island, Num. Nov. 1922. (2) The Copper Tokens of the Bank of Montreal, 1919. The Habitant Tokens of Lower Canada, 1927. The Non-Local Tokens of Canada, Num. May 1924. (2) The St. George Copper Tokens of the Bank of Upper Canada, 1934. The Wellington Tokens Relating to Canada, 1914. (1)
Curry, Michael:	The Anticosti Token Re-examined, CNJ Oct. 1972.
Davis, W.J.:	The Nineteenth Century Token Coinage, 1904. Reprint 1969.
Faulkner, C.:	Breton 999: A Numismatic Record, CNJ Sept. 1984. "Out the Past - An History of Breton 999," from "Aspects of the Numismatics of North American," edited C. Gilboy, published by Regina Coin Club in 1985.
Ferguson, J.D.:	Sun Tavern Blacksmith Token, CNJ Aug. 1966.
Fleming, H.A.:	Halifax Currency in the Collections of the Nova Scotia Historical Society, 1921.
Fougere, J.J.:	Nova Scotia Thistle Tokens 1823-1824, CNJ June 1987.

Gibbs, Jeremiah:	Sir Isaac Brock and the Brock Halfpennies, Num. Nov. 1902, CNJ Jan. 1965.
Jacobs, Wayne:	The Phantom Token, CNJ July 1962.
Kennedy, Earle K.:	The Prince Edward Island Holey Dollar, 1979.
Lees, W.A.D.:	The Ships, Colonies and Commerce Tokens, Num. Jan. 1917. Reprinted 1961. Addenda in Num. Dec. 1919 and May 1926.
Leroux, Dr. Jos.:	The Canadian Coin Cabinet, First Edition, 1888. The Canadian Coin Cabinet, Second Edition, 1892. Supplements to the Canadian Coin Cabinet, 1890 and 1897.
Linecar, H.W.A.:	A Catalogue of Canadian Coins and Tokens in the British Museum, CNJ Jan.-Feb. 1960. British Commonwealth Coins, 1959.
Lorrain, M.:	A Newly Found Variety of the 1832 Nova Scotia Halfpenny Token, CNJ Nov. 1968.
Low, Lyman H.:	Hard Times Tokens, 1900.
McCullough, A.B.:	Money and Exchange in Canada to 1900. Dundurn Press, 1984.
McLachlan, R.W.:	Address to the ANA Convention, Num. Sept. 1912. A Descriptive Catalogue of Coins, Tokens and Medals Issued in or Relating to the Dominion of Canada and Newfoundland, 1886. Reprint 1975. A Hoard of Canadian Coppers, CA 1890. Annals of the Nova Scotian Currency, 1892. Coins Struck in Canada Previous to 1840, 1892. The Copper Currency of the Canadian Banks, 1903. The Copper Tokens of Upper Canada, 1916. Reprint 1964. Fabrications in Canadian Coins, CA 1893-1894. Is the Mysterious Bust on Canadian Coins Really That of Wellington? Num. June 1916. Jean-Marie Arnault, Num. Mar. 1914. The Magdalen Islands Coinage, CA Apr. 1886. The Money of Canada From An Historical Standpoint, 1915. The Real Date of the Canadian 1820 Bust and Harp ANJ 1907. Some Recent Frauds in Canadian Coins, CA 1892. The Wellington Tokens Relating to Canada: A Review, Num. Nov. 1915. When Was the Vexator Canadinsis Issued? CA Apr. 1915.
Metcalf, J.:	Prince Edward Island Hard Times Currency, CA 1889-1890.
Nichols, G. and Faulkner, C.:	Ships, Colonies & Commerce, CNJ Jan/Feb 1998.
Prenoveau, J.J.:	Le Jeton de John Shaw, CNJ Dec. 1962. Le Sou de J. Roy, CNJ Apr. 1963.
Pridmore, Fred:	The Coins of the British Commonwealth of Nations, Part III, The West Indies, 1965. The Holey Dollar and Plug of Prince Edward Island, NC Nov.-Dec. 1960. Notes on Colonial Coins, NC Oct.-Nov. 1964.
Reid, R.L.:	The Holey Dollar of Prince Edward Island, Num. Feb. 1929.
Russell, Dr. Peter A.:	Canadian Colonial Tokens Struck by Boulton & Watt 1838-1845, CNJ May 1982.

Sandham, A.:	Coins, Tokens and Medals of the Dominion of Canada, 1869, Reprint 1962.
	Montreal Trade Tokens, 1872. Numismata Canadiana. CA 1880-1881.
Shortt, Adam:	Documents Relating to Currency Exchange and Finance During the French Regime, 1925.
	Documents Relating to Currency Exchange and Finance in Nova Scotia, 1933.
	The History of Canadian Metallic Currency. Transactions of the Canadian Institute, 1912.
Thomson, Geo. H.:	Die Varieties of Breton 715, CNJ, May 1997.
Willey, R.C.:	The Boston Sou, CNJ Mar. 1974.
	The Colonial Coinages of Canada, CNJ Jan. 1979 to July/Aug. 1983.
	Ships Colonies and Commerce Halfpennies of Lower Canada, CNJ Dec. 1974.
Wood, Howland:	The Canadian Blacksmith Coppers, Num. June 1910.
Abbreviations:	CNJ - The Canadian Numismatic Journal
	Num. - The Numismatist (ANA)
	NC - Spink's Numismatic Circular
	CA - The Canadian Antiquarian and Numismatic Journal
	AJN - American Journal of Numismatics (American Numismatic Association)
Notes:	**(1)** Reprinted in Dr. Joseph Leroux's "Canadian Coin Cabinet" - a 1964 reprint by Canadian Numismatic Publishing Institution.
	(2) Reprinted in "Canadian Tokens and Medals," an anthology by A.D. Hock, Quarterman Publications, Inc.

LEGEND INDEX TO COLONIAL TOKENS

The legends on tokens are an important numismatic characteristic. They either domiciled the token to a particular colony or carried a message which had either monetary or political significance to the colony. Thus the beginner token collector can also use this index to locate a token by means of the legend it carries.

Legends may be incorporated into the design of a token in one of four different ways:

1. Tokens with both a reverse and obverse legend
2. Tokens with only a reverse legend
3. Tokens with only an obverse legend
4. Tokens with no legends

On Canadian tokens the reverse legend usually indicates the name of the issuer. It is for this reason that we chose to use the reverse legend first in our heading listing.

Each token heading in this catalogue carries a token number followed by the legend on the token as illustrated by one of these four examples.

Chapter heads and sub-heads are shown in normal type while all token legends are italicized.

EXAMPLES

1. Tokens with both a reverse and obverse legend

NS-14   *PAYABLE BY JOHN ALEXR BARRY HALIFAX—*
1815 HALFPENNY TOKEN

Reverse legend   Obverse legend

2. Tokens with only a reverse legend

LC-46   *HALFPENNY TOKEN 1812— (BUST DESIGN)*

Reverse legend   No obverse legend

3. Tokens with only an obverse legend

NF-1A   *— R & I.S. RUTHERFORD NEWFOUNDLAND ST. JOHN'S*

No reverse legend   Obverse legend

4. Token with no legends

LC-55   *— (SEATED JUSTICE DESIGN) - (SAILING SHIP DESIGN)*

No reverse legend   No obverse legend

COMPLETE LEGEND INDEX OF CANADIAN COLONIAL TOKENS

The following index represents a complete listing of all legends appearing on Canadian colonial tokens as catalogued in the Charlton Standard Catalogue of Canadian Colonial Tokens. This listing is grouped into three divisions as follows:

(a) tokens with a legend on each of the obverse and reverse;

(b) tokens with a legend on only one side; and

(c) tokens with no legends on either side.

Within each of these three groups, legends are ordered in alphabetic sequence to minimize legend search time. Once the desired legend is located, you will have instant access to three additional pieces of information. These include:

(a) page number reference for the token in the Charlton Standard Catalogue of Canadian Colonial Tokens - 4th Edition;

(b) the Charlton token reference number; and

(c) the Breton token reference number.

In some instances a particular legend may have multiple entries for page number references and/or catalogue numbers. For an explanation you may have to consult all of the appropriate pages in this catalogue or the Charlton Colonial Token Workbook.

LEGEND INDEX - CANADIAN COLONIAL TOKENS

TOKENS WITH LEGENDS ON TWO SIDES

LEGENDS	Charlton Standard Page No.	Charlton Catalogue Number	Breton Number
1814 - Wellington Halfpenny Token	165	WE-8	979
1816 - Half Penny Token	73	NS-29	—
1841 - R & I.S. Rutherford Newfoundland St.John's	2	NF-1B	952
1846 - Rutherford Bros. Newfoundland Harbour Grace	3	NF-1C	953
Bank of Montreal Token Un Sous - Trade & Agriculture Lower Canada	86, 87	LC-3	714
Bank Token Half Penny - 1838 Bank of Montreal	97	LC-10A	524
Bank Token Half Penny - 1839 Bank of Montreal	98	LC-10B	524
Bank Token Half Penny 1837 - Province Du Bas Canada Un Sou	91-93	LC-8A to D	522
Bank Token Half Penny 1842 - Province of Canada Bank of Montreal	185	PC-1A	527
Bank Token Half Penny 1844 - Province of Canada Bank of Montreal	186	PC-1B	527
Bank Token Half Penny 1845 - Province of Canada Bank of Montreal	187	PC-1C	527
Bank Token Montreal ½ Penny - Trade & Agriculture Lower Canada	90	LC-7	673
Bank Token Montreal Un Sous - Trade & Agriculture Lower Canada	84, 85	LC-2	713
Bank Token One Half-Penny - 1850 Bank of Upper Canada	190	PC-5A	720
Bank Token One Half-Penny - 1852 Bank of Upper Canada	191	PC-5B	720
Bank Token One Half-Penny - 1854 Bank of Upper Canada	191	PC-5C	720
Bank Token One Half-Penny - 1857 Bank of Upper Canada	192	PC-5D	720
Bank Token One Penny - 1838 Bank of Montreal	99	LC-11A	523
Bank Token One Penny - 1839 Bank of Montreal	99	LC-11B	523
Bank Token One Penny - 1839 Bank of Montreal	100	LC-11C	525
Bank Token One Penny 1837 - Province Du Bas Canada Deux Sous	94-96	LC-9A to D	521
Bank Token One Penny 1837 - Province of Canada Bank of Montreal	187	PC-2A	—
Bank Token One Penny 1842 - Province of Canada Bank of Montreal	188	PC-2B	526
Bank Token One Penny - 1850 Bank of Upper Canada	192	PC-6A	719
Bank Token One Penny - 1852 Bank of Upper Canada	193	PC-6B	719
Bank Token One Penny - 1854 Bank of Upper Canada	194	PC-6C	719
Bank Token One Penny - 1857 Bank of Upper Canada	194	PC-6D	719
Banque Du Peuple Montreal Un Sou - Agriculture & Commerce Bas-Canada	88	LC-4	716
Banque Du Peuple Montreal Un Sou - Agriculture & Commerce Bas Canada	89	LC-5	715
Britannia 1814 - Broke Halifax Nova Scotia	54, 55	NS-7A-B	879
Canada Half Penny Token - For Public Accommodation	102	LC-14	533
Cash Paid For All Sorts of Grain 1837			
- THS & WM Molson Montreal Brewers Distillers &&& Un Sou	103	LC-16	562
Commerce & Trade - 1840 Prince Edward's Island Halfpenny	10	PE-4	916
Commerce - 1781 North American Token	197	AM-5	1013
Commerce - 1813 Marquis Wellington	164	WE-7	978
Commerce Rules The Main - 1812 Success to Trade	196	AM-3	983
Commercial Change 1815 - Halfpenny Token Upper Canada	179	UC-8	726
Commercial Change 1820 - Halfpenny Token Upper Canada	180	UC-9	727
Commercial Change 1821 Upper Canada - Halfpenny Token Upper Canada	181	UC-10	728
Commercial Change 1821 Jamaica - Halfpenny Token Upper Canada	181	UC-11	729
Commerical Change 1833 - Halfpenny Token Upper Canada	183	UC-13	731
Copper Company of Upper Canada One Half Penny - 1794	173	UC-1	721
Cossack Penny Token - Vimiera Talavera Busaco Badajoz Salamanca	170	WE-13	985
Fisheries and Agriculture - 1855 One Cent	12	PE-6	920
Fisheries and Agriculture - Halfpenny Token	16	PE-8	921
F. McDermott Importer of English, French & German Fancy Goods, King St.			
Saint John, N.B. - Depository of Arts	79	NB-3	914
For Public Accommodation One Penny - 1805 Hibernia	196	AM-2	975
For Publick Accommodation - 1815 Ships Colonies and Commerce	17	PE-9B	996
For the Convenience of Trade - 1814 Half Penny Token	56	NS-8	880
Francis Mullins & Son Montreal Importers of Ship Chandlery &c.			
- Commerce Token	104	LC-17	563
Genuine British Copper (Seated Britannia Design)			
- 1815 Half Penny Token	71	NS-25	886
H - 1816 Halfpenny Token	74	NS-30	—
Halfpenny - 1815 Genuine British Copper	72	NS-26	887

LEGENDS	Charlton Standard Page No.	Charlton Catalogue Number	Breton Number
Half Penny - 1830 Canada	101	LC-13A	532
Half Penny - 1841 Canada	101	LC-13B	532
Halfpenny Token - Field Marshal Wellington	160	WE-2A	971
Halfpenny Token - Field Marshal Wellington	161	WE-2B	972
Halfpenny Token - Nova Scotia and New Brunswick Success	73	NS-28	895
Halfpenny Token - Victoria Nobis Est	140	LC-49	982
Halfpenny Token 1813 - Field Marshal Wellington	160	WE-1	969
Halfpenny Token 1832 - Province of Nova Scotia	49	NS-3B	872
Halfpenny Token 1823 - Province of Nova-Scotia	38	NS-1A	867
Halfpenny Token 1823 - Province of Nova Scotia	39	NS-1B	867
Halfpenny Token 1824 - Province of Nova Scotia	40	NS-1C	869
Halfpenny Token 1832 - Province of Nova Scotia	41	NS-1D	871
	48	NS-3A	871
	49	NS-3C	871
	50	NS-3D	871
Halfpenny Token 1840 - Province of Nova Scotia	42	NS-1E	874
Halfpenny Token 1832 - Province of Upper Canada	183	UC-14	732
Halfpenny Token 1843 - Province of Nova Scotia	43	NS-1F	874
Halfpenny Token Nova Scotia - 1815 Commercial Change	58	NS-12	885
Halfpenny Token Nova Scotia - 1815 Starr & Shannon Halifax	58	NS-11	884
Halifax - 1815 Halfpenny Token	72	NS-27	889
Halifax Nova Scotia - 1816 Wholesale & Retail Hardware Store	61	NS-15A	892
Hibernia 1805 - Field Marshal Wellington	163	WE-5	976
JB (Script Initials) - Halfpenny (Warehouse Design)	218	BL-31	—
J. Roy Montreal Un Sou - Commerce Bas-Canada	106	LC-20	671
Montreal - 1816 Half Penny Token	100	LC-12	531
New Brunswick Half Penny Token - 1843 Victoria Dei Gratia Regina	77	NB-1A	910
New Brunswick Half Penny Currency - 1854 Victoria Dei Gratia Regina	77	NB-1B	912
New Brunswick One Penny Token - 1843 Victoria Dei Gratia Regina	78	NB-2A	909
New Brunswick One Penny Currency - 1854 Victoria Dei Gratia Regina	78	NB-2B	911
One Half Penny Token - 1815 Ships Colonies and Commerce	17	PE-9A	995
One Halfpenny Token 1820 - Trade & Navigation	70	NS-24	894
One Penny Token - 1812	133	LC-47B	958
One Penny Token - 1813	134	LC-47C	958
One Penny Token - 1813 Field Marshal Wellington	162	WE-3	974
One Penny Token - 1812 Bon Pour Deux Sous	136	LC-47E	—
One Penny Token - Field Marshal Wellington	162	WE-4A	970
	162	WE-4B	—
One Penny Token 1812 - 1812	132	LC-47A	957
One Penny Token 1813			
- Vimiera Talavera Badajoz Salamanca Vittoria	170	WE-12	984
One Penny Token 1824 - Province of Nova Scotia	44	NS-2A	868
One Penny Token 1832 - Province of Nova Scotia	45	NS-2B	870
	51	NS-4	870
One Penny Token 1840 - Province of Nova Scotia	46	NS-2C	873
One Penny Token 1843 - Province of Nova Scotia	47	NS-2D	873
Payable at the Store of J Brown - Nemo Me Impune Lacessit	62	NS-16	896
Payable at W.A. & S.Black's Halifax N.S.			
- 1816 Wholesale & Retail Hardware Store	61	NS-15B	893
Payable by Carritt & Alport Halifax - 1814 Half Penny Token	56	NS-9	881
Payable by Hosterman & Etter Halifax - 1814 Halfpenny Token	57	NS-10A	882
Payable by Hosterman & Etter Halifax - 1815 Halfpenny Token	57	NS-10B	883
Payable by John Alexr. Barry Halifax - 1815 Halfpenny Token	60	NS-14	891
Payable by Miles W. White Halifax NS - 1815 Halfpenny Token	59	NS-13	890
Pro Bono Publico Montreal ½ Penny Token 1837			
- Trade & Agriculture Lower Canada	90	LC-6	672
Prosperity to Canada La Prudence et la Candeur Token Halfpenny			
- Lesslie & Sons York Kingston & Dundas	174	UC-2	718
Prosperity to Canada La Prudence et la Candeur Token 2d Currency			
- 1822 Lesslie & Sons Toronto & Dundass	175	UC-3	717
Province of Nova Scotia Halfpenny Token			
- 1856 Victoria D:G:Britanniar:Reg:F:D:	52	NS-5	876

LEGENDS	Charlton Standard Page No.	Charlton Catalogue Number	Breton Number
Province of Nova Scotia One Penny Token			
- 1856 Victoria D:G:Britanniar:Reg:F:D:	53	NS-6	875
Pure Copper Preferable to Paper Half Penny Token -			
For General Accommodation	195	AM-1	966
Pure Copper Preferable to Paper Half Penny Token			
- 1812 Trade & Navigation	64	NS-19A	963
Pure Copper Preferable to Paper Half Penny Token			
- 1813 Trade & Navigation (Seated Britannia Design)	64	NS-19B	963
Pure Copper Preferable to Paper Half Penny Token			
- 1813 Trade & Navigation (Ship Design)	67	NS-21	965
Pure Copper Preferable to Paper One Farthing			
- 1813 Trade & Navigation	63	NS-18	964
Pure Copper Preferable to Paper One Penny Token			
- 1813 Trade & Navigation	65	NS-20A	962
Pure Copper Preferable to Paper One Penny Token			
- 1814 Trade & Navigation	66	NS-20B	962
Quebec Bank Token Half Penny 1852			
- Province Du Canada Un Sou	189	PC-3	529
Quebec Bank Token One Penny 1852			
- Province Du Canada Deux Sous	189	PC-4	528
Responsible Government and Free Trade			
- 1860 Fishery Rights for Newfoundland	5	NF-4	955
RH (Script Initials) - 1812 Farthing Token	141	LC-50	991
RH (Script Initials) - 1814 Half Penny Token	141	LC-51	990
RH (Script Initials) - 1814 One Penny Token	142	LC-52	989
Self Government and Free Trade - 1855 Prince Edward Island	14	PE-7B	919
Self Government and Free Trade - 1855 Prince Edward's Island	13	PE-7A	918
Self Government and Free Trade - 1857 Prince Edward Island	15	PE-7C	919
Sells All Sorts of Shop & Store Goods			
- Peter McAuslane St. John's Newfoundland	4	NF-2	956
Sir Isaac Brook Bart. The Hero of Upper Canada 1812			
- Success to the Commerce of Uppr & Lowr Canada	177	UC-5	723
Speed the Plough - Success to the Fisheries	11	PE-5A,B	917
Speed The Plough Halfpenny Token - No Labour No Bread	176	UC-4	1010
St. John New Brunswick Half Penny Token - For Public Accommodation	79	NB-4	913
Success to Commerce & Peace to the World 1816			
- Sr. Isaac Brock The Hero of Upr Canada Fell Oct 13 1812	178	UC-6	724
Success to Navigation & Trade - 1815 Halfpenny Token	69	NS-23	888
Success to Commerce and Peace to the World 1816			
- Success to the Commerce of Uppr & Lowr Canada	179	UC-7	725
Success to the Fishery One Penny - 1815 Magdalen Island Token	83	LC-1	520
T. Duseaman Butcher Belleville - Agriculture & Commerce Bas-Canada	130	LC-45	670
To Facilitate Trade 1823 - Halfpenny Token Upper Canada	182	UC-12A	730
To Facilitate Trade 1833 - Halfpenny Token Upper Canada	182	UC-12B	730
Token Montreal Un Sou - Agriculture & Commerce Bas-Canada	109-123,127-130	LC-21 to LC-36	674-708
	125, 126	LC-38 to LC-39	710-712
Token Montreal Un Sou - Trade & Agriculture Lower Canada	124	LC-37	709
Trade & Navigation 1838 - Pure Copper Preferable to Paper	68	NS-22	967
Vexator Canadinsis 1811	199	VC-1	558
Vexator (or Venator) Canadinsis 1811	199	VC-2	558
Vexator (or Venator) Canadiensis ML 1811	199	VC-3	559
Vimiera Talavera Almeida - Hispaniam et Lvsitaniam Restitvit Wellington	167-169	WE-11A-D	986-988
W.L. Whites Halifax House Halifax Cheap Dry Goods Store			
- One Farthing Payable at White's Halifax House Halifax	62	NS-17	899
Waterloo Halfpenny 1816 - The Illustrious Wellington	166	WE-10	981

TOKENS WITH LEGENDS ON ONE SIDE ONLY

LEGENDS	Charlton Standard Page No.	Charlton Catalogue Number	Breton Number
1812 (Seated Justice Design) - (Bust Design)	140	LC-48C	961
1820 (Harp Design) - (Bust Design)	152-157	LC-60B to F	1012
1825 (Harp Design) - (Bust Design)	152	LC-60A	1012
1858 - (Sailing Ship Design)	4	NF-3	954
Commerce - (Bust Design)	137	LC-47G	—
Commerce 1814 - (Bust Design)	136	LC-47F	—
Commercial Change - (Bust Design)	151	LC-59A,B	1007
DMC P.E.I Uniface (McCarthy Penny Token)	9	PE-3	—
Field Marshal Wellington - (Seated Britannia Design)	161	WE-2C	973
Half Penny Token (Bust of George III)	217	BL-29	—
Halfpenny Token - (Sailing Ship Design)	147	LC-56C	1005
Halfpenny Token 1815 - (Sailing Ship Design)	147	LC-56B	1004
Halfpenny Token 1812 - (Bust Design)	131	LC-46	960
	138	LC48A	960
	139	LC-48B	960
Halfpenny Token 1812 - (Sailing Ship Design)	146	LC-56A	1004
Halfpenny Token 1813 - (Seated Britannia Design)	143, 144	LC-54A,B	994
Halfpenny Token 1814 - (Seated Britannia Design)	144	LC-54C	994
Halfpenny Token 1815 - (Seated Britannia Design)	145	LC-54D	994
J. Shaw & Co. Importers of Hardwares Upper Town Quebec -	105	LC-19	565
One Penny Token 1812 - (Bust Design)	135	LC-47D	959
P.E.I Uniface (McCausland Penny Token)	9	PE-2	—
Pure Copper Preferable to Paper - (Irishman Design)	197	AM-4	1009
R.W. Owen Montreal Ropery - (Sailing Ship Design)	104	LC-18	564
Ships Colonies & Commerce - (Harp Design)	216	BL-28	998
Ships Colonies & Commerce - (Bust Design)	149, 150	LC-58A,B	1002
Ships Colonies & Commerce - (Laureate Bust Design)	215	BL-26	997
Ships Colonies & Commerce - (Sailing Ship Design)	21-36	PE-10-1 to 10-44	997, 1000
	213-214	BL-24 A-C	997,999
St. John's N.B. Halfpenny Token -	80	NB-5	—
T.S. Brown & Co. Importers of Hardwares Montreal -	102	LC-15	561
To Facilitate Trade 1825 - (Civilian Bust Design)	143	LC-53B	—
To Facilitate Trade 1825 - (Military Bust Design)	142	LC-53A	992
Trade & Commerce 1811 - (Bust Design)	163	WE-6	977
Wellington Halfpenny Token - (Seated Britannia Design)	166	WE-9	980
Wellington Waterloo 1815 - (Large Bust Design)	171	WE-15	1006
Wellington Waterloo 1815 - (Sailing Ship Design)	171	WE-14	1003
(Seated Justice Design) - 1820 (Bust of George III)	148	LC-57	1011
(Harp Design) - Halfpenny (Warehouse Design)	217	BL-30	—
- R & I.S. Rutherford Newfoundland St.John's	2	NF-1A	952

TOKENS WITH NO LEGENDS

LEGENDS	Charlton Standard Page No.	Charlton Catalogue Number	Breton Number
(Harp Design) - (Bust Design)	158	LC-61	—
(Sailing Ship Design) - (Laureate Bust Design)	215	BL-25	—
(Seated Justice Design) - (Sailing Ship Design)	146	LC-55	1001

TOKENS OF NEWFOUNDLAND

In 1838 the British government abandoned the idea of introducing Sterling into British North America.

Meanwhile, local halfpenny tokens began to appear to satisfy the need for currency. The first of these were the Rutherford halfpennies, in use from about 1840 to 1850. Due to the vast numbers of P.E.I. halfpennies being brought into St. John's, further importation was forbidden by the government in 1851. To further complicate the situation, French coppers were also circulating at this time.

A proposed issue of 500 Pounds in pennies and halfpennies of distinctive design failed and in 1860 the government again forbade the importation of all private tokens.

In 1863 the decimal system was adopted and old coppers of all kinds were recalled and redeemed at weight.

BRETON CROSS REFERENCE TABLE FOR NEWFOUNDLAND TOKENS

Breton No.	Charlton Cat. No.	Page No.	Breton No.	Charlton Cat. No.	Page No.
952	NF-1A, B	2	955	NF-4	5
953	NF-1C	3	956	NF-2	4
954	NF-3	4			

PRIVATE TOKENS

NF-1   *RUTHERFORD TOKENS*

In 1840 George, Andrew, Robert and I.S. Rutherford left England to set up as general merchants. Robert and I.S. Rutherford settled in St. John's, with George and Andrew settling in Harbour Grace. The first tokens were issued shortly thereafter from St. John's and were struck by Boulton & Watt.

NF-1A   *— R & I.S. RUTHERFORD NEWFOUNDLAND ST. JOHN'S*

Composition: Copper, brass
Weight: 8.7 to 10.6 gms
Diameter: 28.7 to 28.9 mm
Die Axis: ↑↑ ↑↓
Edge: Plain
Ref.Nos.: Br 952; Co 1NF; W 180

Varieties: Composition and die axis
     A1   Copper; Coinage
     A2   Copper; Medal
     A3   Brass; Medal
     A4   Brass; Coinage

Variations: An undated variety exists where the apostrophe in St. John's touches the fleece of the right hind foot, W 181.

Cat.No.	Date	Description	VG	F	VF	EF	AU	UNC
NF-1A1	Undated	Copper; Coinage	4.00	8.00	30.00	125.00	225.00	-
NF 1A2	Undated	Copper; Medal	4.00	8.00	30.00	125.00	225.00	-
NF-1A3	Undated	Brass; Medal	5.00	10.00	40.00	150.00	250.00	-
NF-1A4	Undated	Brass; Coinage	5.00	10.00	40.00	150.00	250.00	-

NF-1B   *1841 — R & I.S. RUTHERFORD NEWFOUNDLAND ST. JOHN'S*

Composition: Copper, brass
Weight: 9.0 to 10.4 gms
Diameter: 28.8 to 29.5 mm
Die Axis: ↑↑ ↑↓
Edge: Plain
Ref.Nos.: Br 952; Co 2NF; W 182

Varieties: Composition and die axis
     B1   Copper, Coinage
     B2   Copper, Medal
     B3   Brass, Medal

Cat.No.	Date	Description	VG	F	VF	EF	AU	UNC
NF-1B1	1841	Copper, Coinage	3.00	10.00	40.00	150.00	300.00	-
NF-1B2	1841	Copper, Medal	3.00	10.00	40.00	150.00	300.00	-
NF-1B3	1841	Brass, Medal	3.00	10.00	40.00	150.00	300.00	-

NF-1C   *1846 — RUTHERFORD BROS. NEWFOUNDLAND HARBOUR GRACE*

In 1846 the Harbour Grace Store issued halfpenny tokens. While the initials R.H. appear below the arms on the reverse it is doubtful that these tokens were actually struck by Ralph Heaton and Company as previously believed, as they did not receive the coining equipment from Boulton and Watt until the late 1840s.

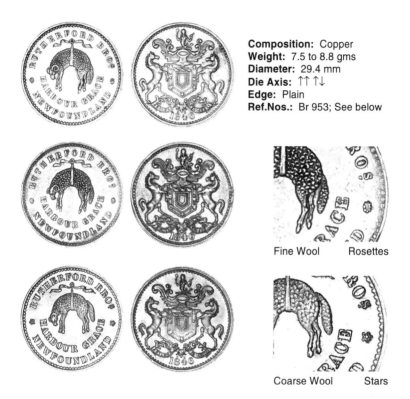

Composition: Copper
Weight: 7.5 to 8.8 gms
Diameter: 29.4 mm
Die Axis: ↑↑ ↑↓
Edge: Plain
Ref.Nos.: Br 953; See below

Fine Wool   Rosettes

Coarse Wool   Stars

Varieties: Obverse and die axis
C1 Fine Wool, Rosettes, Medal; Co 3, 5NF; W 183, 184
C2 Coarse Wool, Rosettes, Medal; Co 7NF; W 185
C3 Coarse Wool, Stars, Medal; Co 8NF; W 186
C4 Coarse Wool, Stars, Coinage; Co 8NF; W 186

Variations: Minor varieties exist as a result of worn and retouched dies.

Cat.No.	Date	Description	VG	F	VF	EF	AU	UNC
NF-1C1	1846	Fine, Rosettes, Medal	3.00	6.00	15.00	45.00	125.00	225.00
NF-1C2	1846	Coarse, Rosettes, Medal	3.00	8.00	20.00	45.00	125.00	225.00
NF-1C3	1846	Coarse, Stars, Medal	5.00	12.00	25.00	55.00	150.00	-
NF-1C4	1846	Coarse, Stars, Coinage	5.00	12.00	25.00	55.00	150.00	-

NF-2   *SELLS ALL SORTS OF SHOP & STORE GOODS*
           — PETER McAUSLANE ST. JOHN'S NEWFOUNDLAND

Peter McAuslane, a blacksmith by trade, opened a dry goods store on Water Street in St. John's about 1844. It is believed that McAuslane struck one hundred of these pieces which once were thought to be intended as farthings due to their size. Most were probably lost in the fire of 1846 that destroyed his establishment.

Composition: Brass
Weight: N/A
Diameter: 20.0 to 20.6 mm
Die Axis: ↑↑
Edge: Plain
Ref.Nos.: Br 956

Cat.No.	Date	Description	VG	F	VF	EF	AU	UNC
NF-2	Undated				Extremely Rare			

ANONYMOUS TOKENS

NF-3   *1858 — (SAILING SHIP DESIGN)*

A rare halfpenny was issued anonymously at St. John's in 1858. It was struck by Ralph Heaton and Company using Halliday's Ships Colonies and Commerce obverse design.

Composition: Copper
Weight: 5.0 to 6.1 gms
Diameter: 25.4 to 25.6 mm
Die Axis: ↑↑
Edge: Plain
Ref.No.: Br 954; Co 9NF

Open "5"   Closed "5"

Varieties: Reverse
A1 Open "5"; W 188
A2 Closed "5"; W 187

Cat.No.	Date	Description	VG	F	VF	EF	AU	UNC
NF-3A1	1858	Open "5"	350.00	500.00	900.00	1,200.00	1,750.00	-
NF-3A2	1858	Closed "5"	350.00	500.00	900.00	1,200.00	1,750.00	-

NF-4   *RESPONSIBLE GOVERNMENT AND FREE TRADE*
    — 1860 FISHERY RIGHTS FOR NEWFOUNDLAND

This token was issued in 1860 to commemorate the signing of a treaty by the major fishing nations to regulate the fisheries and establish fishing limits. The treaty also took steps to control the actions of foreign fishermen while on Newfoundland waters and in Newfoundland ports. The tokens were struck by Ralph Heaton and Company.

Composition: Copper
Weight: 4.8 to 5.8 gms
Diameter: 26.0 to 26.2 mm
Die Axis: ↑↑
Edge: Plain
Ref.Nos.: Br 955; Co 10NF;
        W 189

Cat.No.	Date	Description	VG	F	VF	EF	AU	UNC
NF-4	1860		40.00	60.00	100.00	200.00	400.00	-

TOKENS OF PRINCE EDWARD ISLAND

Prince Edward Island formed part of the French colony of Acadia but was not ceded to Great Britain when mainland Acadia was lost by France in 1713. The Island was acquired by Britain with the Treaty of Paris and received its present name in 1798 in honour of Queen Victoria's father. Prince Edward Island was governed from Nova Scotia until 1769 when it was made a separate colony. The first act to regulate its currency was passed in 1785 when the Spanish dollar was rated at five shillings (5/-), the same as Nova Scotia. Currency depreciation began when the first of the redeemable treasury notes was issued. By 1827 the Spanish dollar was circulating at five shillings and six pence (5/6). In 1829 an act was passed by the legislative assembly but it was later rejected, probably due to its odd valuation of gold coins. By 1833 the dollar was circulating at six shillings (6/-), a premium of 20% over its intrinsic value due to the increasing volume of treasury notes. This was done in order to keep the coins circulating in Prince Edward Island and not elsewhere.

According to Pridmore, the late British colonial token authority, the treasury ordered the countermarking of coins with the letters "P.E.I.," also to keep them in local circulation. Today these coins are extremely rare.

By 1847, when an inquiry into local currency was ordered, the situation was still very unsettled as most government departments were valuing the dollar at six shillings (6/-), while the Customs department valued it at six shillings and three pence (6/3).

In 1849 the recommendations of the Committee of Inquiry were accepted and an act was passed regulating the currency and fixing the Spanish dollar at six shillings and threepence (6/3). This rating prevailed until the adoption of the decimal system in 1871.

BRETON CROSS REFERENCE TABLE FOR PRINCE EDWARD ISLAND TOKENS

Breton No.	Charlton Cat. No.	Page No.	Breton No.	Charlton Cat. No.	Page No.
916	PE-4	10	997	PE-10-10 to 13	24
917	PE-5A, B	11	997	PE-10-14 to 17	26
918	PE-7A	13	997	PE-10-18 to 22	27
919	PE-7B, C	14, 15	997	PE-10-23, 24, 26	29
920	PE-6	12	997	PE-10-25	30
921	PE-8	16	997	PE-10-27, 33	30
995	PE-9A	17	997	PE-10-28 to 32	31
996	PE-9B	17	997	PE-10-34, 35, 40	33
997	PE-10-1	21	997	PE-10-36, 37, 42, 45, 46	34
997	PE-10-2	21	997	PE-10-38, 39	35
997	PE-10-3	22, 213	997	PE-10-41A, 41B, 43, 44	36
997	PE-10-4	22, 214	999	PE-10-5A	22, 214
997	PE-10-5	22, 215	1000	PE-5B	22
997	PE-10-6 to 9	23			

SEMI-REGAL TOKENS

PE-1 *"HOLEY" DOLLAR AND PLUG OF 1813*

PE1A *TREASURY ISSUE*

The principal coin used on Prince Edward Island in the early 19th century was the Spanish-American dollar. When a new governor arrived there in 1813 to take up his post however, he found that all coins were very scarce creating something of a commercial crisis. The scarcity was due to the tendency of local businessmen to hoard coins for the purpose of sending them abroad to pay for purchases of goods.

The governor decided that a remedy to the problem was the creation of a local coinage from mutilated Spanish-American coins, similar to that taking place in the West Indies and Australia. He ordered that a quantity of Spanish-American dollars be perforated to form two kinds of coins. The piece punched out of the centre (the plug) was to be a shilling and the large ring that remained ("holey" dollar) was to be a five shilling piece.

Each plug and holey dollar was given an official counterstamp. The nature of this counterstamp seems not to have been specified. Circumstantial evidence suggests it consisted of ten triangles arranged in a circle, like a symbol for the sun. On the holey dollar the triangles are well separated from each other and the symbol touches the king's forehead. However, on the plug the triangles are larger and run together at the corners.

The reasoning behind the creation of the plug and holey dollar coinage was that the coins would remain on the island, being overvalued (as they were by some 20 percent) compared to the unmutilated coins. Anyone using the mutilated coins for payments abroad would thus sustain a loss of 20 percent because the coins would only be accepted at the inflated rate on the island. This proved to be correct. The merchants saw a chance to make a quick profit by creating their own holey dollars. This forced the government to withdraw the official issue in 1814, leaving the merchants' forgeries behind. The merchants' pieces are thought to have continued in circulation for about another ten years.

Authenticating a holey dollar or plug is not an easy matter. Provenance, the appearance and placement of the counterstamp and the appearance of the hole in the centre of the dollar are all important. Differentiating the original issue from the merchants' imitations is made doubly difficult by the fact that from about 1890 onward forgeries have been made to sell to collectors. Most are made from genuine Spanish-American dollars. The forgeries made for collectors are, of course, worth much less than an original or merchants' imitation. Recently, lightweight counterfeits of the holey dollar and plug have also begun to appear. At the present time it is not possible to positively differentiate the originals from the contemporary merchants' imitations. It is assumed that certain of the holey dollars with counterstamps consisting of small squares or radiating lines instead of triangles are merchants' imitations, but it is also possible that the counterstamp on the merchants' imitations were always more like the originals and that all pieces with squares, lines, etc. are later forgeries for collectors. For this reason, we have listed the merchants' forgeries along with the originals. Pieces of particularly good appearance and with a good pedigree are worth a premium over the prices given below.

PE-1B *MERCHANTS' ISSUE*

A thousand pieces proved insufficient in light of subsequent forgeries and on May 7, 1814, the government warned against such forgeries and announced that only the original treasury issue would be honoured by the treasury. On June 14, 1814, the government announced that these holey dollars and plugs were to be withdrawn and redeemed at the value at which they were issued. In August of 1814 it was announced that the exchange of official dollars and plugs would cease on September 28 of that year.

On withdrawal of the official issue, the local merchants, accustomed to an adequare supply of silver, agreed among themselves to accept forgeries for trade at the official value of 5/- the for the ring and 1/- for the plug. As a result, forgeries were raised to the status of private tokens. They were used for the next ten years.

PE-1   *"HOLEY" DOLLAR AND PLUG OF 1813*

Composition: Silver
Weight: Ring: 21.8 gms
Plug: N/A
Diameter: Ring: 39.2 mm
Plug: 16.0 mm
Die Axis: ↑↑
Edge: Lettered
Ref.Nos.: W 201, 202

Note: There is currently no way of authenticating the counterstamp used for the treasury issues. Thus, the merchant and treasury issues, while listed separately, are priced the same.

Cat.No.	Date	Description	VG	F	VF	AU	EF	UNC
PE-1A1		Treasury Ring	-	-	3,500.00	-	-	-
PE-1A2		Merchant Ring	-	-	3,500.00	-	-	-
PE-1B1		Treasury Plug	-	-	4,500.00	-	-	-
PE-1B2		Merchant Plug	-	-	4,500.00	-	-	-

Modern Copies

A crude eleven-point radiate counterstamp was applied to white metal cast copies of rings and plugs of Spanish-American Dollars made in the early 1960s by Regency Coin and Stamp Co. of Winnipeg. There was no intent to deceive collectors. These copies are easily recognized by the fact all rings are dated 1793, by the distinctiveness of the counterstamp, and by the fact that it is applied to the field in front of the king's nose on the ring and away from the throat on the plug.

PRIVATE TOKENS

PE-2 *P.E.I UNIFACE (McCAUSLAND PENNY TOKEN)*

This piece was issued as a penny token by Peter McCausland, a prosperous farmer and fisherman who owned the island of Rustico. The pennies were crude with extreme variation in weight. The specimen illustrated weighs only 125 grains, so light that it is difficult to believe that it would have been accepted as a penny even with the depreciated standard of the local currency.

Composition: Copper
Weight: 8.1 to 9.3 gms
Diameter: 33.8 mm
Die Axis: Uniface
Edge: Plain
Ref.Nos.: W 236

Cat.No.	Date	Description	VG	F	VF	EF	AU	UNC
PE-2	Undated		J. Hoare Auction, October 1999, Lot 587, AVE - $1,980.00					

PE-3 *DMC P.E.I UNIFACE (McCARTHY PENNY TOKEN)*

This token is said to have been issued by Dennis McCarthy, a tinsmith from Charlottetown. It first came to notice over fifty years ago when a specimen was listed in the Wilson sale. A specimen was also offered in 1976 in the McKay-Clements sale.

Composition: Copper
Weight: N/A
Diameter: 34.4 mm
Die Axis: Uniface
Edge: Plain
Ref.Nos.: See below

Varieties: Uniface
3A DMC; W 237
3B DMC P.E.I; W 237a

Note: PE-2 and PE-3 are linked to the same maker by the punches used to form P.E.I.

Cat.No.	Date	Description	VG	F	VF	EF	AU	UNC
PE-3A	Undated	DMC			Rare			
PE-3B	Undated	DMC P.E.I			Extremely Rare			

PE-4

COMMERCE & TRADE—
1840 PRINCE EDWARD'S ISLAND HALFPENNY

The James Millner Sheaf of Wheat token was the first halfpenny struck and issued in Prince Edward Island. In 1840, Millner, with permission from the Colonial government, imported dies and presses from the United States.

Most specimens known are crudely struck on inferior planchets. This token was issued in poor condition which explains why so few were issued and why his production equipment was eventually sold for scrap.

Composition: Copper
Weight: 5.5 to 7.0 gms
Diameter: 27.0 to 28.4 mm
Die Axis: ↑↓
Edge: Plain
Ref.Nos.: Br 916; Co 3PEI; W 238

Cat.No.	Date	Description	Fair	G	VG	F	VF
PE-4	1840		100.00	250.00	500.00	700.00	1,250.00

PE-5   *SPEED THE PLOUGH - SUCCESS TO THE FISHERIES*

Clift, Wood & Co. of Charlottetown are credited with first importing this token into Prince Edward Island. The hook variety was struck by Ralph Heaton & Sons around 1860 and large quantities were subsequently exported to Newfoundland.

The two major varieties, the clevis and the hook, were issued around 1859 and 1860 respectively.

PE-5A   *CLEVIS REVERSE Ca. 1859*

Composition: Copper
Weight: 5.2 to 6.0 gms
Diameter: 25.9 to 26.1 mm
Die Axis: ↑↑
Edge: Plain
Ref.Nos.: Br 917; Co 4 to 8PEI;
                  W 239 to 243

Clevis

Variations: Minor obverse variations exist in the fillet, the size and shaping of the tail and the lower fin. On the reverse, variations exist in the placement of the crossbar on the clevis.

Cat.No.	Date	Description	VG	F	VF	EF	AU	UNC
PE-5A	(1859)		6.00	10.00	25.00	50.00	175.00	300.00

PE-5B   *HOOK REVERSE Ca. 1860*

Composition: Copper
Weight: 5.5 to 6.0 gms
Diameter: 25.9 to 26.1 mm
Die Axis: ↑↑ ↑↓
Edge: Plain
Ref.Nos.: Br 917; Co 9 to 12PEI;
                  W 244 to 246

Hook

Varieties: Die Axis
      B1   Medal
      B2   Coinage

Variations: The same obverse variations exist as for PE-5A.

Cat.No.	Date	Description	VG	F	VF	EF	AU	UNC
PE-5B1	(1860)	Medal	3.00	7.00	12.00	30.00	100.00	200.00
PE-5B2	(1860)	Coinage	4.00	8.00	18.00	35.00	125.00	250.00

PE-6 *FISHERIES AND AGRICULTURE — 1855 ONE CENT*

James Duncan, a hardware merchant in Charlottetown, issued the first Canadian decimal piece, the "cent" of 1855. Competing with other halfpenny tokens which went at 150 to the Spanish dollar (Duncan's piece went at 100 to the dollar) it is doubtful that they were accepted. Later issues on thick flans were probably an attempt to regain acceptance at the higher value.

Composition: Copper
Weight: 5.0 to 6.2 gms
Diameter: 26.0 mm
Die Axis: ↑↑ ↑↓
Edge: Plain
Ref.Nos.: Br 920; See below

Plain fives   Recut fives

Varieties: Obverse and Die Axis
A1 Plain fives, Medal; Co 41, 42PEI; W 247, 248
A2 Recut fives, Medal; Co 43PEI; W 249
A3 Recut fives, Coinage, Thick flan; Co 44PEI, W 250

Cat.No.	Date	Description	VG	F	VF	EF	AU	UNC
PE-6A1	1855	Plain fives, Medal	3.00	6.00	12.00	40.00	125.00	250.00
PE-6A2	1855	Recut fives, Medal	5.00	8.00	20.00	50.00	150.00	300.00
PE-6A3	1855	Recut fives, Coinage	4.00	7.00	15.00	40.00	125.00	250.00

PE-7   *SELF GOVERNMENT AND FREE TRADE —*

The Self Government and Free Trade tokens of 1855 and 1857 were issued by George and Simeon Davies and Henry Haszard. Besides having two distinct issue dates, the most noticeable difference between varieties is in the obverse legends which display the island name spelt two different ways.

PE-7A   *— 1855 PRINCE EDWARD'S ISLAND*

Composition: Copper
Weight: 4.8 to 5.2 gms
Diameter: 26.0 to 26.1 mm
Die Axis: ↑↓
Edge: Plain
Ref.Nos.: Br 918; See below

Thick top fives

Thin top fives

Varieties: Obverse
    A1   Thick top fives; Co 13, 14PEI; W 251, 252
    A2   Thin top fives; Co 15PEI; W 253

Cat.No.	Date	Description	VG	F	VF	EF	AU	UNC
PE-7A1	1855	Thick top fives	3.00	6.00	12.00	30.00	125.00	250.00
PE-7A2	1855	Thin top fives	4.00	7.00	18.00	35.00	125.00	250.00

PE-7B — *1855 PRINCE EDWARD ISLAND*

Composition: Copper
Weight: 4.7 to 5.1 gms
Diameter: 26.0 to 26.3 mm
Die Axis: ↑↓ ↑↑
Edge: Plain
Ref.Nos.: Br 919; See below

Five points
to "S"

Five points
between "I" and "S"

Varieties: Obverse
B1 Top of "5" pointing to "S" of ISLAND; Co 16, 17PEI; W 254, 255
B2 Top of "5" pointing between "I" and "S" of ISLAND; Co 18PEI; W 256

Variations: Courteau variations exist with date numbers slightly closer together.

Cat.No.	Date	Description	VG	F	VF	EF	AU	UNC
PE-7B1	1855	Pointing to "S"	3.00	6.00	15.00	30.00	100.00	200.00
PE-7B2	1855	Pointing between "I" and "S"	3.00	6.00	15.00	30.00	100.00	200.00

PE-7C   *— 1857 PRINCE EDWARD ISLAND*

Composition: Copper
Weight: 4.9 to 5.3 gms
Diameter: 26.0 to 26.3 mm
Die Axis: ↑↑ ↑↓
Edge: Plain
Ref.Nos.: Br 919; See below

| Large "AND" | Small "AND" | Large Quatrefoil | Small Quatrefoil |

Varieties: Obverse, reverse and die axis
C1 Large Quatrefoil, large "AND", Medal; Co 19 to 23, 33PEI; W 257 to 263
C2 Large Quatrefoil, large "AND", Coinage; Co 27, 28; W 257, 262
C3 Large Quatrefoil, small "AND", Medal; Co 25, 26, 34PEI; W 264 to 266
C4 Small Quatrefoil, small "AND", Medal; Co 35 to 40PEI; W 267 to 269

Variations: Varieties exist where the date points to different letters in the legend as in PE-7B. Variations also exist in die alignment, plain or hooked "E" and dot between 8 and 5 of the date.

Cat.No.	Date	Description	VG	F	VF	EF	AU	UNC
PE-7C1	1857	L Quatrefoil, L "AND", Medal	3.00	6.00	15.00	40.00	125.00	200.00
PE-7C2	1857	L Quatrefoil, L "AND", Coinage	3.00	6.00	15.00	40.00	125.00	200.00
PE-7C3	1857	L Quatrefoil, S "AND", Medal	4.00	7.00	18.00	50.00	150.00	225.00
PE-7C4	1857	S Quatrefoil, S "AND", Medal	4.00	7.00	18.00	50.00	150.00	225.00

PE-8   *FISHERIES AND AGRICULTURE — HALFPENNY TOKEN*

The last token of Prince Edward Island was issued about 1858. It is the heaviest of the local tokens which suggests that it represented another attempt by a merchant to circulate cents. It was probably issued by James Duncan as the obverse is similar to that of Duncan's tokens of 1855. It seems that after 1858 Prince Edward Island was amply supplied with copper for there were no further halfpenny issues. The official adoption of the decimal system in 1871 rendered the tokens obsolete and they were replaced by the cents of 1871.

Composition: Copper
Weight: 5.5 to 6.5 gms
Diameter: 26.4 to 26.6 mm
Die Axis: ↑↑
Edge: Plain
Ref.Nos.: Br 921; Co 45PEI;
          W 272

Variations: Specimens exist on thick and thin flans. The thin flans are the scarcer.

Cat.No.	Date	Description	VG	F	VF	EF	AU	UNC
PE-8	(1858)		5.00	10.00	20.00	50.00	125.00	250.00

ANONYMOUS TOKENS

SHIPS COLONIES AND COMMERCE TOKENS

This is an extensive series of halfpenny tokens that circulated chiefly in Prince Edward Island between 1830 and the early 1860s. However, some of the varieties are known to have circulated in Lower Canada and Newfoundland. They are all listed under Prince Edward Island for ease of identification and pricing.

PE-9 — *1815 SHIPS COLONIES AND COMMERCE*

The two tokens dated 1815 were struck after 1830 and antedated to evade the laws prohibiting anonymous tokens. PE-9B has the reverse of a private token issued in the Isle of Man after 1830.

PE-9A   *ONE HALF PENNY TOKEN -*

Composition: Brass
Weight: 4.5 to 4.8 gms
Diameter: 27.9 to 28.1 mm
Die Axis: ↑↑
Edge: Plain
Ref.Nos.: Br 995; Co 1PEI; W 206

Cat.No.	Date	Description	VG	F	VF	EF	AU	UNC
PE-9A	1815		15.00	30.00	75.00	150.00	250.00	-

Note: These dies were poorly prepared resulting in lack of detail. Look for surface wear to help in grading.

PE-9B   *FOR PUBLICK ACCOMMODATION -*

Composition: Brass, Copper
Weight: 4.5 to 4.7 gms
Diameter: 28.0 to 28.1 mm
Die Axis: ↑↑
Edge: Plain
Ref.Nos.: Br 996; Co 2PEI; W 20796; Co 2PEI; W 207

Cat.No.	Date	Description	VG	F	VF	EF	AU	UNC
PE-9B	1815	Brass	20.00	35.00	90.00	175.00	300.00	-
PE-9B	1815	Copper	J. Hoare Auction, June 1996, Lot 1228; EF - $190.00					

PE-10 *SHIPS COLONIES & COMMERCE — (SAILING SHIP DESIGN)*

The following tokens were designed by Thomas Halliday whose initial "H" appears on most of them. W.A.D. Lees in his list published in "The Numismatist" of January 1917, recorded fifty-four varieties of this token dividing the series into three groups: No "H," Single "H" and Double "H." R.C. Willey in his "The Colonial Coinage of Canada" (CNA Journal 1979-1983) followed suit with the exception of an unsigned group, and the Wright & Bale issues which were assigned to Lower Canada. We have grouped the complete series into one and listed all varieties under Prince Edward Island knowing that some of the tokens also circulated in Lower Canada and Newfoundland as well as Prince Edward Island.

IDENTIFICATION OF SHIPS COLONIES & COMMERCE TOKENS

The ships colonies and commerce tokens are divided into four major categories and within these are arranged in order by the numbering sequence used by Lee. These tokens are among the most difficult to identify. The flow charts on pages 20, 25, 28 and 32, plus the illustrations should help in the process of identification.

A: No mint mark — No guys; see flowchart 1 on page 20
B: No mint mark — Guys; see flowchart 2 on page 25
C: Single H mint mark; see flowchart 3 on page 28
D: Double H mint mark; see flowchart 4 on page 32

REVERSE

The ampersand on the token reverse is the major identifying feature. The next is the size and location of the reverse legend.

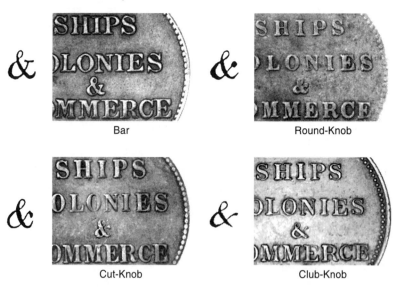

Bar

Round-Knob

Cut-Knob

Club-Knob

OBVERSE

The obverse characteristics of this token are used to help identify the major and minor varieties. The main characteristics are:

1. No mint mark
2. Single "H" mint mark
3. Double "H" mint mark
4. Wright & Bale mint mark

5. British flag, straight or curved
6. U.S. flag
7. No guys to the spritsail
8. Guys to the spritsail

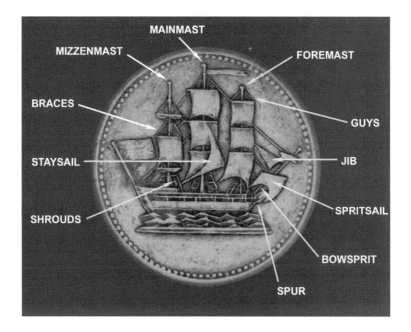

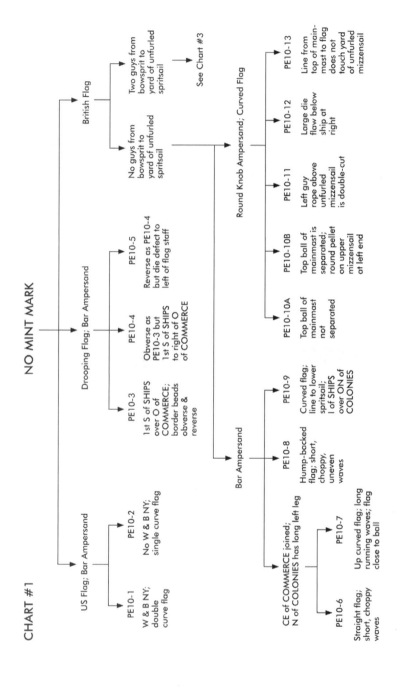

CHART #1

NO MINT MARK

US Flag: Bar Ampersand

PE10-1
W & B NY;
double
curve flag

PE10-2
No W & B NY;
single curve flag

Drooping Flag; Bar Ampersand

PE10-3
1st S of SHIPS
over O of
COMMERCE;
border beads
obverse &
reverse

PE10-4
Obverse as
PE10-3 but
1st S of SHIPS
to right of O
of COMMERCE

PE10-5
Reverse as PE10-4
but die defect to
left of flag staff

British Flag

No guys from
bowsprit to
yard of unfurled
spritsail

Two guys from
bowsprit to
yard of unfurled
spritsail

See Chart #3

Bar Ampersand

CE of COMMERCE joined;
N of COLONIES has long left leg

PE10-6
Straight flag;
short, choppy
waves

PE10-7
Up curved flag; long
running waves; flag
close to ball

PE10-8
Hump-backed
flag; short,
choppy,
uneven
waves

PE10-9
Curved flag;
line to lower
spritsail;
I of SHIPS
over ON of
COLONIES

Round Knob Ampersand; Curved Flag

PE10-10A
Top ball of
mainmast
not
separated

PE10-10B
Top ball of
mainmast is
separated;
round pellet
on upper
mizzensail
at left end

PE10-11
Left guy
rope above
unfurled
mizzensail
is double-cut

PE10-12
Large die
flaw below
ship at
right

PE10-13
Line from
top of main-
mast to flag
does not
touch yard
of unfurled
mizzensail

PE10-1 and 2   *NO MINTMARK: UNITED STATES FLAG*
                      BAR AMPERSAND

   The New York firm of Wright & Bale cut the dies and struck the following tokens which circulated in Lower Canada. The ship is flying a striped flag resembling the flag of the United States. While it was first thought that these tokens were issued in 1829, their light weight could have made acceptance doubtful. Six years later they more likely would have been accepted. These tokens circulated in Lower Canada.

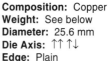
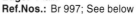

Composition: Copper
Weight: See below
Diameter: 25.6 mm
Die Axis: ↑↑ ↑↓
Edge: Plain
Ref.Nos.: Br 997; See below

With
"W & B N.Y."

Without
"W & B N.Y."

Varieties: Obverse, weight and die axis
   10-1 With "W & B N.Y.," Coinage, 3.1 to 4.1 gms; Lees 1; W 557
   10-2 Without "W & B N.Y.," Coinage, 3.1 to 4.2 gms; Lees 2; W 556

Cat.No.	Date	Description	VG	F	VF	EF	AU	UNC
PE10-1	(1829)	With "W & B N.Y.," Coinage	15.00	30.00	75.00	150.00	300.00	-
PE10-2	(1829)	Without "W & B N.Y.," Coinage	7.00	15.00	35.00	75.00	150.00	-

PE10-3 to 5A   *NO MINTMARK: BRITISH FLAG DROOPING*
                              BAR AMPERSAND

The tokens, PE10-3 to 5A, are listed here in order to complete the PEI section. These tokens are also listed in the Blacksmith section as they are also considered part of that series. For illustrations and technical data in greater detail see BL-24, 25 and 26, pages 213 to 215.

Varieties:

3 Obv. and rev. border beads; First "S" of SHIPS over "O" of COMMERCE; Br 997; Lees 3; W 655

4 Obv. border beads, First "S" of SHIPS to right of "O" of COMMERCE; Br 997; Lees 4; W 654

5 Rectangular pennant with no balls where the guys join the main mast; Br 997; Lees 5; W 653

5A No obv. or rev. border beads; Br 999; Lees 5A

Cat.No.	Date	Description	G	VG	F	VF	EF	AU
PE10-3		Obv. and rev, border beads	25.00	50.00	100.00	-	-	-
PE10-4		Obv. border beads	J. Hoare Auction, October 1995, Lot 1942, F - $715.00					
PE10-5		Rectangular pennant	700.00	1,000.00	1,250.00	1,500.00	-	-
PE10-5A		No obv. or rev. border beads	J. Hoare Auction, February 1995, Lot 1858, VF - $4,800.00					

PE10-5B   *LONG SHIP, UNION JACK FLAG*

Composition: Copper
Weight: 5.9 gms
Diameter: 25.9 mm
Thickness: 1.4 mm
Die Axis: ↑↑
Edge: Plain
Ref.Nos.: Br 1000, Lees 5B, W 558

Cat.No.	Date	Description	VG	F	VF	EF	AU	UNC
PE10-5B		Long Ship		Only two known, Extremely Rare				

PE10-6 to 9   *NO MINTMARK: BRITISH FLAG*
                            NO GUYS
                            BAR AMPERSAND

The first series of the Ships Colonies and Commerce tokens (undated) cannot be attributed to a single minter. The first three tokens circulated in Lower Canada and the others in Prince Edward Island. There is no designer's initial or minter's mark on this series.

Composition: Copper
Weight: 5.0 to 6.2 gms
Diameter: 25.9 to 26.2 mm
Die Axis: ↑↑ ↑↓
Edge: Plain
Ref.Nos.: Br 997; See below

10-6 Choppy even waves

10-7 Long running even waves   **10-8** Short choppy uneven waves

10-9 Long running uneven waves   Bar ampersand

Varieties: Obverse, reverse and die axis
    10-6 Choppy even waves, Straight flag, "CE" of COMMERCE joined, "N" of COLONIES has long left leg; Lees 6; W 559
    10-7 Long running even waves, Up curved flag close to ball, "CE" of COMMERCE joined; Lees 7; W 560
    10-8 Short choppy uneven waves, Hump-backed flag, Coinage; Lees 8; W 555
    10-9 Long running uneven waves, Curved flag; Lees 9; W 208

Cat.No.	Date	Description	VG	F	VF	EF	AU	UNC
PE10-6		Choppy even waves	15.00	30.00	75.00	90.00	150.00	300.00
PE10-7		Long running even waves	7.00	15.00	30.00	60.00	125.00	250.00
PE10-8		Uneven waves	5.00	10.00	15.00	40.00	100.00	250.00
PE10-9		Long uneven waves, knob	7.00	15.00	30.00	60.00	125.00	400.00

PE10-10A to 13   ***NO MINTMARK: BRITISH FLAG (CURVED)***
                    NO GUYS
                    ROUND KNOB AMPERSAND

Composition: Copper
Weight: 5.0 to 6.2 gms
Diameter: 25.9 to 26.2 mm
Die Axis: ↑↑ ↑↓
Edge: Plain
Ref.Nos.: Br 997; W 209 to 211;
            See below

Round-knob ampersand

Varieties: Obverse, reverse and die axis
  10-10A Top ball of main-mast not separated; Lees 10
  10-10B Top ball of main-mast is separated, Round pellet on upper
            mizzen-sail at left end; Lees 10A
  10-11 Left guy rope above unfurled mizzen-sail is doublecut; Lees 11
  10-12 Large die flaw below ship at right; Lees 12
  10-13 Line from top of main-mast to flag does not touch yard of
           unfurled mizzen-sail; Lees 13

Cat.No.	Date	Description	VG	F	VF	EF	AU	UNC
PE10-10A		Top ball not separated	7.00	15.00	30.00	60.00	125.00	-
PE10-10B		Top ball is separated	60.00	100.00	150.00	-	-	-
PE10-11		Double cut guy rope	90.00	150.00	300.00	-	-	-
PE10-12		Flaw below ship	10.00	20.00	40.00	90.00	200.00	300.00
PE10-13		Line does not touch	350.00	500.00	-	-	-	-

CHART #2

NO MINT MARK

TWO GUYS FROM BOWSPRIT TO YARD OF UNFURLED SPRITSAIL; CURVED FLAG

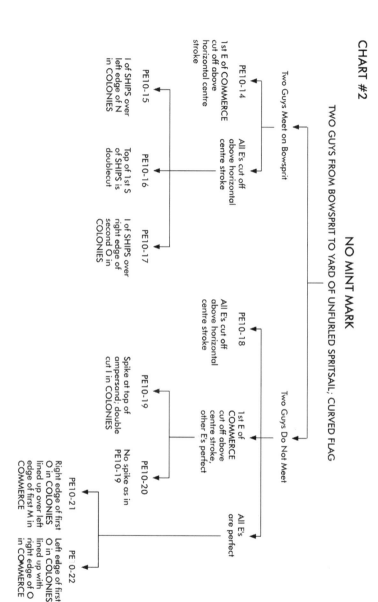

Two Guys Meet on Bowsprit

Two Guys Do Not Meet

PE10-14
1st E of COMMERCE
cut off above
horizontal centre
stroke

All E's cut off
above horizontal
centre stroke

PE10-18
1st E of
COMMERCE
cut off above
centre stroke,
other E's perfect

All E's cut off
above horizontal
centre stroke

All E's
are perfect

PE10-15
I of SHIPS over
left edge of N
in COLONIES

PE10-16
Top of 1st S
of SHIPS is
doublecut

PE10-17
I of SHIPS over
right edge of
second O in
COLONIES

PE10-19
Spike at top of
ampersand; double
cut I in COLONIES

PE10-20
No spike as in
PE10-19

PE10-21
Right edge of first
O in COLONIES
lined up over left
edge of first M in
COMMERCE

Left edge of first
O in COLONIES
lined up with
right edge of O
in COMMERCE

PE 0-22

PE10-14 to 17   *NO MINTMARK: BRITISH FLAG (CURVED)*
TWO GUYS MEET
BAR AMPERSAND

Composition: Copper
Weight: 4.7 to 5.2 gms
Diameter: 25.9 to 26.2 mm
Die Axis: ↑↑
Ref.Nos.: Br 997; W 212;
See Below

Two guys meet   Bar ampersand

Varieties: Obverse
  10-14 First "E" in COMMERCE cut off above horizontal centre stroke; Lees 14
  10-15 All "E's" cut off, first upright as in D15; Lees 15
  10-16 Top of first "S" of SHIPS is doublecut; first upright as in D16; Lees 16
  10-17 All "E's" cut off, first upright as in D17; Lees 17

Cat.No.	Date	Description	VG	F	VF	EF
PE10-14		First "E" cut off	20.00	40.00	75.00	150.00
PE10-15		All "E's" cut off (see Chart 2)	40.00	75.00	125.00	250.00
PE10-16		All "E's" cut off, first "S" doublecut	200.00	300.00	500.00	-
PE10-17		All "E's" cut off (see Chart 2)	30.00	50.00	100.00	175.00

PE10-18 to 22   *NO MINTMARK: BRITISH FLAG (CURVED)*
                  TWO GUYS DO NOT MEET
                  BAR AMPERSAND

Composition: Copper
Weight: 4.7 to 5.2 gms
Diameter: 25.9 to 26.2 mm
Die Axis: ↑↑
Ref.Nos.: Br 997; W 213;
        See Below

Two guys do not meet   Bar ampersand

Varieties: Obverse
10-18 All "E's" cut off above horizontal centre stroke; Lees 18
10-19 First "E" of COMMERCE cut off above centre stroke; Spike at top of ampersand; Lees 19
10-20 First "E" cut off above centre stroke, first upright as in D14; Lees 20
10-21 All "E's" are perfect, first upright as in D21; Lees 21
10-22 All "E's" perfect, first upright as in D17; Lees 22

Note: This group, PE10-18 to 22, is extremely rare in high grade.

Cat.No.	Date	Description	VG	F	VF	EF
PE10-18		All "E's" cut		Extremely Rare		
PE10-19		1st "E" cut off, spike on &	20.00	40.00	75.00	-
PE10-20		1st "E" cut off, no spike	200.00	300.00	500.00	-
PE10-21		All "E's" perfect	100.00	200.00	300.00	500.00
PE10-22		All "E's" perfect (see Chart 2)	J. Hoare Auction, October 1998, Lot 825, F+ $2,860.00			

CHART #3

SINGLE H MINT MARK

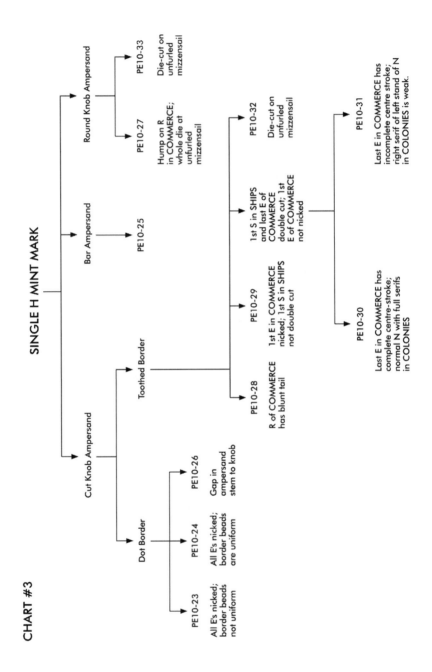

Cut Knob Ampersand

Dot Border

PE10-23
All E's nicked;
border beads
not uniform

PE10-24
All E's nicked;
border beads
are uniform

PE10-26
Gap in
ampersand
stem to knob

Toothed Border

PE10-28
R of COMMERCE
has blunt tail

PE10-29
1st E in COMMERCE
nicked; 1st S in SHIPS
not double cut

PE10-30
Last E in COMMERCE has
complete centre-stroke;
normal N with full serifs
in COLONIES

PE10-32
Die-cut on
unfurled
mizzensail

1st S in SHIPS
and last E of
COMMERCE
double cut; 1st
E of COMMERCE
not nicked

PE10-31
Last E in COMMERCE has
incomplete centre stroke;
right serif of left stand of N
in COLONIES is weak.

Bar Ampersand

PE10-25

Round Knob Ampersand

PE10-27
Hump on R
in COMMERCE;
whole die at
unfurled
mizzensail

PE10-33
Die-cut on
unfurled
mizzensail

PE10-23, 24 and 26

SINGLE H MINTMARK: BRITISH FLAG (STRAIGHT)
CUT KNOB AMPERSAND
DOT BORDER REVERSE

Composition: Copper
Weight: 5.0 to 5.1 gms
Diameter: 25.9 to 26.2 mm
Die Axis: ↑↑
Edge: Plain
Ref.Nos.: Br 997; See below

Single mint mark "H"

Cut knob ampersand

Varieties: Reverse
10-23 All "E's" nicked, Border beads not uniform; Lees 23; W 214
10-24 All "E's" nicked, Border beads are uniform; Lees 24; W 216
10-26 Gap in ampersand stem to knob; Lees 26: W 218

Cat.No.	Date	Description	VG	F	VF	EF	AU	UNC
PE10-23	(1835)	Border beads not uniform	8.00	20.00	35.00	75.00	150.00	-
PE10-24	(1835)	Border beads are uniform	20.00	40.00	75.00	150.00	-	-
PE10-26	(1835)	Gap in ampersand	5.00	10.00	20.00	45.00	100.00	-

PE10-25

SINGLE H MINTMARK: BRITISH FLAG (STRAIGHT)
BAR AMPERSAND

Composition: Copper
Weight: 5.0 to 5.1 gms
Diameter: 25.9 to 26.2 mm
Die Axis: ↑↑
Edge: Plain
Ref.Nos.: Br 997; Lees 25; W 215

Bar ampersand

Cat.No.	Date	Description	VG	F	VF	EF	AU	UNC
PE10-25	(1835)	Bar	J. Hoare Sale, October 1990, Lot 1379, EF+, $1,485.00					

PE10-27
and 33

SINGLE H MINTMARK: BRITISH FLAG (STRAIGHT)
ROUND KNOB AMPERSAND

Composition: Copper
Weight: 5.0 to 5.1 gms
Diameter: 25.9 to 26.2 mm
Die Axis: ↑↑
Edge: Plain
Ref.Nos.: Br 997; See below

Round knob ampersand

Varieties: Reverse
10-27 Hump on "R" in COMMERCE; Lees 27; W 217
10-33 Die-cut on unfurled mizzen-sail; Lees 33; W 222

Cat.No.	Date	Description	VG	F	VF	EF	AU	UNC
PE10-27	(1835)	Hump on "R" in COMMERCE	8.00	20.00	35.00	75.00	150.00	-
PE10-33	(1835)	Die-cut on unfurled mizzen-sail	J. Hoare Auction, October 1996, Lot 1498, VF+ $523.00					

PE10-28
to 32

SINGLE H MINTMARK: BRITISH FLAG (STRAIGHT)
CUT KNOB AMPERSAND
TOOTHED BORDER REVERSE

Composition: Copper
Weight: 5.0 to 5.2 gms
Diameter: 25.9 to 26.2 mm
Die Axis: ↑↑
Edge: Plain
Ref.Nos.: Br 997; See below

Cut knob ampersand

Varieties: Reverse
  10-28 Blunt tail to "R" of COMMERCE; Lees 28; W 218
  10-29 First "E" in COMMERCE nicked; First "S" in SHIPS not
       double-cut; Lees 29; W 219
  10-30 First "S" of SHIPS and last "E" of COMMERCE double-cut;
       Last "E" in COMMERCE has complete centre-stroke; Lees 30; W 220
  10-31 First "S" of SHIPS and last "E" of COMMERCE double-cut;
       Last "E" in COMMERCE incomplete centre-stroke; Lees 31; W 221
  10-32 Die-cut on unfurled mizzen-sail; Lees 32

Cat.No.	Date	Description	VG	F	VF	EF	AU	UNC
PE10-28	(1835)	Blunt tail to "R"	4.00	8.00	15.00	35.00	90.00	150.00
PE10-29	(1835)	First "E" in COMMERCE nicked	4.00	8.00	15.00	35.00	90.00	150.00
PE10-30	(1835)	Complete centrestroke "E"	3.00	6.00	12.00	20.00	60.00	125.00
PE10-31	(1835)	Incomplete centrestroke "E"	3.00	6.00	12.00	20.00	60.00	125.00
PE10-32	(1835)	Die-cut on mizzen-sail	4.00	8.00	15.00	30.00	65.00	135.00

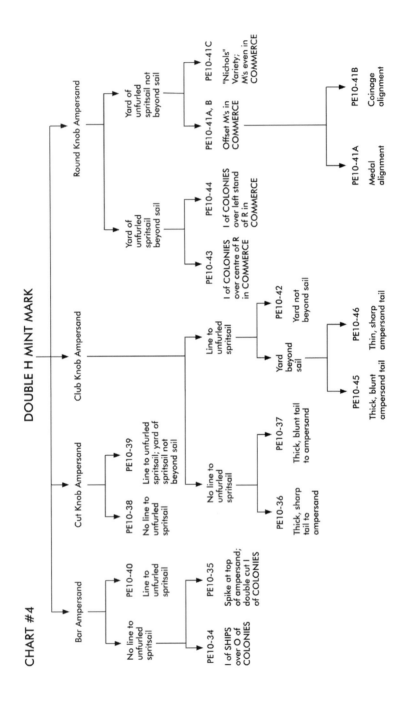

PE10-34, 35
and 40

DOUBLE H MINTMARK: BAR AMPERSAND

The Double "H" mint mark on this series of tokens is known to have been struck by Ralph Heaton & Sons of Birmingham. The dies with the "H" on the exergue line may have been acquired by the Heaton Mint from the successor of Thomas Halliday. Heaton, in order to distinguish his own strikings from the previous minters, may have punched the additional "H." A distinguishing feature of this group is the different varieties of the ampersand used on the reverse die.

Composition: Copper
Weight: 4.7 to 5.2 gms
Diameter: 25.9 to 26.2 mm
Die Axis: ↑↑ ↑↓
Edge: Plain
Ref.Nos.: Br 997; See below

Double mint mark "H"   Bar ampersand

Varieties: Obverse, reverse and die axis
10-34 No line to unfurled spritsail; "I" of SHIPS over "O" of COLONIES; Lees 34; W 223
10-35 No line to unfurled spritsail; Spike at top of ampersand; Double cut "I" of COLONIES; Lees 35; W 224
10-40 Line to unfurled sprit-sail; Lees 40; W 229

Cat.No.	Date	Description	VG	F	VF	EF	AU	UNC
PE10-34		No line to sail, "I" over "O"	10.00	20.00	35.00	75.00	150.00	-
PE10-35		No line to sail, double cut "I"	10.00	20.00	35.00	75.00	150.00	-
PE10-40		Line to unfurled spritsail	10.00	20.00	35.00	75.00	150.00	-

PE10-36, 37,   **DOUBLE H MINTMARK: CLUB KNOB AMPERSAND**
42, 45
and 46

Composition: Copper
Weight: 4.7 to 5.2 gms
Diameter: 25.9 to 26.2 mm
Die Axis: ↑↑ ↑↓
Edge: Plain
Ref.Nos.: Br 997; See below

Club knob ampersand

Varieties: Obverse, reverse and die axis
10-36 No line to unfurled sprit-sail; Thick, sharp tail on ampersand;
"C" of COLONIES over "C" of COMMERCE; Lees 36; W 225
10-37 No line to unfurled sprit-sail; Thick, blunt tail on ampersand;
"C" of COLONIES slightly to the right of "C" of COMMERCE; Lees 37;
W 226
10-42 Line to unfurled sprit-sail; Yard not beyond sail; Lees 42; W 231
10-45 Line to unfurled sprit-sail; Yard beyond sail; Thick, blunt tail; Lees 45; W 234
10-46 Line to unfurled sprit-sail; Yard beyond sail; Thin, sharp ampersand
tail; Lees 46

Cat.No.	Date	Description	VG	F	VF	EF	AU	UNC
PE10-36		Thick, sharp tail, "C" over "C"	7.00	15.00	30.00	65.00	125.00	-
PE10-37		Thick, blunt tail, "C" to right "C"	8.00	17.00	35.00	75.00	150.00	-
PE10-42		Yard not beyond sail	35.00	75.00	150.00	250.00	400.00	-
PE10-45		Thick, blunt tail, Yard beyond	10.00	20.00	35.00	75.00	150.00	-
PE10-46		Thin, sharp tail, Yard beyond	10.00	20.00	35.00	75.00	150.00	-

PE10-38
and 39

DOUBLE H MINTMARK: CUT KNOB AMPERSAND

Composition: Copper
Weight: 4.7 to 5.2 gms
Diameter: 25.9 to 26.2 mm
Die Axis: ↑↑ ↑↓
Edge: Plain
Ref.Nos.: Br 997; See below

Cut-knob ampersand

Varieties: Obverse, reverse and die axis
10-38 No line to unfurled sprit-sail; Lees 38; W 227
10-39 Line to unfurled sprit-sail; Yard of sprit-sail not beyond; Lees 39; W 228

Cat.No.	Date	Description	VG	F	VF	EF	AU	UNC
PE10-38		No line to sprit-sail	6.00	12.00	25.00	50.00	100.00	-
PE10-39		Line to sprit-sail	12.00	25.00	50.00	100.00	175.00	-

PE10-41, 43
and 44   *DOUBLE H MINTMARK: ROUND KNOB AMPERSAND*

Composition: Copper
Weight: 4.7 to 5.2 gms
Diameter: 25.9 to 26.2 mm
Die Axis: ↑↑ ↑↓
Edge: Plain
Ref.Nos.: Br 997; See below

Round-knob ampersand

Varieties: Reverse and die axis
10-41A Yard of unfurled sprit-sail not beyond sail; Offset "M's" in COMMERCE;
Medal; Lees 41
10-41B Yard of unfurled sprit-sail not beyond sail; Offset "M's" in COMMERCE;
Coinage; Lees 41
10-41C Yard of unfurled sprit-sail not beyond sail; Even "M's" in COMMERCE;
Medal; Lees 41a
10-43 Yard of unfurled sprit-sail beyond sail; Weakly struck "I" in SHIPS
and "L" in COLONIES; Lees 43
10-44 Yard of unfurled sprit-sail beyond sail; Well struck "I" and "L"; Lees 44

Cat.No.	Date	Description	VG	F	VF	EF	AU	UNC
PE10-41A		Not beyond sail, medal	15.00	30.00	60.00	125.00	-	-
PE10-41B		Not beyond sail, coinage	6.00	12.00	25.00	50.00	100.00	-
PE10-41C		Not beyond sail, even "M's"	20.00	35.00	75.00	150.00	-	-
PE10-43		Beyond sail, "I" over centre of "R"	20.00	35.00	75.00	150.00	-	-
PE10-44		Beyond sail, "I" over left stand of "R"	10.00	20.00	35.00	75.00	150.00	-

TOKENS OF NOVA SCOTIA

When Halifax was founded in 1749, the governor was instructed to enforce the use of sterling. This proved to be a difficult task for a number of reasons. The Spanish dollar, then rated at 4/4 sterling, was virtually unobtainable unless 5/- was offered. In consequence, the local government paid 5/- for dollars. This rate eventually became the standard for Nova Scotia but in 1753 an attempt to establish this standard by law was disallowed by the British government. Nevertheless, this value of Halifax currency remained in effect.

In 1787 a currency act was passed that rated the British crown at 5/6, the shilling at 1/3 and the sixpence at 6 1/2d, with the Spanish dollar at 5/-. As British silver was overrated, copper began to disappear from circulation.

Many years earlier there had been several shipments of British halfpennies and farthings but legislation of 1787 drove them out of use. Local businessmen took matters into their own hands about 1812 and miscellaneous English pieces often struck over the Bristol Guppy tokens made their way into circulation. Later, issues from 1814 to 1816, of distinctive local design, most being struck in England, began to appear. Due to their variation in weight, size, design and purity of copper, the government ordered their removal in 1817.

No new pieces were issued to replace them but in 1820 a halfpenny appeared. The government issued halfpennies in 1823 and halfpennies and pennies in 1824, 1840, 1843 and 1856.

Plans to issue silver 15d tokens were abandoned in 1823 when it was learned that such a move would constitute a breach of royal prerogative. Had such pieces been coined, local currency could have been depreciated by as much as 25 per cent.

BRETON CROSS REFERENCE TABLE FOR NOVA SCOTIA TOKENS

Breton No.	Charlton Cat. No.	Page No.	Breton No.	Charlton Cat. No.	Page No.
867	NS-1A,B	38, 39	885	NS-12	58
868	NS-2A	44	886	NS-25	71
869	NS-1C	40	887	NS-26	72
870	NS-2B	45	888	NS-23	69
870	NS-4	51	889	NS-27	72
871	NS-1D	41	890	NS-13	59
871	NS-3A, C, D	48, 49, 50	891	NS-14	60
872	NS-3B	49	892	NS-15A	61
873	N3-2C, D	46, 47	893	NS-15B	61
874	NS-1E ,F	42, 43	894	NS-24	70
875	NS-6	53	895	NS-28	73
876	NS-5	52	896	NS-16	62
879	NS-7A, B	54, 55	899	NS-17	62
880	NS-8	56	962	NS-20A, B	65, 66
881	NS-9	56	963	NS-19A, B	64
882	NS-10A	57	964	NS-18	63
883	NS-10B	57	965	NS-21	67
884	NS-11	58	967	NS-22	68

SEMI-REGAL TOKENS

THE THISTLE TOKENS OF 1823-1843

These tokens were issued under the terms of an act of the legislative assembly passed in 1817. The withdrawal of the private issues naturally resulted in a shortage of coppers by the early 1820s. When British coppers could not be obtained the provincial government ordered their own issues through the colonys agent Smith, Forsyth & Co. of Liverpool without the authority of the British Government.

The Act provided that the tokens should bear the British coat of arms on the obverse and the badge of Nova Scotia on the reverse. Michael Wallace, the colonial treasurer, instead ordered a coinage depicting a bust of George IV on the obverse and what was described in his words as A handsome thistle on the reverse.

NS-1
HALFPENNY TOKEN 1823-1843
— PROVINCE OF NOVA SCOTIA

NS-1A
GEORGE IV HALFPENNY TOKEN 1823
WITH HYPHEN IN NOVA SCOTIA

The halfpenny token of 1823 exhibits considerable variation in workmanship, indicating the dies were cut by more than one engraver. The weight was similar to that of the contemporary British halfpenny.

Composition: Copper
Weight: 9.3 to 9.6 gms
Diameter: 28.3 to 28.8 mm
Die Axis: ↑↓
Edge: Plain, engrailed
Ref.Nos.: Br 867; See below

Varieties: Obverse and edge

A1 Laureated with fifteen leaves; Engrailed; Co 251, 252aNS; W 351, 352
A2 Laureated with fifteen leaves, Plain edge
A3 Laureated with fourteen leaves; Engrailed; Co 252NS; W 353
A4 Laureated with thirteen leaves; Engrailed; Co 253NS; W 354
A5 Laureated with twelve leaves, two small and three large locks; Engrailed; Co 256NS; W 357
A6 Laureated with twelve leaves, five locks of equal size; Engrailed; Co 257NS; W 358

Cat.No.	Date	Description	VG	F	VF	EF	AU	UNC
NS-1A1	1823	Fifteen leaves	5.00	10.00	20.00	60.00	150.00	-
NS-1A2	1823	Fifteen leaves, Plain			Very Rare			
NS-1A3	1823	Fourteen leaves	5.00	10.00	20.00	60.00	150.00	-
NS-1A4	1823	Thirteen leaves	8.00	20.00	40.00	100.00	200.00	-
NS-1A5	1823	Twelve leaves, unequal locks	25.00	40.00	75.00	150.00	250.00	-
NS-1A6	1823	Twelve leaves, equal locks	50.00	100.00	150.00	200.00	350.00	-

NS-1B

GEORGE IV HALFPENNY TOKEN 1823
NO HYPHEN IN NOVA SCOTIA

Composition: Copper
Weight: 9.5 gms
Diameter: 28.3 to 28.8 mm
Die Axis: ↑↓
Edge: Engrailed
Ref.Nos.: Br 867; See below

Stem does not   Stem touches
touch top of 8   top of 8

Varieties: Reverse
B1 Stem does not touch top of 8; Co 254NS; W 355
B2 Stem touches top of 8; Co 255NS; W 356

Cat.No.	Date	Description	VG	F	VF	EF	AU	UNC
NS-1B1	1823	Does not touch top of 8	8.00	18.00	40.00	125.00	250.00	-
NS-1B2	1823	Touches top of 8	20.00	40.00	80.00	175.00	350.00	-

NS-1C   *GEORGE IV HALF PENNY TOKEN 1824*

In 1824 an issue of 118,636 halfpennies was struck at the request of the colonial government, with John Walker acting as agent.

Composition: Copper
Weight: 8.6 to 8.7 gms
Diameter: 28.4 to 28.9 mm
Die Axis: ↑↓
Edge: Engrailed
Ref.Nos.: Br 869; See below

Far "P"   Near "P"

Varieties: Obverse
    C1 "P" in PROVINCE far from bust; Co 258NS; W 359
    C2 "P" in PROVINCE near to bust; Co 259NS; W 360

Cat.No.	Date	Description	VG	F	VF	EF	AU	UNC
NS-1C1	1824	Far "P"	7.00	15.00	30.00	80.00	200.00	400.00
NS-1C2	1824	Near "P"	7.00	15.00	30.00	80.00	200.00	400.00

NS-1D   *GEORGE IV HALFPENNY TOKEN 1832*

The colonial government, through their agent John Bainbridge of London, placed an order for 800,000 halfpennies in 1832. The order requested tokens of similar design to those previously sent with a new date added. The manufacturer, following instructions, struck the tokens with an obverse bust of George IV and reverse dated 1832, even though William IV became king two years earlier.

Composition: Copper
Weight: 8.0 to 8.6 gms
Diameter: 28.0 to 28.3 mm
Die Axis: ↑↓
Edge: Engrailed
Ref.Nos.: Br 871; See below

Long left ribbon   Long right ribbon   Ribbons of equal length

Varieties: Obverse
  D1 Long left laurel ribbon; Co 265, 265aNS; W 366, 367
  D2 Long right laurel ribbon; Co 266 to 271NS; W 368 to 373
  D3 Laurel ribbons of equal length; Co 272 to 276NS; W 374 to 380

Variations: Eight other variations exist with only very minor obverse and reverse differences.

Cat.No.	Date	Description	VG	F	VF	EF	AU	UNC
NS-1D1	1832	Long left ribbon	4.00	8.00	15.00	50.00	125.00	200.00
NS-1D2	1832	Long right ribbon	3.00	7.00	15.00	40.00	125.00	200.00
NS-1D3	1832	Equal ribbons	3.00	5.00	10.00	35.00	100.00	175.00

NS-1E   *VICTORIA HALFPENNY TOKEN 1840*

An issue of some 300,000 halfpennies was released in 1840 and another issue of the same amount in 1843. As with earlier issues, these coins were circulated without Imperial authority. Some of the 1840 halfpennies are on slightly broader and thinner flans and are struck in a style suggesting that more than one engraver produced the dies. Crude cast forgeries exist.

Composition: Copper
Weight: 8.6 to 8.8 gms
Diameter: 28.0 to 28.8 mm
Die Axis: ↑↓
Edge: Plain, engrailed
Ref.Nos.: Br 874; See below

1840 Large "0"   1840 Medium "0"   1840 Small "0"

Varieties: Reverse and edge
  E1 Large "0" in date; Co 290, 291NS; W 394, 395
  E2 Medium "0" in date; Co 292 to 294NS; W 396 to 398
  E3 Small "0" in date, Plain; Co 296NS; W 400
  E4 Small "0" in date, Engrailed; Co 295 to 298NS; W 399 to 402

Variations: Minor variations exist for these four tokens. These have resulted from touching up the dies. Differences occur in the form and shape of the mouth and nose, where the coil is attached to the chignon on the obverse and with the size of the thistle on the reverse.

Cat.No.	Date	Description	VG	F	VF	EF	AU	UNC
NS-1E1	1840	Large "0" in date	7.00	15.00	40.00	100.00	200.00	-
NS-1E2	1840	Medium "0" in date	5.00	10.00	25.00	50.00	150.00	-
NS-1E3	1840	Small "0" in date, Plain			Very Rare			
NS-1E4	1840	Small "0" in date, Engrailed	6.00	12.00	35.00	80.00	200.00	-

NS-1F *VICTORIA HALFPENNY TOKEN 1843*

Composition: Copper
Weight: 8.6 gms
Diameter: 28.0 to 28.8 mm
Die Axis: ↑↓
Edge: Engrailed
Ref.Nos.: Br 874; See below

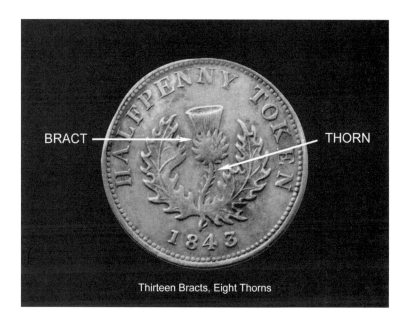

BRACT   THORN

Thirteen Bracts, Eight Thorns

Varieties: Reverse
F1 Fifteen Bracts, Ten Thorns; Co 302, 303NS; W 406, 407
F2 Fourteen Bracts, Fourteen Thorns; Co 299, 301NS; W 403, 405
F3 Thirteen Bracts, Fourteen Thorns; Co 300NS; W 404
F4 Thirteen Bracts, Nine Thorns; Co 304, 304a, 305NS; W 408 to 410
F5 Thirteen Bracts, Eight Thorns; Co 306 to 308 NS; W 411 to 413

Cat.No.	Date	Description	VG	F	VF	EF	AU	UNC
NS-1F1	1843	Fifteen Ten	5.00	10.00	30.00	75.00	150.00	250.00
NS-1F2	1843	Fourteen-Fourteen	5.00	10.00	30.00	75.00	150.00	250.00
NS-1F3	1843	Thirteen-Fourteen	8.00	18.00	45.00	100.00	200.00	350.00
NS-1F4	1843	Thirteen-Nine	12.00	30.00	60.00	125.00	225.00	350.00
NS-1F5	1843	Thirteen-Eight	5.00	10.00	30.00	75.00	150.00	250.00

NS-2   *ONE PENNY TOKEN 1824-1843 —*
PROVINCE OF NOVA SCOTIA

NS-2A   *GEORGE IV PENNY TOKEN 1824*

John Walker & Co. of Birmingham acting as agent for the colonial government procured the striking of the 1824 penny. The mintage of this issue was 217,776.

Composition: Copper
Weight: 17.0 to 17.4 gms
Diameter: 34.1 to 34.3 mm
Die Axis: ↑↓
Edge: Engrailed
Ref.Nos.: Br 868; See below

Three thin top leaves   Three thick top leaves

Varieties: Obverse
A1 Laurel with four top leaves; Co 260NS; W 361
A2 Laurel with three thin top leaves;
Reverse has double cut "K" in TOKEN; Co 261NS; W 362
A3 Laurel with three thick top leaves;
"E" in PROVINCE is defective; Co 262NS; W 363
A4 Laurel with top leaf touching "F" in OF; Co 263NS; W 364
A5 Mule of A4 obverse and A2 reverse; Co 264NS; W 365

Cat.No.	Date	Description	VG	F	VF	EF	AU	UNC
NS-2A1	1824	Four top leaves	35.00	60.00	100.00	150.00	300.00	-
NS-2A2	1824	Three thin top leaves	6.00	15.00	30.00	80.00	200.00	-
NS-2A3	1824	Three thick top leaves	12.00	25.00	50.00	100.00	225.00	-
NS-2A4	1824	Top leaf touching "F"	6.00	15.00	30.00	70.00	200.00	-
NS-2A5	1824	Mule	15.00	30.00	70.00	125.00	250.00	-

NS-2B   *GEORGE IV PENNY TOKEN 1832*

The mintage of 1832 was 200,000 pennies.

Composition: Copper
Weight: 17.0 to 17.1 gms
Diameter: 33.7 to 34.3 mm
Die Axis: ↑↓
Edge: Engrailed
Ref.Nos.: Br 870; See below

Bow far from head   Bow near head   Bow touching head

Varieties: Obverse
B1 Bow far from head; Ribbon ends square, equal length; Co 284NS; W 381
B2 Bow near head; Left ribbon longer; Co 285NS; W 382
B3 Bow touching head; Co 285aNS; W 383

Cat.No.	Date	Description	VG	F	VF	EF	AU	UNC
NS-2B1	1832	Bow far from head	6.00	12.00	25.00	50.00	125.00	300.00
NS-2B2	1832	Bow near head	6.00	12.00	25.00	50.00	125.00	300.00
NS-2B3	1832	Bow touching head	25.00	40.00	85.00	110.00	200.00	400.00

NS-2C   *VICTORIA ONE PENNY TOKEN 1840*

This issue consisted of 150,000 pennies. Crude cast forgeries are known.

Composition: Copper
Weight: 16.4 to 17.2 gms
Diameter: 34.0 to 34.5 mm
Die Axis: ↑↓
Edge: Engrailed
Ref.Nos.: Br 873; See below

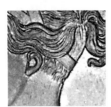

Seven fringes   Five fringes   Four fringes

Varieties: Obverse and die axis
C1 Seven fringes of hair; Co 311NS; W 417
C2 Five fringes of hair; Co 309NS; W 415
C3 Four fringes of hair; Co 310NS; W 416

Cat.No.	Date	Description	VG	F	VF	EF	AU	UNC
NS-2C1	1840	Seven fringes of hair	5.00	10.00	25.00	75.00	200.00	400.00
NS-2C2	1840	Five fringes of hair	12.00	25.00	45.00	100.00	225.00	450.00
NS-2C3	1840	Four fringes of hair, Medal	30.00	50.00	85.00	175.00	350.00	-

NS-2D   *VICTORIA ONE PENNY TOKEN 1843*

In 1843 another 150,000 pennies were issued.

Composition: Copper
Weight: 16.4 to 17.2 gms
Diameter: 34.3 to 34.5 mm
Die Axis: ↑↓
Edge: Engrailed
Ref.Nos.: Br 873; See below

Varieties: Obverse
D1 Seven fringes of hair; Co 314NS; W 420
D2 Four fringes of hair; Co 312NS; W 418
D3 Four fringes of hair, 3 over 0; Co 313NS; W 419

Cat.No.	Date	Description	VG	F	VF	EF	AU	UNC
NS-2D1	1843	Seven fringes of hair	7.00	15.00	30.00	75.00	150.00	350.00
NS-2D2	1843	Four finges of hair	15.00	25.00	60.00	100.00	200.00	400.00
NS-2D3	1843	Four fringes of hair; 3 over 0	80.00	100.00	250.00	-	-	-

THE COUNTERFEIT THISTLE TOKENS OF 1832

About 1835, large numbers of counterfeit tokens were struck in Montreal and shipped to Nova Scotia. They were sent to Saint John, New Brunswick, taken across the Bay of Fundy, and used to pay fishermen of the outports of Nova Scotia for their catch. In spite of their light weight and impure metal, the false coins were freely used because Nova Scotia was once again short of copper by 1835.

Both halfpenny and penny tokens were counterfeited and cast forgeries exist of each denomination.

NS-3
HALFPENNY TOKEN 1832—
PROVINCE OF NOVA SCOTIA-

NS-3A
GEORGE IV HALFPENNY TOKEN 1832

Composition: Copper, brass
Weight: 6.2 to 7.5 gms
Diameter: 28.2 to 28.6 mm
Die Axis: ↑↓
Edge: Engrailed, Plain
Ref.Nos.: Br 871; See below

Hair touches "F"   Hair touches "O"

Varieties: Obverse and composition
  A1 Upper lock of hair touches "F" of OF, Copper; Co 277NS; W 386
  A2 Upper lock of hair touches "O" of OF, Copper; Co 278NS; W 384
  A3 Upper lock of hair touches "O" of OF, Brass; Co 279NS; W 384

Cat.No.	Date	Description	VG	F	VF	EF	AU	UNC
NS-3A1	1832	Hair touches "F"	12.00	25.00	60.00	150.00	-	-
NS-3A2	1832	Hair touches "O"; Copper	5.00	15.00	35.00	110.00	-	-
NS-3A3	1832	Hair touches "O"; Brass	10.00	20.00	60.00	150.00	-	-

NS-3B   *GEORGE IV HALFPENNY TOKEN 1382 (DATE ERROR)*

Composition: Copper
Weight: 6.9 to 7.0 gms
Diameter: 28.2 mm
Die Axis: ↑↓
Edge: Engrailed
Ref.Nos.: Br 872; Co 280NS;
W 385

1382

Cat.No.	Date	Description	G	VG	F	VF
NS-3B	1382	J. Hoare Auction, February 1995, Lot 1775, VF - $2,200.00				

NS-3C   *GEORGE IV HALFPENNY TOKEN 1832 (CORRECTED DATE)*

The die used to strike the error date was corrected by sinking an 83 over the 38. The overdating is most noticeable on the 8 over 3. The date at first glance appears to read 1882. The left leaf has sixteen notches.

  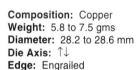

Composition: Copper
Weight: 5.8 to 7.5 gms
Diameter: 28.2 to 28.6 mm
Die Axis: ↑↓
Edge: Engrailed
Ref.Nos.: Br 871; Co 281NS;
W 388

"83" over the "38"
Pointed stem

Cat.No.	Date	Description	VG	F	VF	EF	AU	UNC
NS-3C	1832		12.00	30.00	90.00	200.00	-	-

NS-3D   *GEORGE IV HALFPENNY TOKEN 1832*

Composition: Copper
Weight: 5.8 to 7.5 gms
Diameter: 28.2 to 28.6 mm
Die Axis: ↑↓
Edge: Engrailed
Ref.Nos.: Br 871; See below

Fifteen points,
square stem

Thirteen points,
square stem

Varieties: Reverse
D1 Left leaf has fifteen notches; Co 282NS; W 389
D2 Left leaf has thirteen notches; Co 283NS; W 390

Cat.No.	Date	Description	VG	F	VF	EF	AU	UNC
NS-3D1	1832	Fifteen notches	5.00	15.00	35.00	80.00	225.00	-
NS-3D2	1832	Thirteen notches	10.00	20.00	45.00	110.00	300.00	-

NS-4

ONE PENNY TOKEN 1832 —
PROVINCE OF NOVA SCOTIA

Pennies were counterfeited at the same time and brought to Nova Scotia from the same source as the halfpennies. As with the halfpennies, the counterfeits were a variable copper/brass composition of inferior fabric. Cast forgeries are known.

Composition: Copper, brass
Weight: 12.8 to 16.6 gms
Diameter: 33.5 to 34.0 mm
Die Axis: ↑↓
Edge: Engrailed
Ref.Nos.: Br 870; See below

Left top one   Flat top one   Right top one

Varieties: Reverse and composition
  A1 Flat top one; Co 286NS; W 391
  A2 Left top one; Copper; Co 287NS; W 392
  A3 Left top one; Brass; Co 288NS; W 392
  A4 Right top one; Copper; Co 289NS; W 393
  A5 Right top one; Brass; Co 289aNS; W 393

Cat.No.	Date	Description	VG	F	VF	EF	UNC
NS-4A1	1832	Flat top one; Copper	5.00	10.00	35.00	90.00	-
NS-4A2	1832	Left top one; Copper	5.00	10.00	35.00	90.00	-
NS-4A3	1832	Left top one; Brass	15.00	30.00	75.00	150.00	-
NS-4A4	1832	Right top one; Copper	8.00	15.00	45.00	100.00	-
NS-4A5	1832	Right top one; Brass	15.00	30.00	75.00	150.00	-

VICTORIA MAYFLOWER COINAGE

From 1823 to 1843 the government of Nova Scotia imported a series of unauthorized pence and halfpence which collectors have come to call the Thistle series.

In the 1850s, when the British Government was more willing to allow local coinages in the colonies, the Nova Scotia government officially applied for and received a true coinage, its first. These pence and halfpence feature a sprig of mayflower, now the provincial flower, on their reverses and are considered by many to be among the most beautiful coins ever made for North America. They were produced at Heatons Mint in Birmingham (without the H mint mark), but the master tools were made by the Royal Mint.

NS-5   *PROVINCE OF NOVA SCOTIA HALFPENNY TOKEN*
— 1856 VICTORIA D:G:BRITANNIAR:REG:F:D:

This denomination is represented by two obverse varieties, one with and the other without the designers initials (L.C.W.) below the queen's bust. It appears that the variety with" L.C.W." was struck only as a proof. Proofs of the No L.C.W. variety were also struck; it is most interesting that a rare variety of the No L.C.W. proof was struck from a blundered die where an "A" punch was used to repair a defective "V" in PROVINCE in one of the reverse dies, resulting in PRO∀INCE.

A scarce variety of the circulation strikes of the No L.C.W. halfpenny was coined in brass instead of the normal bronze. It can be recognized by its lighter yellow colour.

Composition: Bronze, brass
Weight: 7.6 to 7.9 gms
Diameter: 27.7 to 27.8 mm
Die Axis: ↑↑
Edge: Plain
Ref.Nos.: Br 876; See below

Varieties: Composition
     A1 Bronze; Co 315NS; W 421
     A2 Brass; Co 316NS; W 421

Variations: Patterns exist with "L.C.W." under truncation. Minor variations exist in the obverse legend, W 422.

Cat.No.	Date	Description	VG	F	VF	EF	AU	UNC
NS-5A1	1856	Bronze	4.00	6.00	12.00	40.00	100.00	250.00
NS-5A2	1856	Brass	100.00	150.00	300.00	450.00	-	-

NS-6 ***PROVINCE OF NOVA SCOTIA ONE PENNY TOKEN***
— 1856 VICTORIA D:G:BRITANNIAR:REG:F:D:

Composition: Bronze
Weight: 15.1 gms
Diameter: 33.3 mm
Die Axis: ↑↑
Edge: Plain
Ref.Nos.: Br 875, Co 318NS,
Co 319NS, W 423

With "LCW"   Without "LCW"

Varieties: Obverse
  A1 With initials "L.C.W." under truncation; Co 319NS
  A2 Without initials "L.C.W."; Co 318NS

Note: Cast counterfeits exist in brass and copper.

Cat.No.	Date	Description	VG	F	VF	EF	AU	UNC
NS-6A1	1856	"L.C.W."	5.00	10.00	20.00	50.00	125.00	300.00
NS-6A2	1856	No "L.C.W."	6.00	12.00	25.00	60.00	150.00	350.00

PRIVATE TOKENS

Most of the local tokens were designed, engraved and struck by Thomas Halliday. The halfpenny inscribed "For The Convenience of Trade" is the work of William Stephen Mossop. A few pieces were struck locally and are very crude in fabric. Most of these are very rare as their crudity made the majority of them unacceptable.

NS-7   *BRITANNIA 1814— BROKE HALIFAX NOVA SCOTIA*

Captain P.B. Vere Broke, Commander of the H.M.S. Shannon, captured the U.S.S. Chesapeake in 1813 in what was the first British naval victory of the War of 1812. The 'Prize of War' was towed to Halifax and sold. The following year this token was struck honouring both Captain Broke and his victory.

Die preparation was very poor resulting in tokens of inferior quality.

NS-7A   *LONG BUST OF CAPTAIN BROKE*

Composition: Copper
Weight: 7.7 to 8.1 gms
Diameter: 26.8 to 27.1 mm
Die Axis: ↑↓
Edge: Reeded
Ref.Nos.: Br 879; Co 325NS;
         W 313

Cat.No.	Date	Description	VG	F	VF	EF	AU	UNC
NS-7A	1814		7.00	15.00	50.00	125.00	225.00	-

NS-7B   *SHORT BUST OF CAPTAIN BROKE*

Composition: Copper
Weight: 7.1 to 7.3 gms
Diameter: 26.6 to 26.8 mm
Die Axis: ↑↑
Edge: Reeded
Ref.Nos.: Br 879; See below

Three buttons   Four buttons

Mainmast left   Mainmast even
ship lower

Varieties: Obverse and reverse
Four buttons — heavy die break through "OTI" in SCOTIA
Three buttons — "S" almost touches "C" in SCOTIA
B1 Four coat buttons, Two ships of equal height; Co 326NS; W 314
B2 Four coat buttons, Left ship smaller; Co 329NS; W 317
B3 Three coat buttons, Two ships of equal height; Co 328NS; W 316
B4 Three coat buttons, Left ship smaller; Co 327NS; W 315

Cat.No.	Date	Description	VG	F	VF	EF	AU	UNC
NS-7B1	1814	Four buttons, Equal height	20.00	30.00	60.00	110.00	225.00	-
NS-7B2	1814	Four buttons, Left ship small	40.00	80.00	150.00	250.00	400.00	-
NS-7B3	1814	Three buttons, Equal height	25.00	35.00	65.00	125.00	250.00	-
NS-7B4	1814	Three buttons, Left ship smaller	5.00	10.00	30.00	80.00	175.00	-

NS-8   *FOR THE CONVENIENCE OF TRADE—*
1814 HALF PENNY TOKEN

Possibly issued by Carritt and Alport of Halifax, this halfpenny token was struck by William Stephen Mossop of Dublin. The reverse is from an anonymous Irish token of 1804.

Composition: Copper, brass
Weight: 5.4 to 5.8 gms
Diameter: 27.7 to 28.8 mm
Die Axis: ↑↓
Edge: Plain
Ref.Nos.: Br 880; See below

Varieties: Composition
    A1 Copper; Co 333NS; W 318
    A2 Brass; Co 334NS; W 318

Cat.No.	Date	Description	G	VG	F	VF	EF	AU	UNC
NS-8A1	1814	Copper	15.00	25.00	50.00	100.00	225.00	400.00	-
NS-8A2	1814	Brass				Very Rare			

NS-9   *PAYABLE BY CARRITT & ALPORT HALIFAX—*
1814 HALF PENNY TOKEN

The Carritt & Alport tokens were produced by either Peter Wyon or Thomas Wyon the Elder. The reverse type is that of the Gloucester and Berkeley Canal Company halfpenny of 1797, designed by Thomas Wyon the Elder and struck by Peter Kempson, with new inscriptions.

Two different patterns exist of this token. One pattern is in the Bank of Canada Collection (CO 332NS; W 320) and shows the bowsprit pointing directly to the "O" in ALPORT and the other is in the British Museum (W 320a) which shows the obverse legend starting at 9 o'clock and finishing at 3 o'clock. Both are extremely rare.

Composition: Copper
Weight: 6.9 to 7.1 gms
Diameter: 28.8 mm to 28.9 mm
Die Axis: ↑↓
Edge: Engrailed
Ref.Nos.: Br 881; Co 331NS;
    W 319

Variations: There are two minor edge variations in the engrailing, northwest to southeast and northeast to southwest, the latter being the rarer of the two.

Cat.No.	Date	Description	VG	F	VF	EF	AU	UNC
NS-9	1814		12.00	25.00	65.00	150.00	300.00	-

NS-10   *PAYABLE BY HOSTERMAN & ETTER HALIFAX*—

Hosterman & Etter were jewellers in Halifax. Their halfpennies are believed to have been produced by Thomas Halliday. Their workmanship is somewhat inferior to what Halliday usually produced, suggesting the halfpennies may have been the work of an apprentice.

NS-10A   *- 1814 HALFPENNY TOKEN*

Composition: Copper
Weight: 8.4 to 8.5 gms
Diameter: 27.7 to 27.8 mm
Die Axis: ↑↑
Edge: Plain
Ref.Nos.: Br 882; Co 335NS; W 321

Cat.No.	Date	Description	VG	F	VF	EF	AU	UNC
NS-10A	1814	Inner circle	6.00	15.00	30.00	65.00	150.00	300.00

NS-10B   *— 1815 HALFPENNY TOKEN*

Composition: Copper
Weight: 5.7 to 6.5 gms
Diameter: 25.8 to 26.0 mm
Die Axis: ↑↓
Edge: Plain
Ref.Nos.: Br 883; See below

Sashed windows   Plain windows

Varieties: Reverse
   B1 All windows are sashed; Co 336NS; W 322
   B2 Not all windows sashed; Co 337NS: W 323

Note: Contemporary forgeries exist in brass and are very rare.

Cat.No.	Date	Description	VG	F	VF	EF	AU	UNC
NS-10B1	1815	Sashed windows	5.00	10.00	30.00	65.00	125.00	250.00
NS-10B2	1815	Plain windows	7.00	15.00	35.00	80.00	150.00	300.00

NS-11 ***HALFPENNY TOKEN NOVA SCOTIA —***
1815 STARR & SHANNON HALIFAX

Starr and Shannon were hardware merchants whose halfpennies were well-known in colonial Nova Scotia. The tokens were produced by John Sheriff of Liverpool, who cut the dies. The designs were probably a suggestion of the issuer.

Composition: Copper
Weight: Thin Flan: 5.8 to 6.0 gms
Thick Flan: 7.2 to 7.8 gms
Thickness: Thin Flan: 1.2 mm
Thick Flan: 1.6 mm
Diameter: 27.7 to 28.1 mm
Die Axis: ↑↓
Edge: Plain, engrailed
Ref.Nos.: Br 884; See below

Varieties: Weight and edge
A1 Thin flan, Plain edge; Co 339NS; W 340
A2 Thick flan, Plain edge
A3 Thick flan, Engrailed edge; Co 338NS; W 340

Cat.No.	Date	Description	VG	F	VF	EF	AU	UNC
NS-11A1	1815	Thin flan, Plain edge	5.00	12.00	30.00	75.00	150.00	300.00
NS-11A2	1815	Thick flan, Plain edge			Rare			
NS-11A3	1815	Thick flan, Engrailed edge	5.00	12.00	30.00	75.00	150.00	300.00

NS-12 ***HALFPENNY TOKEN NOVA SCOTIA —***
1815 COMMERCIAL CHANGE

The obverse die of this token was muled, in worn condition, with an Upper Canada sloop obverse to produce UC-8.

Composition: Copper
Weight: 5.8 gms
Diameter: 27.9 to 28.0 mm
Die Axis: ↑↓
Edge: Plain
Ref.Nos.: Br 885; Co 340NS
W 341

Cat.No.	Date	Description	VG	F	VF	EF	AU	UNC
NS-12	1815		6.00	15.00	40.00	110.00	250.00	-

NS-13   *PAYABLE BY MILES W. WHITE HALIFAX NS —*
1815 HALFPENNY TOKEN

Miles W. White's halfpenny of 1815 was issued in Halifax. White, a hardware merchant in business between 1812 and 1822, issued tokens of full weight, a practice seldom followed by his contemporaries.

Composition: Copper
Weight: 7.3 to 7.9 gms.
Diameter: 27.7 to 28.1 mm
Die Axis: ↑↑ ↑↓ ↑→
Edge: Plain
Ref.Nos.: Br 890; See below

Varieties: Die axis
  A1 Medal; Co 341NS; W 342
  A2 Ninety degrees east; Co 341NS; W 342
  A3 Coinage; Co 341NS; W 342

Cat.No.	Date	Description	VG	F	VF	EF	AU	UNC
NS-13A1	1815	Medal	5.00	15.00	45.00	100.00	225.00	350.00
NS-13A2	1815	Ninety degrees	8.00	20.00	60.00	125.00	275.00	400.00
NS-13A3	1815	Coinage	5.00	15.00	45.00	100.00	225.00	350.00

NS-14   *PAYABLE BY JOHN ALEXR. BARRY HALIFAX—*
              1815 HALFPENNY TOKEN

John Alexander Barry was a Halifax dry goods merchant who also enjoyed a very stormy political career. He issued a halfpenny token in 1815, the work of Thomas Halliday and his apprentices.

Composition: Copper, brass
Weight: 6.2 to 6.7 gms
Diameter: 25.9 to 26.1 mm
Die Axis: ↑↑ ↑↓
Edge: Plain
Ref.Nos.: Br 891; See below

Large Bust	Slender Bust	Small bust
Eight Leaves	Seven Leaves	

Varieties: Obverse, composition and die axis
     A1 Large bust, Laurel 8 leaves; Co 342NS; W 326
     A2 Slender bust, Laurel 7 leaves, Copper; Co 343NS; W 327
     A3 Slender bust, Laurel 7 leaves, Brass; Co 344NS; W 327
     A4 Small bust, Laurel 7 leaves, Medal; Co 345NS; W 328
     A5 Small bust, Laurel 7 leaves, Coinage; Co 345NS; W 328

Cat.No.	Date	Description	VG	F	VF	EF	AU	UNC
NS-14A1	1815	Large bust, 8 leaves	6.00	15.00	45.00	90.00	150.00	250.00
NS-14A2	1815	Slender bust, 7 leaves, Copper	8.00	18.00	50.00	100.00	175.00	300.00
NS-14A3	1815	Slender bust, 7 leaves, Brass			Very Rare			
NS-14A4	1815	Small bust, 7 leaves, Medal	5.00	12.00	35.00	75.00	125.00	225.00
NS-14A5	1815	Small bust, 7 leaves, Coinage	5.00	12.00	35.00	75.00	125.00	225.00

NS-15 — *1816 WHOLESALE & RETAIL HARDWARE STORE*

William Anderson and Samuel Black operated a hardware store in Halifax and issued their own tokens in 1816.

NS-15A   *HALIFAX NOVA SCOTIA —*

Composition: Copper
Weight: 5.5 to 6.0 gms
Diameter: 25.5 to 25.6 mm
Die Axis: ↑↑
Edge: Plain
Ref.Nos.: Br 892; Co 358NS;
       W 343

Cat.No.	Date	Description	VG	F	VF	EF	AU	UNC
NS-15A	1816		15.00	25.00	50.00	125.00	225.00	350.00

NS-15B   *PAYABLE AT W.A. & S. BLACK'S HALIFAX N.S. —*

Composition: Copper
Weight: 5.6 to 6.0 gms
Diameter: 25.5 to 25.6 mm
Die Axis: ↑↑
Edge: Plain
Ref.Nos.: Br 893; Co 357NS;
       W 344

Cat.No.	Date	Description	VG	F	VF	EF	AU	UNC
NS-15B	1816		10.00	20.00	45.00	90.00	200.00	300.00

NS-16   *PAYABLE AT THE STORE OF J BROWN—*
NEMO ME IMPUNE LACESSIT

John Brown, a Halifax dry goods merchant, issued a halfpenny token with an obverse showing the national motto and flower of Scotland.

Composition: Copper
Weight: 6.1 to 6.5 gms
Diameter: 25.9 to 26.0 mm
Die Axis: ↑↑
Edge: Reeded
Ref.Nos.: Br 896; Co 359NS;
           W 338

Cat.No.	Date	Description	VG	F	VF	EF	AU	UNC
NS-16			5.00	10.00	30.00	75.00	150.00	300.00

NS-17   *W.L. WHITES HALIFAX HOUSE HALIFAX CHEAP*
DRY GOODS STORE— ONE FARTHING PAYABLE AT
WHITES HALIFAX HOUSE HALIFAX

The one farthing token of W. L. White may have been issued after 1830. The fabric of this token is similar to that of tokens issued in Ireland during the coin shortage of 1830-1840.

Composition: Brass, bronze
Weight: 3.9 to 4.2 gms
Diameter: 21.8 to 21.9 mm
Die Axis: ↑↓
Edge: Plain
Ref.Nos.: Br 899; See below

Varieties: Reverse
     A1 The "D" of DRY is to the left of the "C" of CHEAP; Co 362NS; W 349
     A2 The "D" of DRY is directly under the "C" of CHEAP; Co 363NS; W 350

Cat.No.	Date	Description	VG	F	VF	EF	AU	UNC
NS-17A1	(1830)	"D" left of "C"	20.00	35.00	60.00	100.00	175.00	250.00
NS-17A2	(1830)	"D" under "C"	J. Hoare Auction, June 1995, Lot 700, EF - $3,450.00					

ANONYMOUS TOKENS

TRADE AND NAVIGATION TOKENS 1812-1838

The economy of the Atlantic colonies, especially Nova Scotia, was based on trade and navigation. These tokens bear a slogan very popular in that colony.

The reverse inscription clearly reflects the mistrust of paper money. Most of the population consisted of immigrants from the United States who had come to Nova Scotia to ensure their status as British subjects following the recent American independence. In addition, they had suffered the collapse of various issues of paper money in the original colonies prior to 1783.

SEATED COMMERCE TOKENS 1812-1813

The Seated Commerce Issues of 1812 and 1813 were designed by Thomas Halliday and struck over the existing tokens of Samuel Guppy of Bristol. The farthing token was imported into Halifax by a merchant named Haliburton.

NS-18 *PURE COPPER PREFERABLE TO PAPER ONE FARTHING—*
1813 TRADE & NAVIGATION

Composition: Copper
Weight: 3.6 gms
Diameter: 22.1 to 22.6 mm
Die Axis: ↑↑, ↑↓
Edge: Plain (Engrailed on original)
Ref.Nos.: Br 964; Co 5NS; W 301

Cat.No.	Date	Description	VG	F	VF	EF	AU	UNC
NS-18	1813		25.00	40.00	60.00	100.00	175.00	300.00

NS-19
PURE COPPER PREFERABLE TO PAPER HALF PENNY TOKEN—

NS-19A
— 1812 TRADE & NAVIGATION

Composition: Copper
Weight: 8.8 to 9.2 gms
Diameter: 27.6 to 27.8 mm
Die Axis: ↑↑
Edge: Engrailed
Ref.Nos.: Br 963; Co 6NS; W 302

Variations: Some of these pieces are struck over Guppy halfpennies, on thick and thin flans.

Cat.No.	Date	Description	VG	F	VF	EF	AU	UNC
NS-19A	1812		5.00	10.00	20.00	60.00	125.00	250.00

NS-19B
— 1813 TRADE & NAVIGATION

Composition: Copper
Weight: 8.8 to 9.5 gms
Diameter: 27.4 to 27.8 mm
Die Axis: ↑↑
Edge: Plain, engrailed
Ref.Nos.: Br 963; See below

Varieties: Edge
  B1 Plain; Co 7NS; W 302
  B2 Engrailed; Co 7NS; W 302

Variations: Specimens exist on thick and thin flans.

Cat.No.	Date	Description	VG	F	VF	EF	AU	UNC
NS-19B1	1813	Plain	20.00	35.00	70.00	150.00	250.00	350.00
NS-19B2	1813	Engrailed	7.00	15.00	25.00	60.00	125.00	250.00

NS-20 *PURE COPPER PREFERABLE TO PAPER ONE PENNY TOKEN —*

Pennies dated 1812 are reported to have been sold at auction on several occasions in the past and references to their existence in private collections have appeared from time to time. Nevertheless, no specimen has been seen recently. Courteau did not list the date of 1812 in his monograph on non-local tokens. However, a specimen dated 1812 is listed in the catalogue of the sale of his collection in 1944. The "H" mintmark appears on obverse lower right.

NS-20A — *1813 TRADE & NAVIGATION*

Composition: Copper
Weight: 18.8 to 20.3 gms
Diameter: 33.5 to 33.8 mm
Die Axis: ↑↑
Edge: Engrailed
Ref.Nos.: Br 962; See below

Varieties: Obverse, reverse legend

A1 Large letters, bar ampersand, period in reverse legend high; Co 8NS; W 304

A2 Large letters, bar ampersand, drapery touches water; Co 9NS; W 305

A3 Large letters, bar ampersand, leaves on ground; Co 10NS; W 306

A4 Small letters, round knob ampersand; C0 11NS; W 307

Cat.No.	Date	Description	VG	F	VF	EF	AU	UNC
NS-20A1	1813	High period	10.00	20.00	40.00	90.00	125.00	250.00
NS-20A2	1813	Drapery	30.00	50.00	100.00	250.00	350.00	-
NS-20A3	1813	Leaves	20.00	35.00	55.00	100.00	150.00	300.00
NS-20A4	1813	Round knob	15.00	25.00	40.00	90.00	125.00	250.00

NS-20B   *— 1814 TRADE & NAVIGATION*

The one penny token issues of 1814 were struck over many years in imitation of Thomas Hallidays designs. They are of inferior workmanship and lighter in weight than previous issues and the letter "H" does not appear on the obverse.

Composition: Copper
Weight: 15.6 to 17.6 gms
Diameter: 33.5 to 33.8 mm
Die Axis: ↑↑ ↑↓
Edge: Engrailed, plain
Ref.Nos.: Br 962; See below

1 over 0   Plain 1

Varieties: Obverse, edge and die axis
    B1 Dated 1814, 1 over 0, Engrailed, Medal; Co 12NS; W 308
    B2 Dated 1814, 1 over 0, Engrailed, Coinage; Co 12NS; W 308
    B3 Dated 1814, Plain, Coinage; Co 13NS; W 309

Cat.No.	Date	Description	VG	F	VF	EF	AU	UNC
NS-20B1	1814	1 over 0, Engrailed, Medal	25.00	55.00	80.00	175.00	300.00	-
NS-20B2	1814	1 over 0, Engrailed, Coinage	25.00	55.00	80.00	175.00	300.00	-
NS-20B3	1814	Plain, Coinage	20.00	30.00	50.00	100.00	200.00	-

NS-21   *PURE COPPER PREFERABLE TO PAPER*
                    HALF PENNY TOKEN—
                1813 TRADE & NAVIGATION

Composition: Copper
Weight: 7.5 to 7.9 gms
Diameter: 27.3 to 27.4 mm
Die Axis: ↑↓
Edge: Plain, engrailed
Ref.Nos.: Br 965; See below

Large Central Wave   Third Wave From Right Tallest   Round Right Wave

Varieties: Obverse and edge
   A1 Large central wave, Plain; Co 15NL; W 310
   A2 Large central wave, Engrailed; Co 15NL; W 310
   A3 Third wave from right the tallest; Co 16NL; W 311
   A4 Round right wave, Flaw at date; Co 17NL; W 312

Cat.No.	Date	Description	VG	F	VF	EF	AU	UNC
NS-21A1	1813	Large wave, Plain	7.00	15.00	35.00	85.00	175.00	300.00
NS-21A2	1813	Large wave, Engrailed	4.00	8.00	20.00	60.00	150.00	250.00
NS-21A3	1813	Third wave tallest	4.00	8.00	20.00	60.00	150.00	250.00
NS-21A4	1813	Round wave, Date flaw	5.00	10.00	25.00	75.00	175.00	275.00

NS-22   *TRADE & NAVIGATION 1838—*
                  PURE COPPER PREFERABLE TO PAPER

This one penny token was issued for use in British Guiana (modern Guyana). The reverse die is the same as that used to strike the obverse NS-20B except the date was changed from 1814 to 1838. Also, it was struck over a number of years and comes with varying states of reverse rust spots. It is doubtful, even though the legends on this token are similar to ones circulating in Nova Scotia, that it was imported in quantities. It is more likely that collectors imported the token towards the end of the century.

Penny tokens did circulate in Nova Scotia during and after 1838. Trade between the Province and the West Indies was of great importance.

Composition: Copper
Weight: 17.6 to 17.7 gms
Diameter: 33.2 to 33.3 mm
Die Axis: ↑↓
Edge: Plain
Ref.Nos.: Br 967; Co 14NS;
             W B8

Cat.No.	Date	Description	VG	F	VF	EF	AU	UNC
NS-22	1838		5.00	10.00	20.00	50.00	100.00	200.00

NS-23   *SUCCESS TO NAVIGATION & TRADE —*
                  1815 HALFPENNY TOKEN

Nova Scotia depended on shipbuilding and trade with Great Britain, the United States and the West Indies and tokens issued bearing these legends were readily accepted. Thomas Halliday is credited with the design.

Composition: Copper
Weight: 7.4 to 8.4 gms
Diameter: 27.6 to 27.7 mm
Die Axis: ↑↓
Edge: Plain
Ref.Nos.: Br 888; See below

Large flag

Small flag

2 top leaves

1 top leaf

Varieties: Obverse and reverse
A1 Laurel with 2 top leaves, Large flag; Co 353NS; W 329
A2 Laurel with 2 top leaves, Small flag; Co 354NS; W 330
A3 Laurel with 1 top leaf, Large flag; Co 355NS; W 331
A4 Laurel with 1 top leaf, Small flag; Co 356NS; W 332

Cat.No.	Date	Description	VG	F	VF	EF	AU	UNC
NS-23A1	1815	2 top leaves, L flag	8.00	20.00	40.00	100.00	150.00	250.00
NS-23A2	1815	2 top leaves, S flag	6.00	15.00	50.00	125.00	225.00	400.00
NS-23A3	1815	1 top leaf, L flag	20.00	35.00	75.00	125.00	225.00	400.00
NS-23A4	1815	1 top leaf, S flag	5.00	12.00	35.00	90.00	125.00	200.00

NS-24

ONE HALFPENNY TOKEN 1820 —
TRADE & NAVIGATION

In 1817 the government ordered the removal of all halfpenny tokens from circulation by the year 1820. Nothing was done immediately to provide an alternate supply of copper and attempts began once more to do so privately. In 1820, an anonymous halfpenny of Irish design appeared with legends that link it with Nova Scotia. The detail on this token is very poor.

Composition: Copper, brass
Weight: 6.0 to 7.0 gms
Diameter: 27.4 to 27.6 mm
Die Axis: ↑↓
Edge: Plain
Ref.Nos.: Br 894; See below

Varieties: Composition
A1 Copper; Co 3NL; W 348
A2 Brass; Co 3NL; W 348

Cat.No.	Date	Description	VG	F	VF	EF	AU	UNC
NS-24A1	1820	Copper	7.00	15.00	50.00	100.00	200.00	-
NS-24A2	1820	Brass	10.00	20.00	60.00	125.00	250.00	-

GENUINE BRITISH COPPER TOKENS

Issued anonymously at the peak of private token circulation in Nova Scotia, this token stressed honest copper content and competed against the numerous forgeries which threatened confidence in copper currency. The first token is the work of Thomas Halliday while the others are attributed to his apprentices.

NS-25 *GENUINE BRITISH COPPER — 1815 HALF PENNY TOKEN*

Composition: Copper
Weight: 6.1 to 7.1 gms
Diameter: 25.8 to 26.1mm
Die Axis: ↑↓
Edge: Plain
Ref.Nos.: Br 886; See below

| Large Bust
8 Laurel leaves | Slender Bust
7 Laurel leaves | Slender Bust
6 Laurel leaves | Small Bust
7 Laurel leaves |

Varieties: Obverse
A1 Large bust, Laurel 8 leaves; Co 347NS; W 333
A2 Slender bust, Laurel 7 leaves; Co 348NS; W 334
A3 Slender bust, Laurel 6 leaves; Co 349NS; W 335
A4 Small bust, Laurel 7 leaves; Co 350NS; W 336

Cat.No.	Date	Description	VG	F	VF	EF	AU	UNC
NS-25A1	1815	Large bust, 8 leaves	6.00	12.00	25.00	65.00	175.00	-
NS-25A2	1815	Slender bust, 7 leaves	5.00	10.00	20.00	60.00	150.00	-
NS-25A3	1815	Slender bust, 6 leaves	7.00	15.00	30.00	90.00	200.00	-
NS-25A4	1815	Small bust, 7 leaves	25.00	45.00	80.00	150.00	325.00	-

NS-26   *HALFPENNY — 1815 GENUINE BRITISH COPPER*

Composition: Copper
Weight: 5.5 to 5.8 gms
Diameter: 28.1 to 28.2 mm
Die Axis: ↑↓
Edge: Reeded, engrailed
Ref.Nos.: Br 887; See below

Varieties: Edge
    A1   Reeded; Co 346NS; W 337
    A2   Engrailed; Co 346NS; W 337

Cat.No.	Date	Description	VG	F	VF	EF	AU	UNC
NS-26A1	1815	Reeded	25.00	40.00	75.00	150.00	250.00	-
NS-26A2	1815	Engrailed	25.00	40.00	75.00	150.00	250.00	-

NS-27   *HALIFAX — 1815 HALFPENNY TOKEN*

The Halifax halfpenny token of 1815 is an anonymous issue possibly designed and produced by Thomas Halliday.

Composition: Copper
Weight: 6.2 to 6.5 gms
Diameter: 25.9 to 26.0 mm
Die Axis: ↑↑ ↑↓
Edge: Reeded
Ref.Nos.: Br 889; See below

No hair between
two top leaves

Hair between
top leaves

Varieties: Obverse and die axis
    A1   No hair between two top leaves, Medal; Co 351NS; W 324
    A2   No hair between two top leaves, Coinage; Co 351NS; W 324
    A3   Hair between top leaves, Medal; Co 352NS; W 325

Cat.No.	Date	Description	VG	F	VF	EF	AU	UNC
NS-27A1	1815	No hair, Medal	6.00	12.00	35.00	75.00	125.00	300.00
NS-27A2	1815	No hair, Coinage	6.00	12.00	35.00	75.00	125.00	300.00
NS-27A3	1815	Hair, Medal	7.00	15.00	45.00	125.00	200.00	400.00

NS-28   *HALFPENNY TOKEN—*
           NOVA SCOTIA AND NEW BRUNSWICK SUCCESS

This piece was issued anonymously, the inscription clearly favouring the union of Nova Scotia and New Brunswick.

Composition: Copper, brass
Weight: 5.7 to 6.0 gms
Diameter: 27.9 to 28.1 mm
Die Axis: ↑↑
Edge: Reeded
Ref.Nos.: Br 895; Co 330NS;
           W 339

Note: Cast forgeries are known to exist.

Cat.No.	Date	Description	VG	F	VF	EF	AU	UNC
NS-28A	Undated	Copper	25.00	50.00	90.00	175.00	350.00	500.00
NS-28B	Undated	Brass	50.00	125.00	250.00	-	-	-

NS-29   *1816—HALF PENNY TOKEN*

This Canadian colonial token discovered in 1988 was the first significant find in over 75 years. The piece bears a striking resemblance in design and workmanship to other tokens attributed to Halifax, Nova Scotia. The JB Script/Warehouse Token(BL-31), the W. A. & S. Black Token of 1816 (NS-15), and the Anchor and H Token (NS-30) can all be linked to this token either through their obverse or reverse designs.

Composition: Copper
Weight: 4.9 gms
Diameter: 26.0 mm
Die Axis: ↑↓
Edge: Plain
Ref.Nos.: Previously unlisted

Cat.No.	Date	Description	VG	F	VF	EF	AU	UNC
NS-29	1816		J. Hoare Auction, Fall 1988, Lot 1124, $6,500.00					

NS-30   *H—1816 HALFPENNY TOKEN*

This token was moved from the Anonymous and Miscellaneous section to the Nova Scotia section due to the discovery piece NS-29. That token certainly confirms the Anchor and H as being struck for the Halifax, Nova Scotia trade.

Composition: Copper
Weight: 3.84 to 5.0 gms
Diameter: 26.0 to 26.5 mm
Die Axis: ↑↑
Edge: Plain
Ref.Nos.: Co 35NL; W 154

Note: The Courteau sale of 1944 listed a specimen in very poor condition dated 1814. This piece was probably a worn 1816 piece.

Cat.No.	Date	Description	VG	F	VF	EF	AU	UNC
NS-30	1816	J. Hoare Auction, February 1999, Lot 695, F - $1,870.00						

IMITATIONS OF NOVA SCOTIA TOKENS "BLACKSMITH STYLE"

For listings of imitations of Nova Scotia tokens see page 217 and 218, BL-29 to BL-31.

TOKENS OF NEW BRUNSWICK

Unlike most other pre-Confederation British American colonies, New Brunswick did not have a serious deficiency of copper currency until the late 1830s and early 1840s.

In 1843 the provincial government obtained copper pence and halfpence from Boulton and Watt, a private mint in England. These pieces are technically tokens because they were obtained without the permission of the British government.

In 1853 a further issue of copper was required. The adoption of a decimal currency was being seriously considered but was still up in the air. Therefore, it was decided to order more coppers in the pounds/shillings/pence system. It was at this time that the British government learned of the "spurious" token issue of 1843. The master tools for the 1843 coppers were sent to the Royal Mint in London where the reverses were modified by substituting CURRENCY for TOKEN. Totally new obverses were prepared.

The actual striking of the 1854 coinage took place at Heaton's Mint in Birmingham, but the coins lack the familiar "H" mint mark.

BRETON CROSS REFERENCE TABLE FOR NEW BRUNSWICK TOKENS

Breton No.	Charlton Cat. No.	Page No.	Breton No.	Charlton Cat. No.	Page No.
909	NB-2A	78	912	NB-1B	77
910	NB-1A	77	913	NB-4	79
911	NB-2B	78	914	NB-3	79

SEMI-REGAL TOKENS AND 1854 COINAGE

VICTORIA FRIGATE TOKENS 1843-1854

TOKEN COINAGE OF 1843

After an unsuccessful attempt to circulate British copper the New Brunswick government decided to issue penny and halfpenny tokens and entered into an arrangement with William Hammond of Halifax to procure a coinage. The Colonial Office, on being informed of the plan, was displeased and ordered the New Brunswick authorities to cease at once from proceeding with the proposed coinage. The New Brunswick government then terminated the arrangement with Hammond and informed the Colonial Office. Evidently either Hammond or the New Brunswick government secretly went ahead with the plans as a coinage of pennies and halfpennies was struck by Boulton & Watt and surreptitiously reached circulation. The matrices and punches were sent to New Brunswick after the coinage was completed. It was not known in England that the colonial government had ignored the wishes of the Colonial Office until 1853, when the succeeding governor was corresponding with London concerning the coinage of 1854, and learned to his surprise that there was not supposed to be a coinage of 1843.

COINAGE OF 1854

Under the provisions of the Currency Act of 1852, the government of New Brunswick in June 1853 sought permission to issue a coinage of copper pennies and halfpennies. Imperial sanction was obtained for this coinage and the matrices and punches of the coinage of 1843 were sent to England. The coinage was struck by Ralph Heaton & Co. of Birmingham from modified reverse dies and new obverse dies. The dies were prepared by Leonard Charles Wyon, who used for the obverse the head punch of the contemporary English coinage. These head punches were of the attractive young head designed by William Wyon. The coinage was secured through the agency of John Sears of Saint John and comprised 480,000 pennies and 480,000 halfpennies.

New Brunswick adopted the decimal system in 1860 and had no further need for the pennies and halfpennies of 1843 and 1854.

Pending the arrival of the bronze cents of 1861, New Brunswick imported Canadian cents of 1858 and 1859 to provide a temporary stock of cents. Canada, having difficulty in getting these coins into circulation, were glad to ship some $5,000 worth to New Brunswick. They circulated side by side with the New Brunswick cents of 1861 and 1864 until and after Confederation in 1867.

THE RIGGING OF "H.M.S. NEW BRUNSWICK"

The reverse of the coins shows a frigate with sails furled. There are numerous variations in the rigging of the ship giving rise to many varieties. These varieties are a result of different dies and the polishing as well as retouching of older dies.

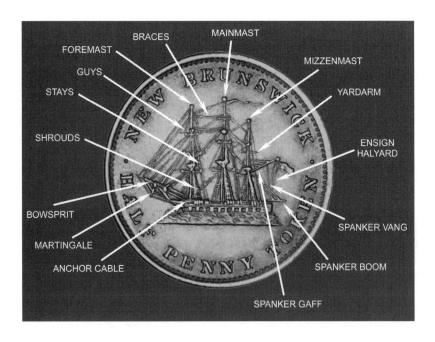

NB-1   *NEW BRUNSWICK HALF PENNY TOKEN/CURRENCY—*
1843/1854 VICTORIA DEI GRATIA REGINA

NB-1A   *HALF PENNY TOKEN 1843*

Composition: Copper
Weight: 8.6 to 9.0 gms
Diameter: 28.2 to 28.3 mm
Die Axis: ↑↑
Edge: Plain
Ref.Nos.: Br 910; See below

Three Complete Groups   Two Complete Groups

Varieties: Obverse
     A1 Three complete groupings of Heraldic flowers in the queen's diadem;
          Co 13 to 20NB; W 458 to 464
     A2 Two complete groupings of Heraldic flowers, the third group has the
          thistle missing; Co 3 to 12NB; W 453 to 457

Variations: New dies or the retouching of old dies has resulted in minor variations
            in the ship's rigging.

Cat.No.	Date	Description	VG	F	VF	EF	AU	UNC
NB-1A1	1843	Three complete groups	4.00	10.00	20.00	50.00	150.00	300.00
NB-1A2	1843	Two complete groups	4.00	10.00	20.00	50.00	150.00	300.00

NB-1B   *HALF PENNY CURRENCY 1854*

Composition: Copper
Weight: 7.6 to 8.2 gms
Diameter: 28.2 to 28.4 mm
Die Axis: ↑↑
Edge: Plain
Ref.Nos.: Br 912; Co 30 to 41NB;
             W 469 to 473

Variations: New dies or the retouching of old dies has resulted in minor variations.
            On the obverse the placement of the 4 in the date varies. On the
            reverse there are four, five or six lines in the mizzenmast.

Cat.No.	Date	Description	VG	F	VF	EF	AU	UNC
NB-1B	1854		4.00	10.00	20.00	50.00	150.00	300.00

NB-2 *NEW BRUNSWICK ONE PENNY TOKEN/CURRENCY—*
1843/1854 VICTORIA DEI GRATIA REGINA

NB-2A   **ONE PENNY TOKEN 1843**

Composition: Copper
Weight: 17.6 gms
Diameter: 34.1 mm
Die Axis: ↑↑
Edge: Plain
Ref.Nos.: Br 909;
        Co 21 to 29NB
        W 465 to 468

Variations: Minor variations exist due to new dies and the retouching of old dies. Reverse variations exist with two, three or four stays to the right of the mizzenmast.

Cat.No.	Date	Description	VG	F	VF	EF	AU	UNC
NB-2A	1843		5.00	12.00	25.00	75.00	150.00	350.00

NB-2B   ***ONE PENNY CURRENCY— 1854***

Composition: Copper
Weight: 15.1 to 15.8 gms
Diameter: 34.2 mm
Die Axis: ↑↑
Edge: Plain
Ref.Nos.: Br 911; See below

Complete Ensign   Incomplete Ensign

Variations: Reverse
    B1 Complete ensign; Co 42 to 45NB; W 474
    B2 Incomplete ensign; Co 46 to 52NB; W 475

Variations: New dies or the retouching of old dies has created minor variations.

Cat.No.	Date	Description	VG	F	VF	EF	AU	UNC
NB-2B1	1854	Complete ensign	5.00	10.00	25.00	75.00	175.00	400.00
NB-2B2	1854	Incomplete ensign	5.00	10.00	25.00	75.00	175.00	400.00

PRIVATE TOKENS

NB-3 *F. MCDERMOTT IMPORTER OF ENGLISH, FRENCH &*
GERMAN FANCY GOODS, KING—ST., SAINT JOHN, N.B. -
DEPOSITORY OF ARTS

This token is a business card and it is doubtful that it circulated as a halfpenny token.

Composition: Copper, brass
Weight: 5.5 gms
Diameter: 23.9 mm
Die Axis: ↑↑
Edge: Plain
Ref.Nos.: Br 914; Co 2NB

Cat.No.	Date	Description	VG	F	VF	EF	AU	UNC
NB-3	(1845)		300.00	350.00	450.00	650.00	1,000.00	-

ANONYMOUS TOKENS

NB-4 *ST. JOHN NEW BRUNSWICK HALF PENNY TOKEN—*
FOR PUBLIC ACCOMMODATION

In New Brunswick the need for currency was never very great because trade across the Bay of Fundy constantly brought Nova Scotia copper into the city and the colony. The first local tokens appeared about 1830.

Composition: Copper
Weight: 5.2 to 5.4 gms
Diameter: 27.9 to 28.1 mm
Die Axis: ↑↑
Edge: Reeded
Ref.Nos.: Br 913; Co 1NB;
W 451

Variations: Minor varieties exist due to rusty dies.

Cat.No.	Date	Description	VG	F	VF	EF	AU	UNC
NB-4	(1830s)		6.00	12.00	30.00	75.00	175.00	-

NB-5   *ST. JOHN'S N.B. HALFPENNY TOKEN—*

This extremely rare piece was not known to Breton or Courteau. This token was refused because the city named was rendered as St. John's which is the capital of Newfoundland, not New Brunswick. Minter and Issuer are unknown.

Photograph not available

Composition: Copper
Weight: 6.2 gms
Diameter: 28.0 to 28.2 mm
Die Axis: ↑↑
Edge: Reeded
Ref.Nos.: W 452

Cat.No.	Date	Description	VG	F	VF	EF	AU	UNC
NB-5	(1830s)			Only two known, Extremely Rare				

TOKENS OF LOWER CANADA

New France was in British hands in 1759 and was renamed the Colony of Quebec when British possession was confirmed in 1763. Its territory included the valley of the St. Lawrence River and the Great Lakes Region south to the Ohio River. After 1783 the Great Lakes, the upper St. Lawrence, the forty-fifth parallel and the water-shed between the St. Lawrence and its drainage basins became the southern boundary. In 1791 the colony was divided into Upper and Lower Canada.

English and American merchants entered the colony soon after 1760 and influenced the local currency. The shortage of coined money was beginning to result in the use of cut money in Montreal. Spanish dollars were being cut into aliquot parts and circulated without any countermarking of value. The practice was short-lived for the Ordinance of 1764 expressly forbade it. As time passed the colony became very short of coinage.

After 1764 the cut legal money used in Montreal was taken out of circulation. Some French coins circulated and were augmented by small amounts of English coin. The only legal copper pieces were English and Irish halfpennies which were in insufficient and dwindling supply. After 1797 some shipments of halfpennies of George III were sent from England but not enough for the needs of trade. After 1812 anonymous tokens were imported from England and Ireland. Very soon afterward locally-made tokens appeared. At first the weight was good but in later years it steadily decreased. After 1825 many pieces in circulation were brass. A law forbidding the further import of private tokens was passed in 1825. It was so loosely worded that it was possible to import tokens dated before 1825.

By 1837 anything the size of a halfpenny would pass for a token and the banks, in the absence of action by the government, refused to take any of the so-called copper currency except by weight and issued their own tokens.

BRETON CROSS REFERENCE TABLE FOR LOWER CANADA

Breton No.	Charlton Cat. No.	Page No.	Breton No.	Charlton Cat. No.	Page No.
520	LC-1	83	680	LC-21	109
521	LC-9A-D	94, 95, 96	681	LC-22C	110
522	LC-8A-D	91, 92, 93	682	LC-22B	110
523	LC-11A-B	99	683	LC-25	113
524	LC-10A-B	97, 98	684	LC-41	128
525	LC-11C	100	685	LC-30C	118
531	LC-12	100	686	LC-30D	118
532	LC-13A-B	101	687	LC-32A	120
533	LC-14	102	688	LC-31A	119
561	LC-15	102	689	LC-43	129
562	LC-16	103	690	LC-44	130
563	LC-17	104	691	LC-27	114
564	LC-18	104	692	LC-32B	120
565	LC-19	105	693	LC-31B	119
670	LC-45	130	694	LC-31C	119
671	LC-20	106	695	LC-29A	115
672	LC-6	90	696	LC-29B	115
673	LC-7	90	697	LC-29E	116
674	LC-40	127	698	LC-30A	117
675	LC-23A	111	699	LC-30B	117
676	LC-22A	110	700	LC-29C	115
677	LC-23B	111	701	LC-29D	116
678	LC-23C	111	702	LC-28	114
679	LC-24	112	703	LC-30F	118

BRETON CROSS REFERENCE TABLE FOR LOWER CANADA

Breton No.	Charlton Cat. No.	Page No.	Breton No.	Charlton Cat. No.	Page No.
704	LC-33A	121	960	LC-46	131
705	LC-33C1	121	960	LC-48A,B	138, 139
706	LC-34	122	961	LC-48C	140
707	LC-35	123	982	LC-49	140
708	LC-36	123	989	LC-52	142
709	LC-37	124	990	LC-51	141
710	LC-38A	125	991	LC-50	141
711	LC-39	126	992	LC-53A	142
712	LC-38B	125	994	LC-54A-D	143, 144, 145
713	LC-2	84, 85	1001	LC-55	146
714	LC-3	86, 87	1002	LC-58A,B	149, 150
715	LC-5	89	1004	LC-56A-B	146, 147
716	LC-4	88	1005	LC-56C	147
957	LC-47A	132	1007	LC-59A-B	151
958	LC-47B-C	133, 134	1011	LC-57	148
959	LC-47D	137	1012	LC-60A-F	152 to 157

SEMI-REGAL TOKENS

MAGDALEN ISLAND TOKEN

The Magdalen Islands were settled by the French who gave them the name Isles de la Madeleine. During the French period the islands were governed from Acadia and after 1713 from Isle Royale. The islands were ceded to Great Britain in 1763 and placed under the control of the government of Newfoundland. When the Quebec Act was passed in 1774 the Magdalen Islands were transferred to the colony of Quebec. In 1791 they were included in the territory of Lower Canada.

After the American Revolution the islands were granted to Sir Isaac Coffin as a reward for loyalty during the war. He visited the islands only once, in 1815, with the intent to set up a feudal barony.

One of the privileges claimed by Sir Isaac Coffin was the right to coin money. He ordered a coinage of pennies from Sir Edward Thomason of Birmingham and planned to issue halfpennies as well. He was reputed to have taken a coining press and dies with him in order to set up a mint on the islands.

The coin was struck by Sir Edward Thomason from dies probably cut by Thomas Halliday who produced several dies for Sir Edward.

After a long history of bad relations, the government of Canada bought out the descendants of Sir Isaac Coffin and resold the land to its inhabitants.

LC-1   *SUCCESS TO THE FISHERY ONE PENNY —*
1815 MAGDALEN ISLAND TOKEN

Composition: Copper
Weight: 17.1 to 17.4 gms
Diameter: 33.4 to 33.6 mm
Die Axis: ↑↑
Edge: Engrailed
Ref.Nos: Br 520; W 500

Variations: Examples struck on extra thick planchets of 23.5 grams are known but are very rare.

Cat.No.	Date	Description	G	VG	F	VF	EF	AU	UNC
LC-1	1815		20.00	40.00	90.00	225.00	550.00	1,250.00	1,750.00

BANK OF MONTREAL UN SOUS TOKENS

About 1835, the Bank of Montreal's directors, alarmed at the state of the copper currency, began to issue tokens. In 1836 the bank was permitted to issue sous inscribed with its name. They probably were struck in Birmingham by Boulton and Watt. Their fabric suggests this but nothing has yet been discovered to confirm their place of manufacture. The engravers, in their ignorance of the French language, cut the value to read UN SOUS. Thus the Bank of Montreal sous of both issues carried the value erroneously rendered in the plural. The misspelling was not a hindrance to their circulation but an easy means of identification when numerous imitations were later imported.

LC-2   *BANK TOKEN MONTREAL UN SOUS — TRADE & AGRICULTURE LOWER CANADA*

This Bank of Montreal token is linked to the Birmingham issue of the bouquet sou LC-37 by the common obverse LC-2A5.

Varieties: Obverse

Composition: Copper
Weight: 7.9 to 9.0 gms
Diameter: 27.4 to 28.2 mm
Die Axis: ↑↑
Edge: Plain
Ref.Nos.: Br 713; See below

A1 The stem of the lower left rosebud is nearly straight with a leaf hanging from a short stem; Co 8B; W 678

A2 The stem of the lower left rosebud curves upward with a leaf with no stem; Co 9B; W 679

Cat.No.	Date	Description	VG	F	VF	EF	AU	UNC
LC-2A1	(1835)	Straight stem	8.00	15.00	30.00	60.00	125.00	250.00
LC-2A2	(1835)	Curved stem	4.00	8.00	20.00	40.00	100.00	200.00

LC-2 cont'd overleaf

LC-2 *BANK TOKEN MONTREAL UN SOUS—*
TRADE & AGRICULTURE LOWER CANADA

A3 The bow on the bouquet is doubled; Co 10B; W 680

A4 The stem of the lower left rosebud is broken; Co 11B; W 681

A5 The stem of the lower left rosebud does not connect directly to the bouquet;
Co 12B; W 682

A6 The stem of the lower left rosebud originates from a leaf, large ampersand;
Co 13B; W 683

Cat.No.	Date	Description	VG	F	VF	EF	AU	UNC
LC-2A3	(1835)	Double bow	4.00	8.00	20.00	60.00	125.00	250.00
LC-2A4	(1835)	Broken stem	5.00	10.00	20.00	60.00	135.00	270.00
LC-2A5	(1835)	Short stem	5.00	10.00	20.00	60.00	135.00	270.00
LC-2A6	(1835)	Large ampersand	10.00	20.00	35.00	75.00	150.00	300.00

LC-3
BANK OF MONTREAL TOKEN UN SOUS —
TRADE AND AGRICULTURE LOWER CANADA

Varieties: Obverse and reverse

Composition: Copper
Weight: 7.9 to 8.6 gms
Diameter: 27.5 to 28.2 mm
Die Axis: ↑↑
Edge: Plain
Ref.Nos.: Br 714; See below

A1 Obverse: Similar to LC-2A1
    Reverse: The first palm leaf under the second letter "S" in SOUS is forked with the left side much shorter that the right one. The three cherry leaves opposite "NK" of BANK have the centre leaf with a short slender stem; Co 3B; W 684

A2 Obverse: The lower left rosebud has a long curved stem
    Reverse: The first palm leaf is forked with sides of equal length. The centre leaf of the group has no stem; Co 4B; W 685

Cat.No.	Date	Description	VG	F	VF	EF	AU	UNC
LC-3A1	(1836)	Short stem	4.00	8.00	20.00	75.00	150.00	300.00
LC-3A2	(1836)	No stem	4.00	8.00	20.00	75.00	150.00	300.00

LC-3 cont'd overleaf

LC-3   ***BANK OF MONTREAL TOKEN UN SOUS —***
TRADE & AGRICULTURE LOWER CANADA

A3 Obverse: Similar to LC-2A2
Reverse: The first palm leaf is forked with the left side short and slender.
All three leaves of the group have clear stems; Co 5B; W 686

A4 Obverse: Similar to LC-2A3
Reverse: The first palm leaf is forked but the two sides are curved. The
group of leaves has only one stem; Co 6B; W 687

A5 Obverse: The lower left rosebud has no stem
Reverse: The group of leaves has three slender long stems; Co 7B; W 688

Cat.No.	Date	Description	VG	F	VF	EF	AU	UNC
LC-3A3	(1836)	Three short stems	4.00	8.00	15.00	60.00	175.00	300.00
LC-3A4	(1836)	One stem	5.00	10.00	20.00	75.00	175.00	300.00
LC-3A5	(1836)	Three long stems	5.00	10.00	20.00	75.00	175.00	300.00

LA BANQUE DU PEUPLE UN SOU TOKENS

The first sous of La Banque du Peuple were issued in 1837. The bank was organized in 1835 by reformists (including French and Scottish) excluded by the conservatives or Tories who dominated the Bank of Montreal's board of directors. La Banque du Peuple never applied for a charter until 1843 and operated as a private bank, Viger, DeWitt & Cie., until it finally was granted a charter in 1844. The bank remained in business until 1895.

The first sou is the famous Rebellion Sou struck by Jean-Marie Arnault, who also cut the dies from designs suggested by the bank. It received its popular name because it was believed that the star and liberty cap were added to the design at the instigation of bank personnel who sympathized with the rebel cause. All the bank's directors were real or suspected rebels late in 1837. (Warrants were issued for their arrest).

The bank also participated in the issue of the 1837 "Habitant" tokens. Later in 1838 the bank was permitted to issue more sous, and released an issue of bouquet sous struck in Belleville, New Jersey. The dies were cut by John Gibbs, a senior partner of the firm.

LC-4 *BANQUE DU PEUPLE MONTREAL UN SOU —*
AGRICULTURE & COMMERCE BAS-CANADA

ARNAULT ISSUE (1837)

Composition: Copper
Weight: 8.3 to 9.0 gms
Diameter: 27.2 to 28.1 mm
Die Axis: ↑↑ ↑↓
Edge: Reeded
Ref.Nos.: Br 716; Co 14B;
W 689

Varieties: Die Axis
A1 Medal
A2 Coinage

Cat.No.	Date	Description	VG	F	VF	EF	AU	UNC
LC-4A1	(1837)	Medal	10.00	20.00	45.00	100.00	200.00	300.00
LC-4A2	(1837)	Coinage	6.00	15.00	40.00	90.00	150.00	250.00

LC-5   *BANQUE DU PEUPLE MONTREAL UN SOU —*
            AGRICULTURE AND COMMERCE BAS CANADA

BELLEVILLE ISSUE (1838)

Composition: Copper, brass
Weight: 8.1 to 9.3 gms
Diameter: 27.3 to 28.0 mm
Die Axis: ↑↑
Edge: Plain, reeded
Ref.Nos.: Br 715; See below

Open Wreath   Closed Wreath

Varieties: Reverse and edge
A1 Open wreath at top, Plain; Co 15B; W 690
A2 Open wreath at top, Reeded; Co 17B; W 690
A3 Closed wreath at top, Reeded; Co 16B, W 691

Note: Many other varieties are described by Geo. Thomson; see Reference Works p.xxiii.

Cat.No.	Date	Description	VG	F	VF	EF	AU	UNC
LC-5A1	(1838)	Open wreath, Plain	150.00	275.00	375.00	475.00	900.00	1,800.00
LC-5A2	(1838)	Open wreath, Reeded	75.00	150.00	300.00	450.00	600.00	750.00
LC-5A3	(1838)	Closed wreath, Reeded	2.00	5.00	10.00	25.00	50.00	100.00

CITY BANK HALF PENNY TOKENS

The City Bank was organized in 1833 for the benefit of businessmen denied the services of the Bank of Montreal because of their political views. The City Bank prospered until 1873 when it suffered a severe strain owing to an unfavourable court decision.

The Bank recovered from this by 1878 when it merged with the Royal Canadian Bank. The combined firm was known as the Consolidated Bank of Canada. The bank collapsed during the financial depression of 1879.

The sous attributed to the City Bank were struck by Jean-Marie Arnault from dies cut by him.

LC-6 PRO BONO PUBLICO MONTREAL ½ PENNY TOKEN 1837— TRADE & AGRICULTURE LOWER CANADA

Composition: Copper
Weight: N/A
Diameter: 26.9 to 27.1 mm
Die Axis: ↑↑
Edge: Plain
Ref.Nos.: Br 672; Co 1B;
W 692

Cat.No.	Date	Description	VG	F	VF	EF	AU	UNC
LC-6	1837				Unique, Bank of Canada Collection			

LC-7 BANK TOKEN MONTREAL ½ PENNY— TRADE & AGRICULTURE LOWER CANADA

Composition: Copper
Weight: 7.8 gms
Diameter: 26.9 to 27.1 mm
Die Axis: ↑↑
Edge: Plain
Ref.Nos.: Br 673; Co 2B
W 693

Cat.No.	Date	Description	VG	F	VF	EF	AU	UNC
LC-7	(1837)					Very Rare		

PROVINCE DU BAS CANADA "HABITANT TOKENS"

In 1837 the Bank of Montreal applied for permission to import halfpennies and pennies. Permission was granted provided the City Bank, Quebec Bank and the Banque du Peuple would also participate. Tokens were ordered through Albert Furniss of Montreal and struck by Boulton & Watt. The obverse design depicted a Canadian Habitant standing in traditional winter costume. The reverse carried the arms of the City of Montreal with the name of the participating bank appearing on the ribbon.

LC-8   ***BANK TOKEN HALF PENNY 1837 —***
                           PROVINCE DU BAS CANADA UN SOU

LC-8A   ***CITY BANK ON RIBBON***

Composition: Copper
Weight: 9.2 to 9.5 gms
Diameter: 28.2 to 28.3 mm
Die Axis: ↑↑
Edge: Plain
Ref.Nos.: Br 522; See below

"V" and "I" in line   "V" lower than top of "I"

Varieties: Obverse
     A1 The right seriph of "V" and the top of "I" in PROVINCE are in line;
          Co 1 to 1nH; W 736 to 739
     A2 The right seriph of "V" is lower that the top of the "I" in PROVINCE;
          Co 2 to 2lH; W 740 to 744

Cat.No.	Date	Description	VG	F	VF	EF	AU	UNC
LC-8A1	1837	In line	2.00	5.00	12.00	35.00	90.00	150.00
LC-8A2	1837	Lower	4.00	8.00	18.00	45.00	100.00	175.00

LC-8B   *QUEBEC BANK ON RIBBON*

Composition: Copper
Weight: 9.0 to 9.4 gms
Diameter: 28.2 to 28.3 mm
Die Axis: ↑↑
Edge: Plain
Ref.Nos.: Br 522; See below

Varieties: Obverse
   B1 The right seriph of "V" and the top of "I" in PROVINCE are in line;
        Co 3 to 3gH; W 749 to 751
   B2 The right seriph of "V" is lower than the top of the "I" in PROVINCE;
        Co 4 to 4iH; W 752 to 756

Note: For variety illustration see page No. 91

Cat.No.	Date	Description	VG	F	VF	EF	AU	UNC
LC-8B1	1837	In Line	2.00	5.00	12.00	35.00	90.00	150.00
LC-8B2	1837	Lower	4.00	8.00	18.00	45.00	100.00	175.00

LC-8C   *LA BANQUE DU PEUPLE ON RIBBON*

Composition: Copper
Weight: 9.5 gms
Diameter: 28.2 to 28.3 mm
Die Axis: ↑↑
Edge: Plain
Ref.Nos.: Br 522; See below

Varieties: Obverse
   C1 The right seriph of "V" and the top of "I" in PROVINCE are in line;
        Co 6 to 6eH; W 760 to 762
   C2 The right seriph of "V" is lower than the top of the "I" in PROVINCE;
        Co 7 to 7bH; W 763

Note: For variety illustration see page No. 91.

Cat.No.	Date	Description	VG	F	VF	EF	AU	UNC
LC-8C1	1837	In line	5.00	10.00	25.00	65.00	125.00	200.00
LC-8C2	1837	Lower	6.00	12.00	30.00	75.00	150.00	225.00

LC-8D   *BANK OF MONTREAL ON RIBBON*

Composition: Copper
Weight: 9.5 gm
Diameter: 28.2 to 28.3 mm
Die Axis: ↑↑
Edge: Plain
Ref.Nos.: Br 522; See below

Varieties: Obverse
   D1 The right seriph of "V" and the top of "I" in PROVINCE are in line;
        Co 14 to 19bBM; W 766 to 769
   D2 The right seriph of "V" is lower than the top of the "I" in PROVINCE;
        Co 20 to 22BM; W 770 to 771

Note: For variety illustration see page No. 91. Proofs exist for LC-8D2.

Cat.No.	Date	Description	VG	F	VF	EF	AU	UNC
LC-8D1	1837	In line	5.00	10.00	25.00	45.00	100.00	175.00
LC-8D2	1837	Lower	5.00	10.00	25.00	45.00	100.00	175.00

LC-9

BANK TOKEN ONE PENNY 1837 —
PROVINCE DU BAS CANADA DEUX SOUS

LC-9A

CITY BANK ON RIBBON

Composition: Copper
Weight: 18.7 to 19.0 gms
Diameter: 34.0 to 34.1 mm
Die Axis: ↑↑ ↑↓
Edge: Plain
Ref.Nos.: Br 521; See below

| Strong or Large Ground | Weak or Small Ground | Period | No Period |

Varieties: Obverse and die axis
Large ground — Left collar below shoulder
Small ground — Left collar at shoulder
A1 Large ground, Period after Canada, Medal; Co 8 to 8cH; W 745
A2 Large ground, No period after Canada, Medal; Co 9 to 9cH; W 746
A3 Small ground, Period after Canada, Medal; Co 11 to 11H; W 747, 748
A4 Small ground, Period after Canada, Coinage; Co 10

Note: Proofs exist for LC-9A1.

Cat.No.	Date	Description	VG	F	VF	EF	AU	UNC
LC-9A1	1837	Large ground, Period, Medal	4.00	8.00	18.00	40.00	100.00	200.00
LC-9A2	1837	Large ground, No period, Medal	3.00	6.00	15.00	35.00	90.00	200.00
LC-9A3	1837	Small ground, Period, Medal	5.00	12.00	25.00	45.00	100.00	225.00
LC-9A4	1837	Small ground, Period, Coinage	10.00	20.00	40.00	65.00	125.00	275.00

LC-9B   *QUEBEC BANK ON RIBBON*

Composition: Copper
Weight: 19.0 gms
Diameter: 34.1 mm
Die Axis: ↑↑
Edge: Plain
Ref.Nos.: Br 521; See below

Varieties: Obverse and die axis
  B1 Large ground, Period after Canada, Medal; Co 12 to 12bH; W 757
  B2 Large ground, No period after Canada, Coinage; Co 13 to 13hH; W 758
  B3 Small ground, Period after Canada, Medal; Co 14 to 14bH; W 759

Note: For variety illustration see page 94.

Cat.No.	Date	Description	VG	F	VF	EF	AU	UNC
LC-9B1	1837	Large ground, Period, Medal	3.00	6.00	15.00	35.00	90.00	200.00
LC-9B2	1837	Large ground, No period, Coinage	4.00	8.00	18.00	40.00	100.00	225.00
LC-9B3	1837	Small ground, Period, Medal	15.00	25.00	50.00	75.00	150.00	300.00

LC-9C   *BANQUE DU PEUPLE ON RIBBON*

Composition: Copper
Weight: 19.0 gms
Diameter: 34.1 mm
Die Axis: ↑↑
Edge: Plain
Ref.Nos.: Br 521; See below

Varieties: Obverse
  C1 Large ground, Period after Canada; Co 16, 16aH; W 764
  C2 Small ground, Period after Canada; Co 17 to 17dH; W 765

Note: For variety illustration see page 94.

Cat.No.	Date	Description	VG	F	VF	EF	AU	UNC
LC-9C1	1837	Large ground, Period	15.00	25.00	60.00	100.00	200.00	300.00
LC-9C2	1837	Small ground, Period	12.00	20.00	50.00	90.00	175.00	300.00

LC-9D   **BANK OF MONTREAL ON RIBBON**

Composition: Copper
Weight: 19.0 gms
Diameter: 34.1 mm
Die Axis: ↑↑
Edge: Plain
Ref.Nos.: Br 521; See below

Varieties: Obverse
    D1 Large ground, No period after Canada; Co 29BM; W 775
    D2 Small ground, Period after Canada; Co 24 to 27BM; W 772, 773
    D3 Small ground, No period after Canada; Co 28BM; W 774

Note: For variety illustration see page 94.

Cat.No.	Date	Description	VG	F	VF	EF	AU	UNC
LC-9D1	1837	Large ground, No period	6.00	12.00	30.00	60.00	125.00	250.00
LC-9D2	1837	Small ground, Period	6.00	12.00	30.00	60.00	125.00	250.00
LC-9D3	1837	Small ground, No period	6.00	12.00	30.00	60.00	125.00	250.00

BANK OF MONTREAL "SIDE VIEW" TOKENS

LC-10   *BANK TOKEN HALF PENNY —*
1838/1839 BANK OF MONTREAL

In 1838 the Bank of Montreal replaced the Habitant tokens with a new issue showing a corner or side view of the bank building on the obverse. The tokens were procured by Cotterill, Hill & Co. of Walsall, Staffordshire and arrived in Montreal in June of 1839. They were short-lived because the manager of the bank did not like their workmanship or weight, and the shipment was returned to England for melting.

LC-10A   *HALF PENNY DATED 1838 BANK OF MONTREAL ON RIBBON*

Composition: Copper, Brass
Weight: 9.9 to 10.4 gms
Diameter: 28.0 to 28.3 mm
Die Axis: ↑↑
Edge: Plain
Ref.Nos.: Br 524; See below

| 13 Palings, | 11 Palings, | 8 Palings, |
| 8 Left of tree | 6 Left of tree | 3 Left of tree |

Varieties: Obverse

A1 Left fence has thirteen palings, eight to left of tree, Copper; Co 30BM; W 776

A2 Left fence has thirteen palings, eight to left of tree, Brass; Co 30BM; W 776

A3 Left fence has eleven palings, six to left of tree, Copper; Co 31BM; W 777 Also reported in brass.

A4 Right fence has eight palings, three to left of tree, Copper; Co 32BM; W 778

Cat.No.	Date	Description	VG	F	VF	EF	AU	UNC
LC-10A1	1838	Thirteen palings, copper	275.00	375.00	475.00	600.00	1,200.00	1,750.00
LC-10A2	1838	Thirteen palings, brass	300.00	400.00	500.00	700.00	1,350.00	2,000.00
LC-10A3	1838	Eleven palings, copper	275.00	375.00	475.00	600.00	1,200.00	1,750.00
LC-10A4	1838	Eight palings, copper	275.00	375.00	475.00	600.00	1,200.00	1,750.00

LC-10B **HALF PENNY DATED 1839 BANK OF MONTREAL ON RIBBON**

In 1839 the bank asked that the order of 1838 be refilled in the same amount as originally requested. The coinage of 1839 was again procured by Cotterill, Hill & Co., but this time in better copper and in more proper weight. This coinage was refused as well by the banks manager who considered its quality even worse than that of the 1838 issues.

Composition: Copper
Weight: 8.8 gms
Diameter: 28.3 mm
Die Axis: ↑↑
Edge: Plain
Ref.Nos.: Br 524; See below

15 Pallings   14 palings

Tail touches garter

Varieties: Obverse and reverse
     B1 Left fence has fifteen palings; Beaver's tail touches garter; Co 33BM; W 781
     B2 Left fence has fourteen palings; Beaver's tail does not touch garter; Co 34BM; W 782
     B3 Mule of B1 and B2, Left fence has fifteen palings; Beaver's tail does not touch garter; Co 35BM; W 783

Cat.No.	Date	Description	VG	F	VF	EF	AU	UNC
LC-10B1	1839	Fifteen palings	275.00	375.00	500.00	700.00	1,000.00	1,500.00
LC-10B2	1839	Fourteen palings	275.00	375.00	500.00	700.00	1,000.00	1,500.00
LC-10B3	1839	Mule	350.00	450.00	600.00	800.00	1,000.00	1,500.00

LC-11
BANK TOKEN ONE PENNY—
1838/1839 BANK OF MONTREAL

LC-11A   *ONE PENNY DATED 1838 BANK OF MONTREAL ON RIBBON*

Composition: Copper, brass
Weight: 19.2 to 19.8 gms
Diameter: 33.8 mm
Die Axis: ↑↑
Edge: Plain
Ref.Nos.: Br 523; See below

Tail almost touches "M"   Tail points to left
                                              foot of "M"

Varieties: Reverse
     A1   Narrow tail beaver almost touches "M"; Co 36BM; W 779
     A2   Wide tail beaver points to left foot of "M"; Co 37BM; W 780

Cat.No.	Date	Description	VG	F	VF	EF	AU	UNC
LC-11A1	1838	Narrow tail almost touches	550.00	700.00	850.00	1,500.00	2,500.00	4,000.00
LC-11A2	1838	Wide tail does not touch	550.00	700.00	850.00	1,500.00	2,500.00	4,000.00

LC-11B   *ONE PENNY BATED 1839 BANK OF MONTREAL ON RIBBON*

Composition: Copper
Weight: 18.7 gms
Diameter: 34.2 mm
Die Axis: ↑↑
Edge: Plain
Ref.Nos.: Br 523; Co 38BM;
                 W 784

Cat.No.	Date	Description	VG	F	V	EF	AU	UNC
LC-11B	1839	Thirteen palings	550.00	700.00	850.00	1,000.00	2,500.00	4,000.00

LC-11C   *ONE PENNY DATED 1839 BANQUE DU PEUPLE ON RIBBON*

This was once considered an error. It is now thought that the manufacturer struck it deliberately, either at the bank's suggestion or to show to the bank as an example of their work. Either way, nothing came of it as there are less than eight examples known today.

Composition: Copper
Weight: 18.7 gms
Diameter: 33.8 mm
Die Axis: ↑↑
Edge: Plain
Ref.Nos.: Br 525; Co 39BM;
        W 785

Cat.No.	Date	Description	VG	F	VF	EF	AU	UNC
LC-11C	1839				Extremely Rare			

PRIVATE TOKENS

LC-12   *MONTREAL — 1816 HALF PENNY TOKEN*

Composition: Copper
Weight: 5.2 to 5.7 gms
Diameter: 27.9 to 28.2 mm
Die Axis: ↑↑
Edge: Plain
Ref.Nos.: Br 531; Co 47W;
        W 541

Variations: Varying degrees of rust areas, especially on the reverse, are in evidence on most pieces. Very shallow die engraving has resulted in poor detail in the struck token.

Cat.No.	Date Description	VG	F	VF	EF	AU	UNC
LC-12	1816	4.00	10.00	40.00	100.00	200.00	400.00

LC-13   *HALF PENNY — 1830/1841 CANADA*

These tokens were issued by Duncan & Co., a Montreal hardware firm. Specimens were put into circulation in Prince Edward Island by James Duncan, brother of the owner, who later issued his own tokens.

LC-13A   *— 1830 CANADA*

Composition: Copper
Weight: 5.8 gms
Diameter: 25.7 to 26.1 mm
Die Axis: ↑↑
Edge: Plain
Ref.Nos.: Br 532; W 575

Cat.No.	Date	Description	VG	F	VF	EF	AU	UNC
LC-13A	1830		5.00	12.00	30.00	75.00	150.00	300.00

LC-13B   *— 1841 CANADA*

Composition: Copper
Weight: 5.3 to 5.8 gms
Diameter: 25.7 to 26.1 mm
Die Axis: ↑↑
Edge: Plain
Ref.Nos.: Br 532; W 575

Cat.No.	Date	Description	VG	F	VF	EF	AU	UNC
LC-13B	1841		5.00	12.00	30.00	65.00	150.00	300.00

LC-14   *CANADA HALF PENNY TOKEN —*
FOR PUBLIC ACCOMMODATION

This token was issued around 1830.

Composition: Copper
Weight: 6.5 to 7.2 gms
Diameter: 27.6 to 28.0 mm
Die Axis: ↑↑
Edge: Plain, reeded
Ref.Nos.: Br 533; W 574

Variations: The obverse comes with large and small periods. This token was struck with rusted dies.

Cat.No.	Date	Description	VG	F	VF	EF	AU	UNC
LC-14	(1830)		5.00	10.00	25.00	60.00	125.00	250.00

LC-15   *T.S. BROWN & CO.*
IMPORTERS OF HARDWARES MONTREAL —

These halfpennies were issued by Thomas Storrow Brown, a Montreal hardware merchant. He led the Fils de la Liberte in the rebellion of 1837 and fled to the United States when the rebellion was put down, remaining there until amnesty was granted in 1844. His coppers were condemned by "Le Populaire" as a profiteering scheme, but are better than the brass pieces then in circulation. The coins were struck in Birmingham. The obverse was also used for a Louisville, Kentucky, business card issued in 1845, and for a Green and Wetmore card, New York.

Composition: Copper
Weight: 7.1 to 7.6 gms
Diameter: 27.9 to 28.3 mm
Die Axis: ↑↑
Edge: Plain, reeded
Ref.Nos.: Br 561

"S" Close to "Co"

"S" Far from "Co"

Varieties: Obverse legends
     A1 "S" of Importers close to "Co"; W 576
     A2 "S" of Importers far from "Co"; W 577

Cat.No.	Date	Description	VG	F	VF	EF	AU	UNC
LC-15A1		Close "S"	5.00	12.00	30.00	75.00	150.00	300.00
LC-15A2		Far "S"	5.00	12.00	35.00	85.00	175.00	350.00

LC-16   CASH PAID FOR ALL SORTS OF GRAIN 1837 — THS & WM MOLSON MONTREAL BREWERS DISTILLERS &&& UN SOU

The dies, which are still owned by the firm, were cut by Jean-Marie Arnault who also struck the coins. Evidently the firm supplied a specimen of a Perthshire halfpenny token of 1797 as a model for the distillery. The reverse of the Molson token is an exact copy, in reverse, of the Perthshire piece.

Composition: Copper, silver
Weight: Thick flan, 11.0 to 11.3 gms
        Thin flan, 8.8 to 9.8 gms
Thickness: Thick flan, 2.1 to 2.3 mm
          Thin flan, 1.7 to 1.9 mm
Diameter: 28.2 to 29.4 mm
Die Axis: ↑↑
Edge: Plain, reeded
Ref.Nos.: Br 562: W 579

Varieties: Weight and edge
     A1 Thick flan, Reeded edge
     A2 Thick flan, Plain edge
     A3 Thin flan, Reeded edge
     A4 Thin flan, Plain edge

Note: A few specimens were struck in silver for presentation purposes.

Cat.No.	Date	Description	VG	F	VF	EF	AU	UNC
LC-16A1	1837	Thick flan, Reeded edge	100.00	175.00	275.00	400.00	800.00	1,000.00
LC-16A2	1837	Thick, Plain edge				Rare		
LC-16A3	1837	Thin, Reeded edge	100.00	175.00	275.00	400.00	800.00	1,000.00
LC-16A4	1837	Thin, Plain edge				Rare		

LC-17 *FRANCIS MULLINS & SON MONTREAL IMPORTERS OF SHIP CHANDLERY &C. — COMMERCE TOKEN*

Francis Mullins, a ship chandler in Montreal, imported these tokens in 1828.

Composition: Copper, brass
Weight: 4.8 to 5.4 gms
Diameter: 26.6 to 26.8 mm
Die Axis: ↑↓
Edge: Plain
Ref.Nos.: Br 563; See below

Varieties: Composition
    A1 Copper; W 573
    A2 Brass; W 573

Cat.No.	Date	Description	VG	F	VF	EF	AU	UNC
LC-17A1	(1828)	Copper	10.00	20.00	40.00	90.00	200.00	400.00
LC-17A2	(1828)	Brass	J. Hoare Auction, February 1996, Lot 1377, VF - $740.00					

LC-18 *R.W. OWEN MONTREAL ROPERY — (SAILING SHIP DESIGN)*

This token was issued in 1824 shortly before R.W. Owen sold out to J.A. Converse, against whose larger, steam-powered ropery he could not compete successfully. As a result very few of these tokens circulated. Forgeries exist.

Composition: Copper
Weight: 7.8 gms
Diameter: 26.7 mm
Die Axis: ↑↑
Edge: Engrailed
Ref.Nos.: Br 564; W 572

Cat.No.	Date	Description	VG	F	VF	EF	AU	UNC
LC-18	(1824)	J. Hoare Auction, October 1999, Lot 576, VG+ - $11,000.00						

LC-19   *J. SHAW & CO. IMPORTERS OF HARDWARES*
             UPPER TOWN QUEBEC—

This token was issued in 1837 by John Shaw. It was denounced as a profiteering fraud by the newspaper "Le Canadien." Shaw at once replied that his halfpennies were issued to provide some supply of small change at a time of a great dearth of copper and that they were redeemable on demand. When the Habitant coppers of the Quebec Bank were released in 1838, Shaw attempted to withdraw his halfpennies.

Composition: Copper
Weight: 6.4 to 7.6 gms
Diameter: 27.9 to 28.3 mm
Die Axis: ↑↑
Edge: Reeded
Ref.Nos.: Br 565; W 578

Cat.No.	Date	Description	VG	F	VF	EF	AU	UNC
LC-19	(1837)		8.00	15.00	35.00	75.00	150.00	300.00

LC-20   *J. ROY MONTREAL UN SOU —*
 COMMERCE BAS-CANADA

Mr. Joseph Roy was a dry goods merchant who operated a business at 70 St. Paul Street in Montreal. During September of 1837 he issued tokens, probably designed by Jean-Marie Arnault.

The shipment to Roy contained tokens of mixed weights even though he had instructed the minter to produce his pieces at the weight of 51 tokens to the pound (which equalled the weight of the current bank tokens.)

A newspaper article published in "Le Populaire" on November 17, 1837, condemned Roy for his lightweight tokens. After a second attempt to have Arnault produce tokens of proper weight, Roy cancelled the order.

Composition: Copper
Weight: See below
Diameter: 27.1 to 28.0 mm
Die Axis: ↑↑
Edge: Plain
Ref.Nos.: Br 671; Co 72B;
          W 580

Varieties: Weight
     A1 Thick flan, weight 8.9 to 9.2 gms
     A2 Thin flan, weight 6.2 to 6.8 gms

Cat.No.	Date	Description	VG	F	VF	EF	AU	UNC
LC-20A1	(1837)	Thick flan	30.00	60.00	125.00	250.00	-	-
LC-20A2	(1837)	Thin flan	30.00	60.00	125.00	250.00	-	-

THE "BOUQUET SOUS"

These tokens feature a bouquet of the heraldic flowers on the obverse. Because of their popularity with the mainly French-speaking opponents of the government of the day they were called the "Sous des Patriotes."

These Patriotes began to boycott English goods and refused English money, relying on the meagre supply of old French coins remaining from the French regime. They also accepted the tokens of the Bank of Montreal, Banque du Peuple and City Bank because they were inscribed in French.

To fill the void caused by this action, a Montreal exchange broker named Dexter Chapin imported a large shipment of sous imitating the design of the sous of the Bank of Montreal from Belleville, New Jersey. Their circulation was very profitable to Chapin because of their lighter weight. Similar imports came from Birmingham and a few were struck in Montreal. By 1837 the Bouquet sous were so numerous that they, in turn, were refused by the banks.

IDENTIFICATION OF "BOUQUET SOUS" TOKENS

The bouquet sous tokens are listed by the number of cherry leaves in the reverse wreath with sublistings according to the number of shamrocks and the position of the bow in the obverse bouquet.

REVERSE

Reverse bow   No reverse bow

OBVERSE

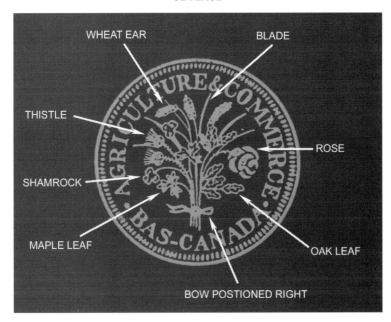

WHEAT EAR

BLADE

THISTLE

ROSE

SHAMROCK

MAPLE LEAF

OAK LEAF

BOW POSTIONED RIGHT

BELLEVILLE ISSUES

Cat.No.	Leaves In Reverse Wreath	Shamrocks In Obverse Bouquet	Position of Obverse Bow	Breton Number	Courteau Number	Willey Number
LC-21	16	2	Right	680	53B	700
LC-22A,B	16	3	Left	676,682	57,59B	695,702
LC-22C	16	3	None	681	60B	701
LC-23	16	4	Left	675	56,58	694,696
				677-678	61-62B	697,698
LC-24	16	7	Left	679	54-55B	699
LC-25	17	2	Right	683	51-52B	703
LC-26	17	3	None	·	·	704
LC-27	18	0	None	691	43-44B	710
LC-28	18	1	None	702	29B	721
LC-29A,D	18	2	Right	695-696	31-32	714-715
				700-701	45-46B	719-720
LC-29E	18	2	None	697	33-34B	716
LC-30A,B	18	3	Left	698-699	35-36B	717-718
LC-30C,F	18	3	None	685-686	30,47	705-706
				703	48B	708,722
LC-31A,B,C	18	5	Right	688,693	37-38	709,712
				694	41B	713
LC-32A.B	18	7	Left	687,692	39,42B	707,711
LC-33A,B	20	2	Left	704	27-28B	723-724
LC-33C	20	2	None	705	26B	725

BIRMINGHAM ISSUES

Cat.No.	Leaves In Reverse Wreath	Shamrocks In Obverse Bouquet	Position of Bow	Breton Number	Courteau Number	Willey Number
LC-34	32	1	None	706	23B	726
LC-35	32	2	None	707	22B	727
LC-36	32	3	None	708	20B	728
LC-37	32	3	Left	709	21B	729
LC-38A,B	39	3	None	710,712	19B	730,G3
LC-39	39	6	None	711	18B	731

MONTREAL ISSUES

Cat.No.	Leaves In Reverse Wreath	Shamrocks In Obverse Bouquet	Position Of Bow	Breton Number	Courteau Number	Willey Number
LC-40	16	5	Left	674	63-70B	734
LC-41	17	6	Right	684	49-50B	732
LC-42	18	2	None	·	·	735
LC-43	21	0	None	689	24B	733

MISCELLANEOUS ISSUES

Cat.No.	Leaves In Reverse Wreath	Shamrocks In Obverse Bouquet	Position Of Bow	Breton Number	Courteau Number	Willey Number
LC-44	18	7	Left	690	40B	G2
LC-45	·	3	None	670	71B	G28

BELLEVILLE ISSUES

TOKEN MONTREAL UN SOU —
AGRICULTURE & COMMERCE BAS-CANADA

These pieces were struck by the Belleville Mint, New Jersey, from dies cut by John Gibbs in imitation of the Bank of Montreal sous.

LC-21   *REVERSE WREATH WITH SIXTEEN CHERRY LEAVES*

OBVERSE BOUQUET WITH TWO SHAMROCKS

Composition: Copper
Weight: 6.9 to 7.5 gms
Diameter: 26.9 to 27.1 mm
Die Axis: ↑↑
Edge: Plain
Ref.Nos.: Br 680; Co 53B;
        W 700

Cat.No.	Date	Description	VG	F	VF	EF	AU	UNC
LC-21		Copper	15.00	30.00	80.00	160.00	-	-

LC-22   *REVERSE WREATH WITH SIXTEEN CHERRY LEAVES*

OBVERSE BOUQUET WITH THREE SHAMROCKS

Varieties: Obverse

Composition: Copper
Weight: 6.9 to 7.5 gms
Diameter: 27.0 to 27.1 mm
Die Axis: ↑↑
Edge: Plain
Ref.Nos.: See below

A Small bow to left; Br 676; Co 57B; W 695

B Small heavy bow to left; Br 682; Co 59B; W 702

C No bow; Br 681; Co 60B; W 701

Cat.No.	Date	Description	VG	F	VF	EF	AU	UNC
LC-22A		Small bow	15.00	30.00	65.00	110.00	-	-
LC-22B		Small heavy bow	8.00	25.00	50.00	90.00	-	-
LC-22C		No bow	J. Hoare Auction, Fall 1989, Lot 2197, VF-EF - $420.00					

LC-23   *REVERSE WREATH WITH SIXTEEN CHERRY LEAVES*

OBVERSE BOUQUET WITH FOUR SHAMROCKS

Varieties: Obverse, reverse and composition

Composition: Copper, brass
Weight: 5.7 to 7.3 gms
Diameter: 26.8 to 27.1 mm
Die Axis: ↑↑
Edge: Plain
Ref.Nos.: See below

A No stalk between thistles; Br 675; Co 61B; W 694

B Stalk between thistles; Br 677; Co 58B; W 696

C No berry left of bow; Br 678; Co 56B; W 697

Note: LC-23C ordinarily comes in copper.

Cat. No.	Date	Description	VG	F	VF	EF	AU	UNC
LC-23A		No stalk between thistles	J. Hoare Auction, Summer 1995, Lot 1594, F-VF $1,450.00					
LC-23B		Stalk between thistles	J. Hoare Auction, Fall 1989, Lot 2193, VF - $700.00					
LC-23C		No berry	5.00	10.00	30.00	100.00	250.00	-

LC-23 cont'd overleaf

LC-23   *REVERSE WREATH WITH SIXTEEN CHERRY LEAVES*

OBVERSE BOUQUET WITH FOUR SHAMROCKS

D Mule with the obverse of LC-23A and the reverse of LC-23C; Co 62 B; W 698

Cat.No.	Date	Description	VG	F	VF	EF	AU	UNC
LC-23D		Mule			Extremely Rare			

LC-24   *REVERSE WREATH WITH SIXTEEN CHERRY LEAVES*

OBVERSE BOUQUET WITH SEVEN SHAMROCKS

Composition: Copper, brass
Weight: 6.4 to 7.5 gms
Diameter: 27.0 to 27.4 mm
Die Axis: ↑↑
Edge: Plain
Ref.Nos.: Br 679; See below

Varieties: Composition
A1 Copper; Co 54B; W 699
A2 Brass; Co 55B; W 699

Cat.No.	Date	Description	VG	F	VF	EF	AU	UNC
LC-24A1		Copper	4.00	8.00	15.00	35.00	65.00	125.00
LC-24A2		Brass			Rare			

LC-25   *REVERSE WREATH WITH SEVENTEEN CHERRY LEAVES*

OBVERSE BOUQUET WITH TWO SHAMROCKS

Composition: Copper, brass
Weight: 5.7 to 6.9 gms
Diameter: 27.0 to 27.1 mm
Die Axis: ↑↑
Edge: Plain
Ref.Nos.: Br 683; See below

Variations: Composition
   A1 Copper; Co 51B; W 703
   A2 Brass; Co 52B; W 703

Cat.No.	Date	Description	VG	F	VF	EF	AU	UNC
LC-25A1		Copper	7.00	15.00	40.00	90.00	200.00	-
LC-25A2		Brass			Rare			

LC-26   *REVERSE WREATH WITH SEVENTEEN CHERRY LEAVES*

OBVERSE BOUQUET WITH THREE SHAMROCKS

Composition: Copper
Weight: 5.7 to 6.9 gms
Diameter: 27.0 to 27.1 mm
Die Axis: ↑↑
Edge: Plain
Ref.Nos.: W 704

Note: This is a muling of the LC-22C obverse with the LC-25 reverse.

Cat.No.	Date	Description	VG	F	VF	EF	AU	UNC
LC-26		Copper			Extremely Rare			

LC-27   *REVERSE WREATH WITH EIGHTEEN CHERRY LEAVES*

OBVERSE BOUQUET WITH NO SHAMROCKS

Composition: Copper, brass
Weight: 5.9 to 7.4 gms
Diameter: 26.9 to 27.2 mm
Die Axis: ↑↑
Edge: Plain
Ref.Nos.: Br 691; See below

Variations: Composition
A1 Copper, Thin and thick flans; Co 43B; W 710
A2 Brass; Co 44B; W 710

Cat.No.	Date	Description	VG	F	VF	EF	AU	UNC
LC-27A1		Copper	3.00	5.00	10.00	30.00	65.00	125.00
LC-27A2		Brass		J. Hoare Auction, February 1999, Lot 667, F+ $375.00				

LC-28   *REVERSE WREATH WITH EIGHTEEN CHERRY LEAVES*

OBVERSE BOUQUET WITH ONE SHAMROCK

Composition: Copper
Weight: 7.2 to 7.8 gms
Diameter: 27.0 to 27.1 mm
Die Axis: ↑↑
Edge: Plain
Ref.Nos.: Br 702; Co 29B;
                     W 721

Cat.No.	Date	Description	VG	F	VF	EF	AU	UNC
LC-28		Copper	4.00	8.00	15.00	40.00	75.00	150.00

LC-29   *REVERSE WREATH WITH EIGHTEEN CHERRY LEAVES*

OBVERSE BOUQUET WITH TWO SHAMROCKS

Composition: Copper, brass
Weight: 6.4 to 8.6 gms
Diameter: 26.9 to 27.2 mm
Die Axis: ↑↑
Edge: Plain
Ref.Nos.: See below

Varieties: The first four varieties have their obverse bow positioned right.

A Small reverse bow flanked by cherries; Br 695; Co 46B; W 714

B Small reverse bow, without flanking cherries; Br 696; Co 45B; W 715

C Large reverse bow without flanking cherries, Obverse bouquet points to "CA" of Canada; Br 700; Co 32B; W 719

Cat.No.	Date	Description	VG	F	VF	EF	AU	UNC
LC-29A		Small bow, Cherries	10.00	25.00	60.00	100.00	175.00	-
LC-29B		Small bow, No cherries	20.00	40.00	100.00	175.00	350.00	-
LC-29C		Large reverse bow, "CA"	5.00	10.00	30.00	65.00	125.00	-

LC-29 cont'd overleaf

LC-29 REVERSE WREATH WITH EIGHTEEN CHERRY LEAVES

OBVERSE BOUQUET WITH TWO SHAMROCKS

D Large reverse bow without flanking cherries, Obverse bouquet points to "N" of Canada; Br 701; Co31B; W 720

E1 No obverse bow, Copper; Br 697; Co 33B; W 716
E2 No obverse bow, Brass; Br 697; Co 34B; W 716

Cat.No.	Date	Description	VG	F	VF	EF	AU	UNC
LC-29D		Large reverse bow, "N"	12.00	25.00	50.00	100.00	200.00	-
LC-29E1		No obverse bow, Copper	10.00	15.00	25.00	50.00	100.00	-
LC-29E2		No obverse bow, brass	J. Hoare Auction, October 1996, Lot 1330, VF - $340.00					

LC-30   *REVERSE WREATH WITH EIGHTEEN CHERRY LEAVES*

OBVERSE BOUQUET WITH THREE SHAMROCKS
OBVERSE BOW POSITIONED LEFT

Composition: Copper
Weight: Bow, 6.2 to 7.1 gms
No bow, 5.6 to 6.6 gms
Diameter: Bow, 26.9 to 27.1 mm
No bow, 27.0 to 27.1 mm
Die Axis: ↑↑
Edge: Plain
Ref.Nos.: See below

Varieties: Obverse and reverse
 A Obverse bow position left; small reverse bow; Br 698; Co 36B; W 717

 B Obverse bow positioned left; large reverse bow; Br 699; Co35B; W 718

Cat. No.	Date	Description	VG	F	VF	EF	AU	UNC
LC-30A		Small bow	15.00	25.00	50.00	100.00	200.00	-
LC-30B		Large bow	6.00	15.00	30.00	60.00	125.00	-

LC-30, No obverse bow cont'd overleaf

LC-30 *REVERSE WREATH WITH EIGHTEEN CHERRY LEAVES*

OBVERSE BOUQUET WITH THREE SHAMROCKS
NO OBVERSE BOW

C No obverse or reverse bows; Open wreath; Br 685; Co 48B; W 705

D No obverse or reverse bows; Normal wreath; Br 686; Co 47; W 706

E No obverse or reverse bows; Closed wreath; W 708

F No obverse bow; Reverse bow; Normal wreath; Br 703; Co 30B; W 722

Cat.No.	Date	Description	VG	F	VF	EF	AU	UNC
LC-30C		No bow, Open wreath	7.00	20.00	50.00	125.00	200.00	-
LC-30D		No bow, Normal wreath	7.00	15.00	35.00	100.00	200.00	-
LC-30E		No bow, Closed wreath			Extremely Rare			
LC-30F		Reverse bow		J. Hoare Auction, Spring 1995, Lot 1610; VF - $3,000.00				

LC-31   *REVERSE WREATH WITH EIGHTEEN CHERRY LEAVES*

OBVERSE BOUQUET WITH FIVE SHAMROCKS

Varieties: Reverse and composition
All varieties have obverse bow positioned right.

Composition: Copper, brass
Weight: 6.0 to 7.1 gms
Diameter: 27.1 to 27.4 mm
Die Axis: ↑↑
Edge: Plain
Ref.Nos.: See below

A On the reverse leaves instead of a bow; Obverse with
three blades of wheat; Br 688; Co 41B; W 709

B1 On the reverse a bow, Obverse with three
blades of wheat, Copper; Br 693; Co 37B; W 712
B2 As above, Brass; Br 693; Co 37B; W 712

C On the reverse a bow, Obverse with two
blades of wheat; Br 694, Co 38B; W 713

Cat.No.	Date Description	VG	F	VF	EF	AU	UNC
LC-31A	Leaves instead of bow	10.00	20.00	50.00	125.00	250.00	-
LC-31B1	Bow, Three blades, Copper	10.00	20.00	45.00	90.00	150.00	-
LC-31B2	Bow, Three blades, Brass			Very Rare			
LC-31C	Bow, Two blades	3.00	5.00	10.00	60.00	125.00	-

LC-32   *REVERSE WREATH WITH EIGHTEEN CHERRY LEAVES*

OBVERSE BOUQUET WITH SEVEN SHAMROCKS

Composition: Copper
Weight: 6.3 to 7.3 gms
Diameter: 27.0 to 27.2 mm
Die Axis: ↑↑
Edge: Plain
Ref.Nos.: See below

Varieties: Reverse, and all varieties have obverse bow positioned left

A No reverse bow; Br 687; Co 42B; W 707

B Reverse bow; Br 692; Co 39B; W 711

Cat.No.	Date	Description	VG	F	VF	EF	AU	UNC
LC-32A		No reverse bow	7.00	14.00	35.00	100.00	200.00	-
LC-32B		Bow	3.00	5.00	15.00	40.00	100.00	200.00

LC-33   *REVERSE WREATH WITH TWENTY CHERRY LEAVES*

OBVERSE BOUQUET WITH TWO SHAMROCKS

Composition: Copper, brass
Weight: 6.6 to 7.8 gms
Diameter: 26.9 to 27.1 mm
Die Axis: ↑↑
Edge: Plain
Ref.Nos.: See below

Varieties: Reverse and composition
A1 Small flat reverse bow, Copper; Br 704; Co 27B; W 723
A2 Small flat reverse bow, Brass; Br 704; Co 28B; W 723

B Large flat reverse bow, Mule, obverse of LC-33A1,
and reverse of LC-33C1; W 724

C1 Without obverse bow, No blade of wheat; Hart variety; Br 705; Co 26B;
W 725
C2 Without obverse bow, Blade of wheat bewteen thistles; Co 25B; W 725

Cat.No.	Date	Description	VG	F	VF	EF	AU	UNC
LC-33A1		Flat bow, Copper	3.00	8.00	20.00	50.00	100.00	250.00
LC-33A2		Flat bow, Brass	J. Hoare Auction, February 1997, Lot 1029, F+ $440.00					
LC-33B		Large flat bow, Mule			Extremely Rare			
LC-33C1		Without bow, No wheat, Hart	5.00	10.00	20.00	80.00	125.00	-
LC-33C2		Without bow	5.00	10.00	20.00	80.00	125.00	-

BIRMINGHAM ISSUES

OBVERSE FRENCH LEGEND

TOKEN MONTREAL UN SOU—
AGRICULTURE & COMMERCE BAS CANADA

As the popularity of the Bouquet sous increased further importations were made anonymously from England, these pieces being struck by the same Birmingham firm that struck the sous of the Bank of Montreal.

LC-34 *REVERSE WREATH WITH THIRTY TWO LAUREL LEAVES*

OBVERSE BOUQUET WITH ONE SHAMROCK

Composition: Copper, brass
Weight: 7.1 to 8.1 gms
Diameter: 27.0 to 27.1 mm
Die Axis: ↑↑
Edge: Plain
Ref.Nos.: Br 706; Co 23B; W 726

Cat.No.	Date	Description	VG	F	VF	EF	AU	UNC
LC-34A1		Copper	15.00	40.00	90.00	150.00	225.00	400.00
LC-34A2		Brass	15.00	40.00	90.00	150.00	225.00	400.00

LC-35   *REVERSE WREATH WITH THIRTY TWO LAUREL LEAVES*

OBVERSE BOUQUET WITH TWO SHAMROCKS

Composition: Copper, brass
Weight: 7.1 to 8.1 gms
Diameter: 27.0 to 27.2 mm
Die Axis: ↑↑
Edge: Plain
Ref.Nos.: See below

Varieties: Composition
    A1 Copper; Br 707; Co 22B; W 727
    A2 Brass; Br 707; Co 22B

Cat.No.	Date	Description	VG	F	VF	EF	AU	UNC
LC-35A1		Copper	4.00	8.00	15.00	50.00	100.00	-
LC-35A2		Brass	5.00	10.00	20.00	80.00	150.00	-

LC-36   *REVERSE WREATH WITH THIRTY TWO LAUREL LEAVES*

OBVERSE BOUQUET WITH THREE SHAMROCKS

Composition: Copper
Weight: 7.1 to 8.1 gms
Diameter: 27.0 to 27.1 mm
Die Axis: ↑↑
Edge: Plain
Ref.Nos.: Br 708; Co 20B; W 728

Cat.No.	Date	Description	VG	F	VF	EF	AU	UNC
LC-36		Copper	15.00	25.00	35.00	85.00	175.00	-

OBVERSE ENGLISH LEGEND

LC-37

TOKEN MONTREAL UN SOU —
TRADE & AGRICULTURE LOWER CANADA

REVERSE WREATH WITH THIRTY TWO LAUREL LEAVES
OBVERSE WITH THREE SHAMROCKS

The obverse of this token is the same as that of the Bank of Montreal token (LC-2A5). The obverse die was retouched and mated with the thirty-two-leaf reverse, thus linking the Birmingham issues to the Bank of Montreal tokens.

Composition: Copper
Weight: 7.1 to 7.8 gms
Diameter: 27.0 mm
Die Axis: ↑↑
Edge: Plain
Ref.Nos.: Br 709; Co 21B; W 729

Cat.No.	Date	Description	VG	F	VF	EF	AU	UNC
LC-37		Three shamrocks	20.00	35.00	50.00	100.00	250.00	-

OBVERSE FRENCH LEGEND

LC-38

TOKEN MONTREAL UN SOU—
AGRICULTURE & COMMERCE BAS CANADA
REVERSE WREATH WITH THIRTY NINE LAUREL LEAVES

OBVERSE BOUQUET WITH THREE SHAMROCKS

Composition: Copper
Weight: 7.4 to 7.8 gms
Diameter: 26.9 to 27.0 mm
Die Axis: ↑↑
Edge: Plain
Ref.Nos.: See below

Varieties: Obverse
    A No obverse bow; Br 710; Co 19B; W 730

    B Obverse bow; Br 712; W G3

Note: McLachlan, in a paper presented before the American Numismatic Association in 1912, illustrated how the two copper examples of this token (LC-38B) were considered by him to be fraudulent.

Cat.No.	Date	Description	VG	F	VF	EF	AU	UNC
LC-38A		No bow	20.00	35.00	75.00	125.00	-	-
LC-38B		Bow		Possibly three or four known, Very Rare				

LC-39   *REVERSE WREATH WITH THIRTY NINE LAUREL LEAVES*

OBVERSE BOUQUET WITH SIX SHAMROCKS

Composition: Copper
Weight: 7.5 to 7.8 gms
Diameter: 26.9 to 27.0 mm
Die Axis: ↑↑
Edge: Plain
Ref.Nos.: Br 711, Co 18B;
                W 731

Cat.No.	Date	Description	VG	F	VF	EF	AU	UNC
LC-39		Six shamrocks	15.00	25.00	40.00	90.00	200.00	-

MONTREAL ISSUES

Some varieties were produced in Montreal as the demand for sous continued. These pieces vary considerably in fabric, size and weight. All have the bouquet of the heraldic flowers shown in various ways, with the usual reverse design. Jean-Marie Arnault cut the dies and struck the token LC-40.

LC-40   *TOKEN MONTREAL UN SOU*
            — AGRICULTURE & COMMERCE BAS CANADA

REVERSE WREATH WITH SIXTEEN CHERRY LEAVES
OBVERSE BOUQUET WITH FIVE SHAMROCKS

All varieties have obverse bow positioned to the left and are found struck over all the following pieces.

Copper: Various Blacksmith Tokens, The Sloop Tokens of Upper Canada, The Ships Colonies & Commerce Halfpennies of Lower Canada and The Commercial Change Farthing Token

Brass: Various Blacksmith Tokens, Bust & Harp Tokens and Tiffin Tokens

Composition: Copper, brass
Weight: 5.0 to 5.3 gms
Diameter: 26.4 to 27.1 mm
Die Axis: ↑↑
Edge: See varieties
Ref.Nos.: Br 674; W 734;
        See below

Varieties: Composition and Edge

A1 Copper, Coarsely reeded edge; Co 63B
A2 Copper, Finely reeded edge; Co 64B
A3 Copper, Plain edge; Co 65B
A4 Copper, Thin flan, Reeded edge; Co 66B
A5 Copper, Overstruck on various tokens

A6 Brass, Coarsely reeded edge; Co 67B
A7 Brass, Finely reeded edge; Co 68B
A8 Brass, Plain edge; Co 69B
A9 Brass, Thin flan, Reeded edge; Co 70B
A10 Brass, Overstruck on various tokens

Cat.No.	Date Description	VG	F	VF	EF	AU	UNC
LC-40A1	Copper, Coarsely reeded	12.00	25.00	60.00	125.00	-	-
LC-40A2	Copper, Finely reeded	8.00	15.00	45.00	100.00	-	-
LC-40A3	Copper, Plain	8.00	15.00	45.00	100.00	-	-
LC-40A4	Copper, Thin, reeded	10.00	20.00	50.00	100.00	-	-
LC-40A5	Copper, Overstruck	25.00	50.00	75.00	150.00	-	-
LC-40A6	Brass, Coarsely reeded	10.00	20.00	60.00	125.00	-	-
LC-40A7	Brass, Finely reeded	10.00	20.00	60.00	125.00	-	-
LC-40A8	Brass, Plain	10.00	20.00	60.00	125.00	-	-
LC-40A9	Brass, Thin, Reeded	10.00	20.00	60.00	125.00	-	-
LC-40A10	Brass, Overstruck	25.00	50.00	75.00	150.00	-	-

LC-41　*REVERSE WREATH WITH SEVENTEEN CHERRY LEAVES*

OBVERSE BOUQUET WITH SIX SHAMROCKS

Composition: Copper, brass
Weight: 5.9 to 6.7 gms
Diameter: 27.6 to 28.3 mm
Die Axis: ↑↑ ↑↓
Edge: Plain
Ref.Nos.: Br 684; W 732

Varieties: Composition and die axis
All varieties have obverse bow positioned right
A1 Copper, Medal; Co 49B
A2 Copper, Coinage; Co 49B
A3 Brass, Co 50B

Cat.No.	Date	Description	VG	F	VF	EF	AU	UNC
LC-41A1		Copper, Medal	5.00	10.00	35.00	90.00	200.00	-
LC-41A2		Copper, Coinage	10.00	20.00	50.00	110.00	250.00	-
LC-41A3		Brass, Medal			Rare			

LC-42　*REVERSE WREATH WITH EIGHTEEN CHERRY LEAVES*

OBVERSE BOUQUET WITH TWO SHAMROCKS

This token is only known struck over UC-12B. The undertype obscures much of the design. The striking appears to be the work of Jean-Marie Arnault.

Photograph not available

Composition: Copper
Weight: 6.5 gms
Diameter: 27.6 mm
Die Axis: ↑↑
Edge: Plain
Ref.Nos.: W 735

Cat.No.	Date	Description	VG	F	VF	EF	AU	UNC
LC-42					Unique			

LC-43 *REVERSE WREATH WITH TWENTY ONE CHERRY LEAVES*

OBVERSE BOUQUET WITH NO SHAMROCKS

The dies for this sou were found in Montreal in 1863 and presented to the Antiquarian and Numismatic Society of Montreal which struck a few specimens and then had the dies turned down to receive a collar. Later re-strikes were struck with a collar and exist in copper, brass and lead. A few were struck on square flans and over American cents.

Composition: Copper, brass, lead
Weight: Variable
Diameter: 28.3 to 28.5 mm
Die Axis: ↑↑
Edge: Plain, reeded
Ref.Nos.: Br 689; Co 24B; W 733

Varieties: Composition and edge
A1 Original, Brass, Reeded
A2 Restrike, Lead/copper/brass without collar
A3 Restrike, Copper/brass with collar, Plain

Cat.No.	Date	Description	VF	EF	AU	UNC
LC-43A1		Original, Brass, Reeded		Extremely Rare		
LC-43A2		Restrike, Lead/copper/brass, No collar		Rare		
LC-43A3		Restrike, Copper/brass with collar, plain	150.00	250.00	300.00	350.00

MISCELLANEOUS ISSUES

LC-44   *REVERSE WREATH WITH EIGHTEEN CHERRY LEAVES*

OBVERSE BOUQUET WITH SEVEN SHAMROCKS

Composition: Copper, Brass
Weight: 6.8 to 7.0 gms
Diameter: 27.5 to 27.7 mm
Die Axis: ↑↓
Edge: Plain
Ref.Nos.: Br 690; Co 40B,
          W G2

Cat.No.	Date	Description	VG	F	VF	EF	AU	UNC
LC-44A		Copper	-	-	150.00	250.00	300.00	375.00
LC-44B		Brass						

J. Hoare Auction, October 1998, Lot 765, EF - $300.00

LC-45   *T. DUSEAMAN BUTCHER BELLEVILLE*

OBVERSE BOUQUET WITH THREE SHAMROCKS

This token was prepared on order for Tobias Seaman, a butcher and hotelier of Belleville, New Jersey, as his business card. After being rejected by him it seems the "U" was added later to create the name Duseaman. This mule of a bouquet and store card die is as heavy as an American Large Cent.

Composition: Copper
Weight: 10.8 to 11.1 gms
Diameter: 27.9 to 28.2 mm
Die Axis: ↑↑
Edge: Plain
Ref.Nos.: Br 670; Co 71B;
          W C28

Cat.No.	Date	Description	VG	F	VF	EF	AU	UNC
LC-45			10.00	25.00	50.00	100.00	200.00	350.00

ANONYMOUS TOKENS OF LOWER CANADA

Most tokens imported into Lower Canada or manufactured in the colony were anonymous. They were usually produced with good weight but as their weight decreased the profit potential for the issuer increased. After 1825, imported tokens were antedated or bore no date whatsoever.

THOMAS HALLIDAY TOKENS 1812-1814

These are an extensive series of anonymous English tokens struck by Thomas Halliday in 1812 and 1813. They are of good weight and were designed by Halliday who also cut the dies. They saw extensive use in England until 1819, when copper tokens were ordered to be withdrawn from circulation, and then circulated in Canada.

LC-46   *HALFPENNY TOKEN*

HALFPENNY TOKEN 1812 — (BUST DESIGN)

The Halliday mintmark "H" must appear on this token.

Composition: Copper
Weight: 8.2 to 8.6 gms
Diameter: 28.3 to 28.9 mm
Die Axis: ↑↓
Edge: Engrailed
Ref.Nos: Br 960; See below

Varieties: Obverse

"H" right of bust   "H" centre of bust   "H" left of bust

A1 "H" to right of bust; Co 25T; W C14
A2 "H" in centre of bust; Co 26T; W C15
A3 "H" to left of bust; Co 27T; W C16

Cat.No.	Date	Description	VG	F	VF	EF	AU	UNC
LC-46A1	1812	"H" Right	5.00	10.00	25.00	50.00	125.00	250.00
LC-46A2	1812	"H" Centre	5.00	10.00	25.00	50.00	125.00	250.00
LC-46A3	1812	"H" Left	5.00	10.00	25.00	50.00	125.00	250.00

LC-47   *ONE PENNY TOKEN*

LC-47A   *ONE PENNY TOKEN 1812 — 1812*

Composition: Copper
Weight: 18.2 gms
Diameter: 34.4 mm
Die Axis: ↑↓
Edge: Engrailed
Ref.Nos.: Br 957; See below

Closed Wreath   Open Wreath

Varieties: Obverse
A1 Closed wreath at top; Co 39T; W C26
A2 Open wreath at top; Co 40T, W C27

Cat.No.	Date	Description	VG	F	VF	EF	AU	UNC
LC-47A1	1812	Closed wreath	10.00	20.00	40.00	90.00	200.00	-
LC-47A2	1812	Open wreath	10.00	20.00	40.00	90.00	200.00	-

LC-47B   *ONE PENNY TOKEN— 1812*

Composition: Copper
Weight: 17.1 to 18.2 gms
Diameter: 34.2 to 34.6 mm
Die Axis: ↑↓
Edge: Engrailed
Ref.Nos.: Br 958; See below

Small Ship   Large Ship

Four leaves in cornucopia

Varieties: Obverse
B1 Small ship, Four leaves in cornucopia; Co 34T; W C22
B2 Large ship, Two leaves in cornucopia; Co 35T; W C23

Cat.No.	Date	Description	VG	F	VF	EF	AU	UNC
LC-47B1	1812	Small ship	10.00	20.00	35.00	75.00	150.00	250.00
LC-47B2	1812	Large ship	J. Hoare Auction, February 1999, Lot 701, VG - $165.00					

LC-47C   *ONE PENNY TOKEN— 1813*

Composition: Copper
Weight: 17.1 to 18.2 gms
Diameter: 34.2 to 34.6 mm
Die Axis: ↑↑ ↑↓
Edge: Engrailed
Ref.Nos.: Br 958; See below

Leaves   Acorns

Varieties: Reverse and die axis
C1 Oak wreath begins with leaves, Medal; Co 37T; W C25
C2 Oak wreath begins with acorns, Coinage; Co 38T; W C24

Cat. No.	Date	Description	VG	F	VF	EF	AU	UNC
LC-47C1	1813	Leaves, Medal	20.00	30.00	50.00	100.00	225.00	350.00
LC-47C2	1813	Acorns, Coinage	20.00	30.00	50.00	100.00	225.00	350.00

LC-47D

ONE PENNY TOKEN 1812 —

Composition: Copper
Weight: 16.5 to 18.2 gms
Diameter: 34.1 to 34.3 mm
Die Axis: ↑↓
Edge: Engrailed, reeded
(diagonally)
Ref.Nos.: Br 959; See below

Seven Leaves

Eight Leaves

Nine Leaves

Twelve Leaves

Varieties: Obverse
D1 Bust laureated with twelve leaves, Engrailed; Co 33T; W C21
D2 Bust laureated with eleven leaves, Engrailed; Co 32T; W C20
D3 Bust laureated with nine leaves, Engrailed; Co 31T; W C19
D4 Bust laureated with eight leaves, Engrailed; Co 29T; W C18
D5 Bust laureated with seven leaves, Engrailed; Co 28T
D6 Bust laureated with seven leaves, Reeded diagonally ; Co 28T; W C17

Cat.No.	Date	Description	VG	F	VF	EF	AU	UNC
LC-47D1	1812	Twelve leaves	12.00	25.00	50.00	125.00	200.00	350.00
LC-47D2	1812	Eleven leaves	8.00	20.00	35.00	90.00	150.00	275.00
LC-47D3	1812	Nine leaves	12.00	25.00	40.00	100.00	175.00	300.00
LC-47D4	1812	Eight leaves			Very Rare			
LC-47D5	1812	Seven leaves	20.00	30.00	50.00	125.00	200.00	350.00
LC-47D6	1812	Seven leaves	20.00	30.00	50.00	125.00	200.00	350.00

LC-47E   *ONE PENNY TOKEN — 1812 BON POUR DEUX SOUS*

This pattern was struck by Halliday possibly as a salesmans sample for the Tiffin series in Canada. The legends giving the value in both English and French were certainly appealing to Lower Canada.

Composition: Copper
Weight: 17.54 gms
Diameter: 34.6 mm
Thickness: 2.5 mm
Die Axis: ↑↓
Edge: Engrailed
Ref.Nos: C 36T; W A1

Cat.No.	Date	Description	VG	F	VF	EF	AU	UNC
LC-47E	1812		Only three known, two of which are with the					
			Bank of Canada Collection, and one in a private collection.					

The following two tokens, while produced by Halliday, are English penny tokens. Breton did not recognise these tokens as Canadian, while Courteau in his Tiffin Token monograph listed them because of their die linkage to other Halliday tokens that circulated in Canada.

LC-47F   *COMMERCE 1814 —*

Composition: Copper
Weight: 16.5 to 18.2 gms
Diameter: 34.1 to 34.3 mm
Die Axis: ↑↓
Edge: Engrailed, reeded
Ref.Nos.: See below

Varieties:
   E1 Engrailed; Co 30T; W C12
   E2 Reeded; Co 30T; W C12

Cat. No.	Date	Description	VG	F	VF	EF	AU	UNC
LC-47F1	1814	Engrailed	25.00	50.00	75.00	125.00	250.00	-
LC-47F2	1814	Reeded	25.00	50.00	75.00	125.00	250.00	-

LC-47G   *COMMERCE* —

Composition: Copper
Weight: 16.5 gms
Diameter: 34.1 to 34.3 mm
Die Axis: ↑↓
Edge: Engrailed
Ref.Nos.: Co 41T; W C13

Cat.No.	Date	Description	VG	F	VF	EF	AU	UNC
LC-47G	(Undated)	Engrailed	40.00	75.00	100.00	150.00	300.00	-

TIFFIN TOKENS

About 1832, Joseph Tiffin, a Montreal grocer, imported a quantity of lightweight halfpenny copper tokens from England. These were copies of an anonymous English halfpenny struck in 1812 from dies cut by Thomas Halliday (LC-46). Tiffin's tokens bore the date 1812 in order to evade the laws forbidding the importation of tokens into Canada. Eventually the banks refused to accept any of these pieces as currency and accepted them only for their scrap metal value.

LC-48   *TIFFIN COPPER ORIGINALS*

Halliday's "H" does not appear on this token. Courteau listed a brass specimen (23T) among the copper originals.

LC-48A   *HALFPENNY TOKEN 1812—*

Composition: Copper, brass
Weight: 5.3 to 6.6 gms
Diameter: 27.3 to 27.7 mm
Die Axis: ↑↓
Edge: Plain
Ref.Nos.: Br 960; See below

Two Leaves   Three Daisies   Two Daisies

Varieties: Obverse, Reverse and Composition
A1 Bust laureated four top leaves, Three daisies crown the cornucopia; Co 24T; W 608
A2 Bust laureated two top leaves, Three daisies crown the cornucopia, Copper; Co 22T; W 607
A3 Bust laureated two top leaves, Three daisies crown the cornucopia, Brass; Co 23T; W 607
A4 Bust laureated two top leaves, Two daisies crown the cornucopia; Co 21T; W 606

Variations: A1 was issued on thick and thin flans.

Cat.No.	Date	Description	VG	F	VF	EF	AU	UNC
LC-48A1	1812	4 leaves, 3 daisies	3.00	6.00	12.00	25.00	50.00	100.00
LC-48A2	1812	2 leaves, 3 daisies, Copper	3.00	6.00	12.00	25.00	50.00	100.00
LC-48A3	1812	2 leaves, 3 daisies, Brass	8.00	15.00	30.00	45.00	90.00	180.00
LC-48A4	1812	2 leaves, 2 daisies	5.00	10.00	20.00	35.00	70.00	140.00

IMITATION TIFFIN TOKENS

Imitations of the Tiffin Tokens appeared in copper and brass from 1832 to 1836. They are of variable workmanship and composition and some varieties are extremely rare.

LC-48B   *HALFPENNY TOKEN 1812 —*

Composition: Brass
Weight: 5.0 to 5.9 gms
Diameter: 27.4 to 27.7 mm
Die Axis: ↑↓
Edge: Plain
Ref.Nos.: Br 960; See below

Varieties: Obverse

B1 Counter-clockwise wreath; Co 10 to 16, 18 to 20T; W 610 to 616, 618 to 620
B2 Clockwise wreath; Co 9,17T; W 609,617

Variations: Obverse variations exist in the size, shape and style of the head.

Cat.No.	Date	Description	VG	F	VF	EF	AU	UNC
LC-48B1	1812	Counter-clockwise wreath	3.00	6.00	12.00	25.00	50.00	100.00
LC-48B2	1812	Clockwise wreath	3.00	6.00	12.00	25.00	50.00	100.00

LC-48C   *1812—*

Composition: Brass
Weight: 5.1 to 5.9 gms
Diameter: 27.4 to 27.7 mm
Die Axis: ↑↓
Edge: Plain
Ref.Nos.: Br 961; See below

Varieties: Obverse

C1 Counter-clockwise wreath; Co 5 to 8T; W 622 to 625
C2 Clockwise wreath; Co 1 to 4T; W 621, 626 to 628

Variations: Obverse variations exist in the size, shape and style of the bust.

Cat.No.	Date	Description	VG	F	VF	EF	AU	UNC
LC-48C1	1812	Counter-clockwise wreath	6.00	12.00	25.00	45.00	90.00	175.00
LC-48C2	1812	Clockwise wreath	5.00	10.00	20.00	35.00	70.00	140.00

IMITATIONS OF TIFFIN TOKENS "BLACKSMITH STYLE"

For the listings of these crude Imitations of Tiffin Tokens see page 218 and 219, Cat. Nos. BL-32 and BL-33.

LC-49   *HALFPENNY TOKEN— VICTORIA NOBIS EST*

This token was usually struck over Guppy halfpennies and possibly other tokens. The portrait is one of the "mysterious busts" discussed by McLachlan, Heal and other numismatists writing at the turn of the century. The portrait has never been satisfactorily identified.

Composition: Copper
Weight: 8.5 to 9.0 gms
Diameter: 28.0 to 28.3 mm
Die Axis: ↑↓
Edge: Engrailed
Ref.Nos.: Br 982; Co 40NL;
                W 542

Cat.No.	Date	Description	VG	F	VF	EF	AU	UNC
LC-49A1		Overstruck	5.00	10.00	20.00	40.00	100.00	-
LC-49A2		Not overstruck	6.00	12.00	25.00	50.00	125.00	-

RH TOKENS 1812-1814

Thomas Halliday designed this series of tokens for use in England. The farthing and penny did not circulate in Canada but were imported by collectors after 1870. Of the halfpenny denomination only the plain edge, light weight specimens were imported by Richard Hurd, a Montreal merchant, for use in Canada.

LC-50   *RH (RICHARD HURD) — 1812 FARTHING TOKEN*

Composition: Copper
Weight: 4.0 to 4.1 gms
Diameter: 22.2 to 22.4 mm
Die Axis: ↑↓
Edge: Engrailed
Ref.Nos.: Br 991; Co 32NL; W C2

Cat.No.	Date	Description	VG	F	VF	EF	AU	UNC
LC-50	1812	Engrailed	30.00	40.00	65.00	90.00	175.00	350.00

LC-51   *RH (RICHARD HURD) — 1814 HALF PENNY TOKEN*

Composition: Copper
Weight: See below
Diameter: 28.0 to 28.2 mm
Die Axis: ↑↓
Edge: Engrailed, plain
Ref.Nos.: Br 990; See below

Varieties: Weight and edge
    A1 Weight: 8.5 gms, Engrailed; Co 33NL; W C3
    A2 Weight: 5.5 gms, Plain; Co 33NL; W 571

Cat.No.	Date	Description	VG	F	VF	EF	AU	UNC
LC-51A1	1814	Engrailed, Thick flan	10.00	20.00	35.00	75.00	200.00	350.00
LC-51A2	1814	Plain, Thin flan	15.00	30.00	60.00	125.00	250.00	400.00

LC-52   *RH (RICHARD HURD)— 1814 ONE PENNY TOKEN*

Composition: Copper
Weight: 16.2 gms
Diameter: 34.2 to 34.4 mm
Die Axis: ↑↓
Edge: Engrailed
Ref.Nos.: Br 989; Co 34NL;
       W C4

Cat.No.	Date Description	VG	F	VF	EF	AU	UNC
LC-52	1814 Engrailed	25.00	65.00	150.00	300.00	500.00	-

LC-53   *TO FACILITATE TRADE 1825—*

These two tokens are believed to portray Col. de Salaberry, who repelled the Americans at Chateauguay and Crysler's Farm during the War of 1812, saving Montreal from the fate of York in Upper Canada. The clothing of the bust resembles that seen in a well-known painting of de Salaberry which undoubtedly led early writers to assume that the colonel's features appear on the tokens.

LC-53A   *— (MILITARY BUST OF SALABERRY)*

Composition: Copper
Weight: 6.2 to 6.8 gms
Diameter: 27.8 to 28.1 mm
Die Axis: ↑↓
Edge: Plain
Ref.Nos.: Br 992; See below

Open Sleeve   Closed Sleeve

Varieties: Obverse
    A1   Open sleeve; Co 47NL; W 561
    A2   Closed sleeve; Co 48NL; W 562

Cat.No.	Date	Description	VG	F	VF	EF	AU	UNC
LC-53A1	1825	Open sleeve	5.00	10.00	30.00	75.00	150.00	250.00
LC-53A2	1825	Closed sleeve	30.00	65.00	150.00	-	-	-

LC-53B   *UNIDENTIFIED — (CIVILIAN BUST)*

Composition: Copper
Weight: 6.8 gms
Diameter: 27.6 to 27.8 mm
Die Axis: ↑↓
Edge: Plain
Ref.Nos.: Co 49NL; W 563

Note: Mule, Obverse of LC-58A1, Reverse of LC-53A.

Cat.No.	Date	Description	VG	F	VF	EF	AU	UNC
LC-53B	1825	Mule			Extremely Rare			

LC-54   *SPREAD EAGLE TOKENS 1813—1815*

The eagle was not a popular symbol for a coin design in 1813. The war of 1812-14 was at its height and during this period with the Canadian colonies in the midst of an American invasion, the original issue was not well received.

ORIGINALS OF 1813

The tokens dated 1813 and struck over the Samuel Guppy tokens of Bristol are the original issue by a Boston merchant who settled in Montreal during 1813.

LC-54A   *HALFPENNY TOKEN 1813 —*

Composition: Copper
Weight: 8.8 gms
Diameter: 27.9 mm
Die Axis: ↑↓
Edge: Engrailed
Ref.Nos.: Br 994; Co 25NL; W 543

Cat.No.	Date	Description	VG	F	VF	EF	AU	UNC
LC-54A	1813		6.00	12.00	20.00	45.00	90.00	150.00

IMITATIONS OF 1813 — 1815

The imitations of the Spread Eagle Token appeared after 1825 and were antedated. They are lighter and crude in design. The reverse lettering on the imitations is larger than the originals.

LC-54B   *HALFPENNY TOKEN 1813 —*

Composition: Copper, brass
Weight: 5.5 to 6.5 gms
Diameter: 27.3 mm
Die Axis: ↑↓
Edge: Engrailed
Ref.Nos.: Br 994; See below

Varieties:
B1 Copper; Co 26NL; W 544
B2 Brass; Co 27NL; W 544

Cat.No.	Date	Description	VG	F	VF	EF	AU	UNC
LC-54B1	1813	Copper	7.00	15.00	30.00	65.00	150.00	250.00
LC-54B2	1813	Brass			Extremely Rare			

LC-54C   *HALFPENNY TOKEN 1814 —*

Composition: Copper
Weight: 6.5 to 7.0 gms
Diameter: 27.5 to 27.6 mm
Die Axis: ↑↓
Edge: Engrailed
Ref.Nos.: Br 994; See below

Large shield with drapery between shield and trident handle

Small shield with drapery left of trident handle

Varieties: Reverse
C1 Large shield; Co 28NL; W 545
C2 Small shield; Co 29NL; W 546

Cat.No.	Date	Description	VG	F	VF	EF	AU	UNC
LC-54C1	1814	Large shield	7.00	15.00	25.00	50.00	150.00	250.00
LC-54C2	1814	Small shield	7.00	15.00	25.00	50.00	150.00	250.00

LC-54D   *HALFPENNY TOKEN 1815 —*

Composition: Copper
Weight: 6.1 to 6.5 gms
Diameter: 27.5 to 27.7 mm
Die Axis: ↑↓
Edge: Engrailed
Ref.Nos.: Br 994; See below

Counterclockwise Wreath   Clockwise Wreath

Varieties: Obverse
    D1 Counter clockwise wreath; Co 30NL; W 547
    D2 Clockwise wreath; Co 31NL; W 548

Cat.No.	Date	Description	VG	F	VF	EF	AU	UNC
LC-54D1	1815	Counter clockwise wreath	10.00	15.00	25.00	50.00	125.00	250.00
LC-54D2	1815	Clockwise wreath	5.00	10.00	15.00	30.00	75.00	100.00

THE SEATED JUSTICE TOKENS

The "Seated Justice" tokens have been found in Lower Canadian hoards. They are all derived from a token designed by Thomas Halliday and struck by Sir Edward Thomason for Shaw, Jobson & Co. of Roscoe Mills in Sheffield, England.

LC-55 *(SEATED JUSTICE DESIGN)— (SAILING SHIP DESIGN)*

Composition: Copper
Weight: 5.3 gms
Diameter: 25.5 mm
Die Axis: ↑↑
Edge: Plain
Ref.Nos.: Br 1001; W 567

Cat.No.	Date	Description	VG	F	VF	EF	AU	UNC
LC-55		No legend	J. Hoare Auction, February 1995, Lot 1859, $4,500.00					

LC-56 *HALFPENNY TOKEN— (SAILING SHIP DESIGN)*

LC-56A   *HALFPENNY TOKEN 1812 —*
                             BALE MARKED

S.J. & CO

Composition: Copper, brass
Weight: 5.3 to 6.2 gms
Diameter: 28.3 to 28.7 mm
Die Axis: ↑↓ ↑↑
Edge: Plain
Ref.Nos.: Br 1004; See below

Short pennant

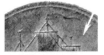

No pennant

Varieties: Obverse, composition and edge
     A1 Short pennant on foremast, Copper, Plain
     A2 Short pennant on foremast, Brass, Plain; Co 20NL; W 569
     A3 No pennant on foremast, Copper, Plain; Co 21NL; W 570
     A4 No pennant on foremast, Brass, Plain; Co 22NL; W 570

Cat.No.	Date	Description	VG	F	VF	EF	AU	UNC
LC-56A1	1812	Short pennant, Copper	Jeffrey Hoare Auction, February 1991, VF+ $385.00					
LC-56A2	1812	Short pennant, Brass	6.00	12.00	25.00	50.00	100.00	200.00
LC-56A3	1812	No pennant, Copper			Very Rare			
LC-56A4	1812	No pennant, Brass	20.00	40.00	60.00	125.00	-	-

LC-56B

HALFPENNY TOKEN 1815—
BALE MARKED S.J. & CO

Composition: Copper, brass
Weight: 5.3 to 6.4 gms
Diameter: 28.3 to 28.9 mm
Die Axis: ↑↓ ↑↓
Edge: Reeded
Ref.Nos.: Br 1004; See below

Varieties: Composition
B1 Copper; Co 23NL; W 570
B2 Brass; Co 24NL; W 570

Cat.No.	Date	Description	VG	F	VF	EF	AU	UNC
LC-56B1	1815	Copper	5.00	10.00	20.00	50.00	125.00	250.00
LC-56B2	1815	Brass	10.00	30.00	125.00	250.00	500.00	-

LC-56C

HALFPENNY TOKEN—

Composition: Copper, brass
Weight: 5.1 to 5.2 gms
Diameter: 27.7 to 28 .0 mm
Die Axis: ↑↓, ↑↑
Edge: Reeded
Ref.Nos.: Br 1005; See below

Varieties: Composition
C1 Copper; Co 19NL; W 568
C2 Brass; Co 19NL; W 568

Cat.No.	Date	Description	VG	F	VF	EF	AU	UNC
LC-56C1		Copper	15.00	40.00	100.00	200.00	400.00	-
LC-56C2		Brass			Very Rare			

LC-57 *(SEATED JUSTICE DESIGN) — 1820 (BUST OF GEORGE III)*

Composition: Copper, brass
Weight: 5.2 to 7.5 gms
Diameter: 27.5 to 27.7 mm
Die Axis: ↑↑ ↑↓
Edge: Plain
Ref.Nos.: Br 1011; See below

Fine Head Obverse

Crude Head Obverse

Varieties: Obverse and composition
A1 Fine head design, Coinage; Co 37NL; W 564
A2 Crude head design, Copper, Coinage; Co 38NL; W 565
A3 Crude head design, Brass, Medal; Co 39NL; W 565

Variations: Issued on thick and thin flans. Willey, referring to Davis, lists another variety without a date W566.

Cat.No.	Date	Description	VG	F	VF	EF	AU	UNC
LC-57A1	1820	Fine head	5.00	10.00	35.00	75.00	150.00	300.00
LC-57A2	1820	Crude head, Copper	15.00	30.00	75.00	150.00	-	-
LC-57A3	1820	Crude head, Brass			Very Rare			

LC-58   *SHIPS COLONIES & COMMERCE — (BUST DESIGN)*

The busts on the following coins have never been identified. The halfpennies bear a bust once identified as that of British Prime Minister Canning but this was an error, as Canning was bald, and the bust on the coin shows plenty of hair. It was identified by McLachlan as a portrait of Papineau but this cannot be substantiated. It is die-linked with the LC-53B "Salaberry" token.

LC-58A   *— (LARGE BUST DESIGN)*

Composition: Copper
Weight: 4.6 to 5.4 gms
Diameter: 26.0 to 26.5 mm
Die Axis: ↑↑
Edge: Plain
Ref.Nos.: Br 1002; See below

Open Sleeve   Closed Sleeve

"S" points to left of "O"   "S" points to right of "O"

Varieties: **A1** Open sleeve, Bottom seriph of the first "S" in SHIPS points to the left of the first "O" in COLONIES; Co 41NL; W 549
A2 Closed sleeve, Bottom seriph of the first "S" in SHIPS points to the right of the first "O" in COLONIES; Co 42NL; W 550
A3 Mule with obverse A1 and reverse A2; Co 43NL; W 551

Cat.No.	Date	Description	VG	F	VF	EF	AU	UNC
LC-58A1		Open sleeve	6.00	12.00	25.00	65.00	125.00	250.00
LC-58A2		Closed sleeve	30.00	60.00	125.00	250.00	-	-
LC-58A3		Mule			Extremely Rare			

LC-58B   *— (SMALL BUST DESIGN)*

This wide rim variety is a mule of LC-59B and LC-58A1. The obverse die was built up to match the diameter of the reverse die, resulting in a wide rim.

Composition: Copper
Weight: 4.9 to 5.4 gms
Diameter: 26.0 to 26.3 mm
Die Axis: ↑↑
Edge: Plain
Ref.Nos: Br 1002, Co 44NL,
                 W 552

Cat.No.	Date	Description	VG	F	VF	EF	AU	UNC
LC-58B			75.00	125.00	250.00	450.00	-	-

LC-59 *COMMERCIAL CHANGE — (BUST DESIGN)*

The obverse die of token number LC-58 was combined with a new reverse die to produce the Commercial Change token. It is clear that both pieces were produced by the same manufacturer.

LC-59A   *— (LARGE BUST DESIGN)*

Composition: Copper
Weight: 4.7 to 4.9 gms
Diameter: 23.9 to 24.1 mm
Die Axis: ↑↓
Edge: Plain
Ref.Nos.: Br 1007; Co 45NL;
       W 554

Cat.No.	Date	Description	VG	F	VF	EF	AU	UNC
LC-59A		J. Hoare Auction, October 1996, Lot 1441, F - $1,700.00						

LC-59B   *— (SMALL BUST DESIGN)*

Composition: Copper
Weight: 4.7 to 4.9 gms
Diameter: 23.9 to 24.1 mm
Die Axis: ↑↓
Edge: Plain
Ref.Nos.: Br 1007; Co 46NL;
       W 553

Variations: Struck on thick and thin flans.

Cat.No.	Date	Description	VG	F	VF	EF	AU	UNC
LC-59B			6.00	10.00	20.00	65.00	150.00	-

BUST AND HARP TOKENS

In 1825 a halfpenny token was struck in Great Britain on Canadian order. It was learned that currency regulations enacted in 1825 forbade the further importation of private tokens into Canada. However, nothing in the regulations interfered with importing tokens dated before 1825. The tokens struck in 1825 are known as the "Bust & Harp" tokens because of their design. They became very popular among the Irish immigrants to Lower Canada. They soon were widely imitated in brass and competed with legitimate colonial coinage for twenty years. The obverse portrays a bust of George IV in a cuirass, a piece of body armour covering the chest and shoulders. Over the shoulders it is divided into several flaps for freedom of movement. The reverse bears a harp with a frame incorporating the body of a winged female facing left.

LC-60 *BUST AND HARP COPPER ORIGINALS*

The originals were struck in 1825 on copper flans. There is a great variation in workmanship and weight.

LC-60A *(HARP DESIGN) 1820 — (BUST DESIGN)*

REVERSE DATED 1825 —
and 1820 OVER 5

Composition: Copper
Weight: 4.7 to 6.8 gms
Diameter: 26.3 to 27.9 mm
Die Axis: ↑↓
Edge: Plain
Ref.Nos.: Br 1012; See below

Seven Flaps

1820/5

Varieties: Obverse and reverse
A1 Dated 1825, Six flaps in the cuirass; Co 21H; W 581
A2 Dated 1820/5, Seven flaps in the cuirass; Co 22H; W 582

Cat.No.	Date	Description	F	VF	EF	AU	UNC
LC-60A1	1825	Six flaps	1,500.00	2,500.00	5,000.00	-	-
LC-60A2	1825	"1820/5", Seven flaps			Extremely Rare		

LC-60B   *DATED 1820*

Composition: Copper
Weight: 4.7 to 6.8 gms
Diameter: 27.4 to 27.7 mm
Die Axis: ↑↓
Edge: Plain
Ref.Nos.: Br 1012; Co 23H;
        W 583

Cat.No.	Date	Description	VG	F	VF	EF	AU	UNC
LC-60B	1820	Seven flaps	25.00	50.00	100.00	200.00	-	-

BUST AND HARP BRASS IMITATIONS

These brass imitations are all dated 1820 and vary greatly in workmanship. Following McLachlan's example, these tokens are divided into four categories depending on the workmanship.

From 1825 to 1837 the quality of tokens circulating in Lower Canada decreased and the blacksmith style was the only piece circulating by the end of this period. See BL-35 and BL-36.

Throughout this series slight obverse variations exist in the size and number of ruffles under the portrait's chin and the number of flaps in the cuirass. Variations on the reverse exist in the size and shape of the chignon, the top, the foot and leaves on the harp.

IMITATIONS ISSUED 1826—1827, DATED 1820

This group is of good quality and style. The bust of George IV is large.

Varieties: Reverse

Composition: Brass
Weight: 5.4 to 6.0 gms
Diameter: 27.5 to 27.9 mm
Die Axis: ↑↓
Edge: Plain
Ref.Nos.: Br 1012; See below

C1 Ten strings on harp; Co 9, 10H; W 584, 585

C2 Nine strings on harp; Co 11 to 13H; W 586 to 588

C3 Eight strings on harp; Co 24H; W 589

Cat.No.	Date	Description	VG	F	VF	EF	AU	UNC
LC-60C1	1820	Ten strings on harp	4.00	8.00	15.00	30.00	75.00	150.00
LC-60C2	1820	Nine strings on harp	4.00	8.00	15.00	30.00	75.00	150.00
LC-60C3	1820	Eight strings on harp	8.00	15.00	30.00	60.00	100.00	200.00

LC-60D   *IMITATIONS ISSUED 1828—1829, DATED 1820*

This group while slightly inferior in workmanship is also lighter in weight. The bust of George IV is smaller than LC-60B.

Varieties: Reverse and composition

Composition: Copper, brass
Weight: 5.2 gms
Diameter: 27.4 to 27.8 mm
Die Axis: ↑↓
Edge: Plain
Ref.Nos.: Br 1012; See below

D1 Ten strings on harp, Copper; Co 8H; W 593
D2 Ten strings on harp, Brass; Co 4 to 7H; W 590 to 593

D3 Nine strings on harp, Brass; Co 18H; W 594

Cat.No.	Date	Description	VG	F	VF	EF	AU	UNC
LC-60D1	1820	Ten strings, Copper	20.00	40.00	100.00	200.00	-	-
LC-60D2	1820	Ten strings, Brass	4.00	8.00	20.00	40.00	90.00	175.00
LC-60D3	1820	Nine strings, Brass	4.00	8.00	20.00	40.00	90.00	175.00

LC-60E   *IMITATIONS ISSUED Ca 1830, DATED 1820*

The workmanship of these tokens was significantly inferior. They are lighter in weight than other tokens of the series and show a larger bust.

Varieties: Reverse

Composition: Brass, Copper
Weight: 4.2 to 5.2 gms
Diameter: 27.5 to 27.8 mm
Die Axis: ↑↓
Edge: Plain
Ref.Nos.: Br 1012; See below

E1   Ten strings on harp, Brass; Co 1, 3H; W 595, 597

E2   Nine strings on harp, Brass; Co 14 to 17; W 596, 598 to 600

Photograph not available

E3   Nine strings on harp, Copper; Co 14

E4   Nine strings on harp, Brass; Co 19; W 601

Cat.No.	Date	Description	VG	F	VF	EF	AU	UNC
LC-60E1	1820	Ten strings on harp, Brass	5.00	10.00	20.00	50.00	100.00	200.00
LC-60E2	1820	Nine strings on harp, Brass	5.00	10.00	25.00	60.00	125.00	250.00
LC-60E3	1820	Nine Strings on harp, Copper			Very Rare			
LC-60E4	1820	Nine Strings on harp, Brass	5.00	10.00	25.00	60.00	125.00	250.00

LC-60F   *IMITATIONS ISSUED 1830-1835, DATED 1820*

This group is the poorest in workmanship.

Composition: Copper, brass
Weight: 5.2 to 5.3 gms
Diameter: 27.5 to 27.8 mm
Die Axis: ↑↓
Edge: Plain
Ref.Nos: Br 1012; Co 2H;
          W 602

Cat.No.	Date	Description	VG	F	VF	EF	AU	UNC
LC-60F	1820	Ten strings, Brass	5.00	10.00	20.00	40.00	80.00	175.00

IMITATIONS OF BUST AND HARP TOKENS "BLACKSMITH STYLE"

For the listing of Imitations of Bust and Harp Tokens see page 219 and 220; Cat. Nos. BL-34 to BL-36

GEORGE ORDS TOKEN

LC-61   *(HARP DESIGN) — (BUST DESIGN)*

This is an Irish halfpenny token struck in 1834 in Dublin. The dies were not deeply cut, resulting in coins of low relief. The legends wore rapidly, making possible the striking of pieces without legend for export to Canada. Large numbers of these were found in the famous hoard of obsolete tokens sent for safety to Quebec from Montreal in the weeks before the rebellion of 1837.

The originals have the obverse legend "George Ords Token" and reverse legend "Ireland 1834."

Composition: Copper, Brass
Weight: 7.3 gms
Diameter: 20 mm
Die Axis: ↑↓
Edge: Plain
Ref.Nos.: W 605

Cat.No.	Date	Description	VG	F	VF	EF	AU	UNC
LC-61A		Brass	15.00	25.00	50.00	150.00	-	-
LC-61B		Copper			Very Scarce			

IMITATIONS OF LOWER CANADA TOKENS "BLACKSMITH STYLE"

For the listings of Lower Canada Tokens see page 228; Cat.Nos. BL-51 and BL-52.

WELLINGTON TOKENS

During the Peninsular Campaign of the Napoleonic War, a series of copper tokens appeared in Yorkshire and elsewhere in England to remedy a shortage of copper. These pieces showed a bust of the Duke of Wellington. They were withdrawn from circulation in England because they became too plentiful. Some pieces were later brought to the Canadian colonies. The famous "Battle Tokens" were struck for J. Picard of Hull in Yorkshire by Sir Edward Thomason, the dies being cut by Thomas Halliday. Picard had specimens struck in silver for presentation at court and ordered a specimen in gold for the Prince Regent. Large numbers of Picard's tokens were later brought to Canada, it is thought, by troops sent out in 1814 to fight the Americans.

Most Wellington pennies had limited circulation in Canada. The halfpennies circulated much more widely, the halfpenny being the basic copper coin in Colonial Canada. The Wellington halfpennies circulated mostly in Lower Canada but found their way in small numbers into Upper Canada. Worn specimens turned up in circulation even after Confederation in remote areas despite the fact that the old Colonial tokens were being taken out of circulation and replaced with cents of the Dominion of Canada.

BRETON CROSS REFERENCE TABLE FOR WELLINGTON TOKENS

Breton No.	Charlton Cat. No	Page No.	Breton No.	Charlton Cat.N o.	Page No.
969	WE-1	160	980	WE-9	166
970	WE-4A	162	981	WE-10	166
971	WE-2A	160	984	WE-12	170
972	WE-2B	161	985	WE-13	170
973	WE-2C	161	986	WE-11B,C	168, 169
974	WE-3	162	987	WE-11A	167
976	WE-5	163	988	WE-11D	169
977	WE-6	163	1003	WE-14	171
978	WE-7	164	1006	WE-15	171
979	WE-8	165			

WE-1   *HALFPENNY TOKEN 1813 — FIELD MARSHAL WELLINGTON*

This token was often struck over Guppy halfpennies.

Composition: Copper
Weight: 7.8 to 11.2 gms
Diameter: 27.9 to 28.1 mm
Die Axis: ↑↑ ↑↓
Edge: Engrailed, plain
Ref.Nos.: Br 969; See below

Varieties: Edge and die axis
    A1 Engrailed, Thin flan, Medal; Co 26W; W 522
    A2 Engrailed, Thin flan, Coinage; Co 26W; W 522
    A3 Engrailed, Thick flan, Coinage; Co 26W; W 522
    A4 Plain, Thick flan, Medal; Co 26W; W 522
    A5 Plain, Thick flan, Coinage; Co 26W; W 522

Cat.No.	Date	Description	VG	F	VF	EF	AU	UNC
WE-1A1	1813	Engrailed, Thin, Medal	20.00	30.00	60.00	125.00	200.00	300.00
WE-1A2	1813	Engrailed, Thin, Coinage	6.00	12.00	30.00	60.00	125.00	225.00
WE-1A3	1813	Engrailed, Thick, Coinage	6.00	12.00	30.00	60.00	125.00	225.00
WE-1A4	1813	Plain, Thick, Medal	3.00	6.00	15.00	35.00	75.00	200.00
WE-1A5	1813	Plain, Thick, Coinage	3.00	6.00	15.00	35.00	75.00	200.00

WE-2   *HALFPENNY TOKEN — FIELD MARSHAL WELLINGTON*

WE-2A   *LEGENDS IN LARGE BOLD LETTERING*

Composition: Copper
Weight: 7.8 to 9.2 gms
Diameter: 27.6 to 28.6 mm
Die Axis: ↑↓
Edge: Plain, engrailed, reeded
Ref.Nos.: Br 971; See below

Varieties: Edge
    A1 Plain; Co 30W; W 526
    A2 Engrailed; Co 30W; W 526
    A3 Reeded; Not previously listed

Cat.No.	Date	Description	VG	F	VF	EF	AU	UNC
WE-2A1		Plain	3.00	6.00	20.00	50.00	125.00	225.00
WE-2A2		Engrailed	3.00	6.00	20.00	50.00	125.00	225.00
WE-2A3		Reeded	3.00	6.00	20.00	50.00	125.00	225.00

WE-2B   *LEGENDS IN SMALL LETTERING*

Composition: Copper
Weight: 7.8 to 10.0 gms
Diameter: 27.7 to 28.2 mm
Die Axis: ↑↓
Edge: Plain, engrailed
Ref.Nos.: Br 972; See below

Trident   Spear

Varieties: Reverse and edge
   B1 Trident, Thick flan, Plain; Co 28W
   B2 Trident, Thick flan, Engrailed; Co 28W; W 523
   B3 Trident, Thin flan, Engrailed; Co 28W; W 523
   B4 Spear, Engrailed; Co 27W; W 524

Cat.No.	Date	Description	VG	F	VF	EF	AU	UNC
WE-2B1		Trident, Thick, Plain	3.00	6.00	20.00	65.00	110.00	225.00
WE-2B2		Trident, Thick, Engrailed	3.00	6.00	20.00	65.00	110.00	225.00
WE-2B3		Trident, Thin, Engrailed	10.00	20.00	40.00	100.00	175.00	300.00
WE-2B4		Spear, Engrailed	20.00	30.00	60.00	150.00	225.00	350.00

WE-2C   *(CONTINUOUS OAK WREATH REVERSE)*

Courteau and Leroux did not list this token. McLachlan denounced it as a fake.

Composition: Copper
Weight: 6.2 gms
Diameter: 26.9 to 27.2 mm
Die Axis: ↑↑ ↑↓
Edge: Plain, engrailed
Ref.Nos.: Br 973; W 528

Varieties: Die axis
   C1 Coinage
   C2 Medal

Cat.No.	Date	Description	VG	F	VF	EF	AU	UNC
WE-2C1		Coinage			Extremely Rare			
WE-2C2		Medal			Extremely Rare			

WE-3 ONE PENNY TOKEN — 1813 FIELD MARSHAL WELLINGTON

Composition: Copper
Weight: 17.8 to 18.8 gms
Diameter: 33.9 to 35.0 mm
Die Axis: ↑↓
Edge: Engrailed
Ref.Nos.: Br 974; Co 29W;
          W 521

Cat.No.	Date	Description	VG	F	VF	EF	AU	UNC
WE-3	1813	Dated, no wreath	35.00	50.00	100.00	200.00	350.00	500.00

WE-4 ONE PENNY TOKEN — FIELD MARSHAL WELLINGTON

The following two varieties are usually found struck over a Bristol penny.

WE-4A   WITH REVERSE WREATH DESIGN

Composition: Copper
Weight: 16.6 to 18.2 gms
Diameter: 33.8 to 34.0 mm
Die Axis: ↑↓
Edge: Engrailed
Ref.Nos.: Br 970; Co 31W;
          W 527

Cat.No.	Date	Description	VG	F	VF	EF	AU	UNC
WE-4A	Undated	Obv. and Rev. wreath	25.00	35.00	65.00	125.00	200.00	350.00

WE-4B   WITHOUT REVERSE WREATH DESIGN

Composition: Copper
Weight: 17.6 to 18.5 gms
Diameter: 33.8 to 34.0 mm
Die Axis: ↑↓
Edge: Engrailed
Ref.Nos.: Co 32W; W 525

Cat.No.	Date	Description	VG	F	VF	EF	AU	UNC
WE-4B	Undated	Obv. wreath	65.00	90.00	150.00	275.00	450.00	650.00

WE-5 *HIBERNIA 1805 — FIELD MARSHAL WELLINGTON*

This token is an anonymous Irish piece from the County of Dublin. It is antedated and the engraver is unknown. The token was found only in small quantities in Canada.

Composition: Copper
Weight: 6.4 to 6.7 gms
Diameter: 28.2 to 28.4 mm
Die Axis: ↑↑ ↑↓
Edge: Reeded (Diagonally)
Ref.Nos.: Br 976; See below

| Double lock | Single lock |
| Large letters | Small letters |

Varieties: Obverse and die axis
A1 Large letters, Double lock, Coinage; Co 1W; W C7
A2 Small letters, Single lock, Medal; Co 2W; W C8
A3 Small letters, Single lock, Coinage; Co 2W; W C8

Variations: Rusted and unrusted dies have caused very minor variations on this token.

Cat.No.	Date	Description	VG	F	VF	EF	AU	UNC
WE-5A1	1805	Large letters, Coinage	15.00	30.00	80.00	175.00	300.00	-
WE-5A2	1805	Small letters, Medal	15.00	30.00	80.00	175.00	300.00	-
WE-5A3	1805	Small letters, Coinage	15.00	30.00	80.00	175.00	300.00	-

WE-6 *TRADE & COMMERCE 1811 — (BUST DESIGN)*

As with the Hibernia 1805 token, this piece is also of Irish origin.

Composition: Copper
Weight: 8.4 to 8.9 gms
Diameter: 28.9 to 29.1 mm
Die Axis: ↑↓
Edge: Reeded (Diagonally)
Ref.Nos.: Br 977; Co 43W;
W C9

Cat.No.	Date	Description	VG	F	VF	EF	AU	UNC
WE-6	1811	Bust design	35.00	65.00	125.00	275.00	500.00	-

WE-7   *COMMERCE — 1813 MARQUIS WELLINGTON*

This Irish token was designed and struck by Isaac Parkes of Dublin. It is antedated since Wellington was not a Marquis until 1814. Small numbers have been found in Canadian hoards.

Composition: Copper
Weight: 8.2 to 8.6 gms
Diameter: 28.4 to 28.5 mm
Die Axis: ↑↓
Edge: Engrailed
Ref.Nos.: Br 978; Co 44W;
        W C10

Cat.No.	Date	Description	VG	F	VF	EF	AU	UNC
WE-7	1813	Marquis	10.00	20.00	40.00	100.00	200.00	300.00

WE-8   *1814 — WELLINGTON HALFPENNY TOKEN*

After 1825, antedated halfpennies began to appear to evade regulations against the import of private tokens. All the lightweight pieces are dated 1814 to 1816 and are clearly antedated.

Composition: Copper
Weight: 5.9 to 6.5 gms
Diameter: 27.1 to 27.5 mm
Die Axis: ↑↓
Edge: Engrailed
Ref.Nos.: Br 979; See below

Middle tine longest   Middle tine shorter

Square epaulette   Round epaulette
Eight leaves   Seven leaves

Large trident
two tines barbed

Varieties: Obverse and reverse
    A1 Square epaulette, Nine leaves, Ship sails in left background, Cannon balls, Middle tine barbed; Co 33W; W 529
    A2 Square epaulette, Nine leaves, No ship, No cannonballs, Middle tine longest; Co 34W; W 530
    A3 Square epaulette, Eight leaves, Ship sails in left background, Large trident with two tines barbed; Co 37W; W 533
    A4 Round epaulette, Eight leaves, Ship sails in left background, Upper tine longer others equal in size none being barbed; Co 35W; W 531
    A5 Mule, Obverse A4, Reverse A2; Co 36W; W 532;
    A6 Round epaulette, Seven leaves, Middle tine shorter; Co 38W; W 534

Cat.No.	Date	Description	VG	F	VF	EF	AU	UNC
WE-8A1	1814	Middle tine barbed	5.00	10.00	20.00	60.00	125.00	250.00
WE-8A2	1814	Middle tine longest	5.00	10.00	20.00	60.00	125.00	250.00
WE-8A3	1814	Trident tine barbed	5.00	10.00	20.00	60.00	125.00	250.00
WE-8A4	1814	Upper tine longer	8.00	15.00	25.00	75.00	150.00	300.00
WE-8A5	1814	Mule	75.00	150.00	300.00	400.00	-	-
WE-8A6	1814	Middle tine shorter	8.00	15.00	25.00	75.00	150.00	300.00

WE-9 — *WELLINGTON HALFPENNY TOKEN*

Composition: Copper
Weight: 5.4 to 6.2 gms
Diameter: 27.1 to 27.5 mm
Die Axis: ↑↓
Edge: Engrailed
Ref.Nos.: Br 980; Co 39W;
W 535

Cat.No.	Date	Description	VG	F	VF	EF	AU	UNC
WE-9	Undated		75.00	150.00	350.00	-	-	-

WE-10 *WATERLOO HALFPENNY 1816 — THE ILLUSTRIOUS WELLINGTON*

Composition: Copper
Weight: 4.1 to 5.8 gms
Diameter: 26.3 to 26.9 mm
Die Axis: ↑↓
Edge: Reeded (Vertically or
Diagonally)
Ref.Nos.: Br 981; See below

Wreath with two top leaves Wreath with one top leaf

Ten Strings Eight Strings

Varieties: Reverse and obverse
A1 Harp with 10 strings; Co 40W; W 538
A2 Harp with 8 strings, Wreath has 2 leaves at top; Co 41W; W 539
A3 Harp with 8 strings, Wreath has 1 leaf at top; Co 42W; W 540

Variations: A1 has diagonal or vertical reeding.

Cat.No.	Date	Description	VG	F	VF	EF	AU	UNC
WE-10A1	1816	Ten strings	5.00	12.00	30.00	75.00	150.00	325.00
WE-10A2	1816	Eight strings, 2 leaves	4.00	10.00	25.00	50.00	125.00	250.00
WE-10A3	1816	Eight strings. 1 leaf	5.00	12.00	30.00	75.00	150.00	325.00

PENINSULAR TOKENS

The Peninsular Tokens were struck for use by Wellington's Army in Portugal and Spain. J.K. Picard of Hull was asked to secure coins of a design distinct from English and Spanish regal copper. The order was placed with Sir Edward Thomason, who secured the services of Thomas Halliday to design the coins and cut the dies. Specimens were brought to Canada by troops sent over to fight the Americans in 1814.

The reverse legends of the halfpennies and the obverse legends of the pennies carry the names of the famous battles Wellington won against Napoleon. Halfpennies circulated to a far greater extent than the penny tokens.

WE-11   *VIMIERA TALAVERA ALMEIDA —*
          HISPANIAM ET LVSITANIAM RESTITVIT WELLINGTON

WE-11A   *CUIDAD RODRIGO, BADAJOZ, SALAMANCA —*

Composition: Copper, brass, silver
Weight: 8.1 to 8.9 gms
Diameter: 27.2 to 27.7 mm
Die Axis: ↑↑
Edge: Plain, reeded
          (Vertically or Diagonal)
Ref.Nos.: Br 987; See below

Varieties: Obverse and composition
  A1 Bust laureated with ten leaves, At the hairline three locks of hair with the centre lock large, Copper, Brass, Silver, Thin and thick flans, Plain, reeded vertically or diagonally; Co 4W; W 502
  A2 Bust laureated with ten leaves, One small lock above two large locks, Copper; Co 5W; Silver; Co 6W; Reeded diagonally; W 503
  A3 Bust laureated with ten leaves, The bottom lock below the ribbon knot pointing to the ear, Copper, Silver, Reeded diagonally; Co 7W; W 504
  A4 Bust laureated with ten leaves, Three short and equal length locks, Copper, Reeded vertically or diagonally; Co 8W; W 505
  A5 Bust laureated with ten leaves, Tied with a single bow, Copper, Reeded vertically or diagonally; Co 9W; W 506
  A6 Bust laureated with ten leaves, Without coat button, Copper, Reeded vertically or diagonally; Co 10W, W 507
  A7 Bust laureated with nine leaves, Without coat button, Brass, Reeded; Co 11W; W 508

Variations: A1, A2 and A3 were issued in silver and are rare. They will command a price in excess of $300.00 in VF.

Note: WE-11A7 is a brass counterfeit. Other brass forgeries exist.

Cat.No.	Date	Description	VG	F	VF	EF	AU	UNC
WE-11A1	Undated	Ten leaves, Large centre lock	4.00	8.00	15.00	25.00	65.00	125.00
WE-11A2	(1812)	Ten leaves, Small lock	4.00	8.00	15.00	25.00	65.00	125.00
WE-11A3		Ten leaves, Lock below ribbon	4.00	8.00	15.00	25.00	65.00	125.00
WE-11A4		Ten leaves, Short equal locks	4.00	8.00	15.00	25.00	65.00	125.00
WE-11A5		Ten leaves, Single bow	4.00	8.00	15.00	25.00	65.00	125.00
WE-11A6		Ten leaves, Without button	4.00	8.00	15.00	25.00	65.00	125.00
WE-11A7		Nine leaves, Without button	30.00	60.00	100.00	175.00	-	-

WE-11B   *CUIDAD RODRIGO, BADAJOZ, SALAMANCA, MADRID—*

Composition: Copper, brass, silver
Weight: 8.2 to 8.4 gms
Diameter: 27.2 to 27.7 mm
Die Axis: ↑↑ ↑↓
Edge: Reeded (Diagonally)
Ref.Nos.: Br 986; See below

Varieties: Obverse
  B1 Bust laureated with ten leaves, Two locks, Copper, Brass, Reeded diagonally; Co 12W; W 509
  B2 Bust laureated with ten leaves, One small lock above two large locks, Similar to WE-11A2, Copper, Reeded diagonally; Co 13W, W 510
  B3 Bust laureated with ten leaves, Three locks of equal length, Similar to WE-11A4, Copper, Reeded diagonally; Co 14W; W 511
  B4 Bust laureated with ten leaves, Without coat button, Similar to WE-11A6, Copper, Reeded diagonally; Co 15W; W 512
  B5 Bust laureated with ten leaves, The locks are small, Coat button near lapel, Copper, Reeded diagonally; Co 16W; W 513
  B6 Bust laureated with nine leaves, Three locks with the centre lock largest, Copper, Reeded diagonally; Co 17W; W 514
  B7 Bust laureated with nine leaves, A single leaf on top, Three locks with the centre lock largest, Copper, Silver, Thin and thick flans, Reeded diagonally; Co 18W; W 515
  B8 Bust laureated with eight leaves, Copper, Thin and thick flans, Coinage, Reeded; Co 19W; W 516

Variations: B7 was issued in silver and is rare. This token commands a price in excess of $300.00 in VF.

Cat.No.	Date	Description	VG	F	VF	EF	AU	UNC
WE-11B1	Undated	Ten leaves, Two locks	5.00	10.00	20.00	40.00	90.00	200.00
WE-11B2	(1812)	Ten leaves, One small lock	5.00	10.00	20.00	40.00	90.00	200.00
WE-11B3		Ten leaves, Three equal locks	5.00	10.00	20.00	40.00	90.00	200.00
WE-11B4		Ten leaves, Without button	6.00	12.00	25.00	45.00	100.00	250.00
WE-11B5		Ten leaves, Button near lapel	5.00	10.00	20.00	40.00	90.00	200.00
WE-11B6		Nine leaves, large centre lock	6.00	12.00	25.00	45.00	100.00	250.00
WE-11B7		Nine leaves, Single leaf on top	6.00	12.00	25.00	45.00	100.00	250.00
WE-11B8		Eight leaves	5.00	10.00	20.00	40.00	90.00	200.00

WE-11C   *CIUDAD, RODRIGO, BADAJOZ, SALAMANCA, MADRID —*

The correct spelling of the Spanish word for city is "Ciudad" not Cuidad. This error on the previous tokens was corrected.

Composition: Copper
Weight: 9.1 gms
Diameter: 27.7 to 27.9 mm
Die Axis: ↑↑
Edge: Reeded (Diagonally)
Ref.Nos.: Br 986; See below

Coat button near collar   Coat button far from collar

Varieties: C1 Coat button near collar; Co 20W; W 517
          C2 Coat button far from collar; Co 21W, W 518

Cat.No.	Date	Description	VG	F	VF	EF	AU	UNC
WE-11C1	(1813)	Button near collar	10.00	20.00	40.00	80.00	150.00	250.00
WE-11C2		Button far from collar	10.00	20.00	40.00	80.00	150.00	250.00

WE-11D   *SALAMANCA, MADRID, ST. SEBASTIAN, PAMPLUNO —*

Composition: Copper
Weight: 7.6 to 9.7 gms
Diameter: 27.2 to 28.1 mm
Die Axis: ↑↑
Edge: Plain, reeded
Ref.Nos.: Br 988; See below

Varieties: Edge
     D1 Plain; Co 22W; W 519
     D2 Reeded; Co 22W; W 519

Variations: Issued on thin and thick flans.

Cat.No.	Date	Description	VG	F	VF	EF	AU	UNC
WE-11D1	(1813)	Plain	40.00	60.00	125.00	-	-	-
WE-11D2		Reeded	10.00	20.00	45.00	100.00	200.00	300.00

WE-12   *ONE PENNY TOKEN 1813 —*
      VIMIERA TALAVERA BADAJOZ SALAMANCA VITTORIA

Composition: Copper
Weight: 17.3 to 18.8 gms
Diameter: 33.9 to 34.0 mm
Die Axis: ↑↑
Edge: Engrailed
Ref.Nos.: Br 984; Co 23W;
          W 520

Cat.No.	Date	Description	VG	F	VF	EF	AU	UNC
WE-12	1813	Vittoria	15.00	25.00	50.00	100.00	200.00	325.00

WE-13   *COSSACK PENNY TOKEN —*
      VIMIERA TALAVERA BUSACO BADAJOZ SALAMANCA

Composition: Copper
Weight: 18.2 to 19.2 gms
Diameter: 33.9 to 34.2 mm
Die Axis: ↑↑
Edge: Engrailed
Ref.Nos.: Br 985; Co 24W;
          W C11

Cat.No.	Date	Description	VG	F	VF	EF	AU	UNC
WE-13	(1813)	Cossack	10.00	20.00	35.00	70.00	125.00	250.00

WE-14 *WELLINGTON WATERLOO 1815 — (SAILING SHIP DESIGN)*

Composition: Copper
Weight: 6.4 to 6.5 gms
Diameter: 26.4 to 26.6 gms
Die Axis: ↑↓
Edge: Plain
Ref.Nos.: Br 1003; Co 46W;
W 537

Note: Forgeries are known in pewter.

Cat.No.	Date	Description	VG	F	VF	EF	AU	UNC
WE-14	1815	Ship	5.00	10.00	25.00	75.00	150.00	325.00

WE-15 *WELLINGTON WATERLOO 1815 — (LARGE BUST DESIGN)*

Composition: Copper
Weight: 4.5 to 6.5 gms
Diameter: 26.1 to 26.4 mm
Die Axis: ↑↓
Edge: Plain
Ref.Nos.: Br 1006; Co 45W;
W 536

Variations: Issued on thin and thick flans.

Cat.No.	Date	Description	VG	F	VF	EF	AU	UNC
WE-15	1815	Large bust	6.00	15.00	30.00	75.00	175.00	300.00

TOKENS OF UPPER CANADA

After the American War of Independence the thousands who remained loyal to the British crown were dispossessed of their property and had to leave the territory of the newly-independent United States. Many came to the Great Lakes region from the state of New York and found themselves in the colony of Quebec and under jurisdiction of the Quebec Act of 1774. In 1791 the British government detached the Great Lakes region from the colony of Quebec, organizing it as the colony of Upper Canada.

Since so many Loyalists had come from New York, the popular mode of reckoning in many areas was the standard of New York State known as York currency. In 1809 the ratings of gold coins were adjusted to keep Spanish and French gold from being exported but no changes were made in the values of silver coin. Silver became the standard as there was no discount on lightweight coin.

York currency continued in use until 1821. About that time the government policy stated that no contracts of any kind in York currency would be permitted to bear interest and no contract would be enforceable in the courts unless expressed in Halifax Currency.

BRETON CROSS REFERENCE TABLE FOR UPPER CANADA TOKENS

Breton No.	Charlton Cat. No.	Page No.	Breton No.	Charlton Cat. No.	Page No.
717	UC-3	175	727	UC-9	180
718	UC-2	174	728	UC-10	181
721	UC-1	173	729	UC-11	181
723	UC-5	177	730	UC-12A-B	182
724	UC-6	178	731	UC-13	183
725	UC-7	179	732	UC-14	183
726	UC-8	179	1010	UC-4	176

PRIVATE TOKENS

UC-1   *COPPER COMPANY OF UPPER CANADA*
ONE HALFPENNY — 1794

Governor Simcoe of Upper Canada through intermediaries requested sample coinage from Boulton & Watt for the new colony of Upper Canada. The Soho Mint, using an obverse design by Noel-Alexandre Ponthon and a simple reverse design, submitted a pattern illustrating their capabilities as minters. The proposed coinage for Upper Canada was abandoned. Restrikes appeared in 1894.

Composition: Silver, copper, white metal
Weight: N/A
Diameter: 29.1 mm
Die Axis: ↑↑, ↑↓
Edge: Plain
Ref.Nos.: Br 721; W A2

Round "O" Letters   Oval "O" Letters
Straight Tail "R"   Curved Tail "R"
Original   1894 Restrike

Varieties: Reverse
A1 All "O" letters are round; All "R" letters have straight tails; Copper; Original
A2 All "O" letters are oval; All "R" letters have curved tails; Copper; Restrike
A3 All "O" letters are oval; All "R" letters have curved tails; Wm.; Restrike
A4 All "O" letters are oval; All "R" letters have curved tails; Silver; Restrike

Cat.No.	Date	Description	VG	F	VF	EF	AU	UNC
UC-1A1	1794	Copper			Extremely Rare			
UC-1A2	1794	Copper			Proof $450.00			
UC-1A3	1794	White metal		J. Hoare Auction, February 1995, Lot 1622; AU - $280.00				
UC-1A4	1794	Silver		J. Hoare Auction, February 1995, Lot 1623; Proof - $800.00				

LESSLIE & SONS TOKENS

The firm of Lesslie & Sons, in the drug and book trade, was established in 1820 with branches at York and Dundas. A third branch was opened in Kingston in 1822. From 1820-1823 William Lyon MacKenzie was John Lesslie's partner in the firm. James Lesslie was a partner from 1822, and William Lesslie later. The tokens of the firm were struck by Boulton & Watt and the dies were cut by Thomas Wells Ingram.

The twopenny piece bears the name Toronto, even though it was issued before Toronto was incorporated under that name in 1834. Ever since it was founded, York was unofficially called Toronto, popularly thought to be the old Indian name for "meeting place," and in 1822 a petition was circulated asking that the town of York be renamed Toronto. Sir Peregrine Maitland, the governor at the time, chose to ignore the petition altogether and York remained the official name until 1834.

UC-2   *PROSPERITY TO CANADA LA PRUDENCE ET LA CANDEUR TOKEN HALFPENNY— LESSLIE & SONS YORK KINGSTON DUNDAS*

Composition: Copper
Weight: 7.0 to 7.3 gms
Diameter: 27.1 to 28.0 mm
Die Axis: ↑↑
Edge: Plain, reeded
Ref.Nos.: Br 718; See below

Plough handle points to period   Plough handle points above "A"

Plough handle points to "A"

Right: No comma after York; Extreme right: Comma after York

Varieties: Obverse and reverse

A1 No comma after York, Lower plough handle points to period, Plain; W 824; Mc 26
A2 No comma after York, Lower plough handle points above final "A" of CANADA, Plain; W 825; Mc 27
A3 Weak comma after York, Lower plough handle points above final "A" of CANADA, Plain; W 826; Mc 28
A4 Comma after York, Lower plough handle points above final "A" of CANADA, Reeded; W 827; Mc 29
A5 Comma after York, Lower plough handle points to final "A" of CANADA, Reeded; W 828; Mc 30

Cat.No.	Date	Description	VG	F	VF	EF	AU	UNC
UC-2A1	(1824)	No comma, To period	8.00	15.00	50.00	150.00	250.00	400.00
UC-2A2	(1824)	No comma, Above "A"	8.00	15.00	50.00	150.00	250.00	400.00
UC-2A3	(1824)	Weak comma, Above "A"	8.00	15.00	50.00	150.00	250.00	400.00
UC-2A4	(1828)	Comma, Above "A"	10.00	20.00	50.00	150.00	250.00	400.00
UC-2A5	(1828)	Comma, To "A"	10.00	20.00	50.00	150.00	250.00	400.00

UC-3   *PROSPERITY TO CANADA LA PRUDENCE*
              ET LA CANDEUR TOKEN 2d CURRENCY —
              1822 LESSLIE & SONS TORONTO & DUNDASS

Composition: Copper
Weight: 27.8 to 28.3 gms
Diameter: 40.2 to 40.5 mm
Die Axis: ↑↑
Edge: Plain
Ref.Nos.: Br 717; W 823;
             Mc 31

Cat.No.	Date	Description	VG	F	VF	EF	AU	UNC
UC-3	(1822)		75.00	150.00	250.00	350.00	500.00	750.00

UC-4   *SPEED THE PLOUGH HALFPENNY TOKEN—*
NO LABOUR NO BREAD

About 1830 these tokens were imported into Toronto by Perrins Bros., a dry goods firm. Under the act outlawing private tokens the customs seized and ordered the tokens melted. However, most escaped the meltdown and were still in circulation as late as 1837.

Varieties: Obverse and reverse

Composition: Copper
Weight: 6.0 to 6.5 gms
Diameter: 26.1 to 26.2 mm
Die Axis: ↑↓
Edge: Plain
Ref.Nos.: Br 1010; See below

A1   Long threshing floor, Wheat table ends vertically, Ground points to middle of "N", Man far from "H"; W 829

A2   Short threshing floor, Wheat table ends diagonally, Ground points to left seriph of "N", Man near "H"; W 830

A3   Mule, obverse A1, reverse A2

Cat.No.	Date	Description	VG	F	VF	EF	AU	UNC
UC-4A1	(1830)	Long, Far from "H"	5.00	10.00	25.00	80.00	200.00	300.00
UC-4A2	(1830)	Short, Near "H"	5.00	10.00	25.00	80.00	200.00	300.00
UC-4A3	(1830)	Mule	30.00	50.00	100.00	300.00	600.00	-

ANONYMOUS TOKENS

THE BROCK TOKENS 1812-1816

The Brock Series of halfpenny tokens was struck in memory of General Sir Isaac Brock, Commander of the British forces in Upper Canada. During July 1812, Brock captured Detroit. On October 13th of that same year, he died during the unsuccessful American invasion at Queenstown, Upper Canada.

The tokens first appeared around 1813. A second issue was released in 1816 but these tokens became too plentiful and were discredited by 1820. They were the lightest Canadian coppers and were in use as early as 1814-1816.

UC-5   *SiR ISAAC BROOK BART.*
           THE HERO OF UPPER CANADA 1812—

Full legend reads:
Reverse: "SIR ISAAC BROOK, BART. THE HERO OF UPPER CANADA WHO
           FELL IN THE GLORIOUS BATTLE OF QUEENSTOWN HEIGHT ON
           THE 13 OCTR 1812."
Obverse: "SUCCESS TO THE COMMERCE OF UPPR & LOWR CANADA."

The spelling "Brook" is incorrect, as it should read "Brock."

Composition: Copper
Weight: 4.9 to 5.1 gms
Diameter: 26.4 to 26.9 mm
Die Axis: ↑↑
Edge: Reeded (diagonally)
Ref.Nos.: Br 723; W 801;
          Mc 10

Cat.No.	Date	Description	VG	F	VF	EF	AU	UNC
UC-5	1812	"Brook"	10.00	20.00	50.00	150.00	275.00	-

Note: A modern mule of obverse UC-6 and reverse UC-5 exists. Struck by Pobjoy Mint.

UC-6

SUCCESS TO COMMERCE & PEACE
TO THE WORLD 1816— SR. ISAAC BROCK
THE HERO OF UPR CANADA FELL OCT 13 1812

Composition: Copper
Weight: 4.5 to 4.9 gms
Diameter: 26.4 to 26.8 mm
Die Axis: ↑↑ ↑↓
Edge: Plain, reeded (diagonally)
Ref.Nos.: Br 724; See below

Varieties: Obverse and die axis

A1 Cherubs heads under "T" and "ER", Wreath is oval, Bottom of urn is curved downwards, Large date, Flat top "1's"; W 802; Mc 4

A2 Cherubs heads under "TH" and "R", Wreath is oval, Bottom of urn is flat, Pedestal has three steps, Flat top "1's"; W 803; Mc 5

A3 Cherubs heads under "T" and "ER", Wreath is round, Bottom of urn is flat, Pedestal has two steps, Flat top "1's"; W 804; Mc 6

A4 Cherubs heads under "T" and "ER", Wreath is round, Bottom of urn is curved upwards, Pedestal has two steps, Flat top "1's"; W 805

A5 Small cherubs heads under "T" and "R", Wreath is round, Bottom of urn is flat, Pedestal has two steps, Flat top "1's"; W 806; Mc 7

A6 Cherubs heads under "TH" and "R", Wreath is round, Bottom of urn is flat, Pedestal has three steps, Top of "1's" slanted; W 807; Mc 8

A7 Cherubs head under "T" and "R", Wreath is oval, Bottom of urn is flat, Pedestal has three steps, Flat top "1's", Coinage; W 808; Mc 9

Cat.No.	Date	Description	VG	F	VF	EF	AU	UNC
UC-6A1	1816	Under "T" and "ER", Flat	5.00	10.00	20.00	45.00	85.00	175.00
UC-6A2	1816	Under "TH" and "R", Flat	5.00	10.00	20.00	45.00	85.00	175.00
UC-6A3	1816	Under "T" and "ER", Flat	5.00	10.00	20.00	45.00	85.00	175.00
UC-6A4	1816	Under "T" and "ER", Flat	5.00	10.00	20.00	45.00	85.00	175.00
UC-6A5	1816	Under "T" and "R", Flat	5.00	10.00	20.00	45.00	85.00	175.00
UC-6A6	1816	Under "TH" and "R", Slanted	5.00	10.00	20.00	45.00	85.00	175.00
UC-6A7	1816	Under "T" and "R", Flat	5.00	10.00	20.00	45.00	85.00	175.00

Note: Gibbs states that "all varieties are diagonally reeded although some are so faint as to appear plain."

UC-7 *SUCCESS TO COMMERCE AND PEACE*
TO THE WORLD 1816 — SUCCESS TO THE
COMMERCE OF UPPR AND LOWR CANADA

This was a mule of the worn obverse of UC-5 and the well worn reverse of UC-6A7.

Composition: Copper
Weight: 4.9 to 5.2 gms
Diameter: 26.5 to 26.9 mm
Die Axis: ↑↑
Edge: Reeded (diagonally)
Ref.Nos.: Br 725; W 809; Mc 11

Cat.No.	Date	Description	VG	F	VF	EF	AU	UNC
UC-7	1816	Mule	35.00	75.00	150.00	350.00	-	-

THE SLOOP TOKENS

These tokens appeared after 1825, some being antedated to evade the law of 1825 against private tokens. In time, the law was openly ignored in Upper Canada by many issuers who were secure in the relative isolation of Upper Canada from the commercial and political centre of Lower Canada.

It is believed that the sloop tokens were produced by John Sheriff of Liverpool from a design sent from Upper Canada. The sloop was the chief means of transportation on the Great Lakes at the time and far more reliable than any form of land transport. The sloop shown on the tokens was said by Rev. Henry Scadding to be a portrayal of the packet "Duke of Richmond," owned by a man named Oates.

UC-8 *COMMERCIAL CHANGE 1815 —*
HALFPENNY TOKEN UPPER CANADA

The Commercial Change 1815 obverse of the Starr & Shannon token, NS-12, becomes the reverse of UC-8 and was mated with the Sloop obverse to produce this halfpenny token of Upper Canada.

Composition: Copper
Weight: 5.8 to 6.5 gms
Diameter: 27.1 to 27.4 mm
Die Axis: ↑↑ ↑↓
Edge: Reeded
Ref.Nos.: Br 726; See below

Varieties: Die axis
A1 Worn die, Medal; W 819; Mc 21
A2 Worn die, very rusted reverse die, Coinage; W 822; Mc 22

Cat.No.	Date	Description	VG	F	VF	EF	AU	UNC
UC-8A1	1815	Medal	35.00	65.00	250.00	-	-	-
UC-8A2	1815	Coinage	40.00	75.00	300.00	-	-	-

UC-9

COMMERCIAL CHANGE 1820 —
HALFPENNY TOKEN UPPER CANADA

Composition: Copper
Weight: 6.4 to 6.7 gms
Diameter: 27.2 to 27.7 mm
Die Axis: ↑↑ ↑↓
Edge: Reeded
Ref.Nos.: Br 727; See below

Bowsprit points to "A"   Bowsprit points between "DA"   Bowsprit points above "A"

Varieties: Obverse and die axis
A1 Bowsprit points to final "A" in CANADA; W 810; Mc 12
A2 Bowsprit points between "DA" of CANADA, Medal; W 811; Mc 13
A3 Bowsprit points between "DA" of CANADA, Coinage; W 811; Mc 13
A4 Bowsprit points above final "A" in CANADA; W 812 to 814; Mc 14 to 16

Variations: Variety UC-9A4 has minor reverse variations including differences in the size of the shovel handle and double punching of the 2nd and 3rd "C" in reverse legend. It was struck with rusted obverse dies.

Cat.No.	Date	Description	VG	F	VF	EF	AU	UNC
UC-9A1	1820	Points to final "A"	5.00	10.00	20.00	45.00	100.00	175.00
UC-9A2	1820	Points between "DA", Medal	5.00	10.00	20.00	50.00	125.00	225.00
UC-9A3	1820	Points between "DA", Coinage	5.00	10.00	20.00	50.00	125.00	225.00
UC-9A4	1820	Points above final "A"	5.00	10.00	20.00	50.00	125.00	225.00

UC-10

COMMERCIAL CHANGE 1821 —
HALFPENNY TOKEN UPPER CANADA

CASK MARKED — UPPER CANADA

Composition: Copper
Weight: 6.0 to 6.5 gms
Diameter: 27.1 to 27.3 mm
Die Axis: ↑↑
Edge: Reeded
Ref.Nos.: Br 728; W 815;
   Mc 17

Cat.No.	Date	Description	VG	F	VF	EF	AU	UNC
UC-10	1821	Upper Canada	45.00	90.00	175.00	300.00	450.00	-

UC-11

COMMERCIAL CHANGE 1821 —
HALFPENNY TOKEN UPPER CANADA

CASK MARKED — JAMAICA

Composition: Copper
Weight: 6.4 to 6.5 gms
Diameter: 27.2 to 27.6 mm
Die Axis: ↑↑
Edge: Reeded
Ref.Nos.: Br 729; W 816;
   Mc 18

Cat.No.	Date	Description	VG	F	VF	EF	AU	UNC
UC-11	1821		400.00	500.00	1,000.00	-	-	-

UC-12 TO FACILITATE TRADE 1823/1833 — HALFPENNY TOKEN UPPER CANADA

UC-12A *TO FACILITATE TRADE 1823 —*

Composition: Copper
Weight: 6.5 gms
Diameter: 27.2 to 27.6 mm
Die Axis: ↑↑ ↑↓
Edge: Reeded
Ref.Nos.: Br 730; See below

Bowsprit points between "DA" of CANADA   Bowsprit points above "A"

Varieties: Obverse and reverse
A1 Bowsprit points between "DA" of CANADA, Medal; W 817; Mc 19
A2 Bowsprit points above final "A", Coinage; W 818; Mc 20

Cat.No.	Date	Description	VG	F	VF	EF	AU	UNC
UC-12A1	1823	Between "DA", Medal	7.00	12.00	30.00	65.00	125.00	250.00
UC-12A2	1823	Above "A", Coinage	8.00	15.00	35.00	75.00	150.00	250.00

UC-12B *TO FACILITATE TRADE 1833 —*

Composition: Copper
Weight: 6.5 to 7.3 gms
Diameter: 27.2 to 27.7
Die Axis: ↑↑ ↑↓
Edge: Reeded
Ref.Nos.: Br 730; W 821; Mc 23

Varieties: Die Axis
B1 Medal
B2 Coinage

Cat.No.	Date	Description	VG	F	VF	EF	AU	UNC
UC-12B1	1833	Above "A", Medal	5.00	10.00	25.00	45.00	100.00	225.00
UC-12B2	1833	Above "A", Coinage	5.00	10.00	25.00	45.00	100.00	225.00

UC-13

COMMERCIAL CHANGE 1833 —
HALFPENNY TOKEN UPPER CANADA

This piece is attributed to Watkins & Harris, a hardware firm in Toronto.

Composition: Brass
Weight: 4.9 to 5.8 gms
Diameter: 27.6 to 27.9 mm
Die Axis: ↑↓
Edge: Plain
Ref.Nos.: Br 731, Mc 24

Cat.No.	Date	Description	VG	F	VF	EF	AU	UNC
UC-13	1833	Plain	8.00	15.00	35.00	100.00	225.00	325.00

UC-14

HALFPENNY TOKEN 1832 —
PROVINCE OF UPPER CANADA

This coin was procured by John Walker & Co. of Birmingham and incorrectly bearing the bust of George IV was used by this firm for the 1832 coinage of Nova Scotia. It is not known whether this token is semi-regal or private.

Composition: Copper
Weight: 8.6 gms
Diameter: 28.1 to 28.3 mm
Die Axis: ↑↓
Edge: Engrailed
Ref.Nos.: Br 732; W 831; Mc 32

Cat.No.	Date	Description	VG	F	VF	EF	AU	UNC
UC-14	1832	Engrailed	10.00	20.00	50.00	125.00	250.00	-

IMITATIONS OF UPPER CANADA TOKENS, "BLACKSMITH STYLE"

For the listings of imitations of Upper Canada Tokens see page No. 227; Cat. Nos. BL-49 and BL-50.

TOKENS OF THE PROVINCE OF CANADA

The rebellions of 1837 in Upper and Lower Canada forced the British government to pay closer attention to conditions in the Canadian colonies. In 1838 Lord Durham was sent out as Governor-in-Chief to inquire into the causes of the revolt and to recommend steps to be taken to insure that such a breach of the peace would not recur. Among his recommendations was the union of Upper and Lower Canada. Union took place in 1841.

The currency was one of the first problems to be dealt with by the new government. In 1841 a new Currency Act superseded the previous currency legislation of both colonies.

In 1857 the decimal system was adopted and took effect at the beginning of the following year. Decimal coins were in use before the end of 1858.

For decimal coins of Canada see the Charlton Standard Catalogue of Canadian Coins.

BRETON CROSS REFERENCE TABLE FOR PROVINCE OF CANADA TOKENS

Breton No.	Charlton Cat. No.	Page No.	Breton No.	Charlton Cat.N o.	Page No.
526	PC-2B	188	529	PC-3	189
527	PC-1A-C	185 to 187	719	PC-6A-D	192 to 194
528	PC-4	189	720	PC-5A-D	190 to 192

SEMI-REGAL TOKENS

BANK OF MONTREAL FRONT VIEW TOKENS

In 1842, after Upper and Lower Canada were united as the Province of Canada, the Bank of Montreal was permitted to import 5,000 Pounds Sterling in copper provided that the entire amount was imported before 1845. The Bank issued 1,000 Pounds in pennies and 1,000 Pounds in halfpennies in 1842, 2,000 Pounds in halfpennies in 1844, and 1,000 Pounds in 1845.

The halfpennies issued in 1845 are all dated 1844. The Bank was permitted to issue another 1,200 Pounds in copper in 1845 but did not do so. Dies dated 1845 were prepared but only two halfpennies are known. Proofs exist and are very rare.

PC-1　　*BANK TOKEN HALF PENNY 1842/1844/1845—*
PROVINCE OF CANADA BANK OF MONTREAL

PC-1A　　*HALFPENNY DATED 1842 BANK OF MONTREAL ON RIBBON*

Composition: Copper
Weight: 9.2 to 9.5 gms
Diameter: 28.2 to 28.6 mm
Die Axis: ↑↑
Edge: Plain
Ref.Nos.: Br 527; See below

Long nose beaver　　　　　Short nose beaver

Varieties: Obverse and reverse
A1　1842, Tall trees, Short nose beaver; Co 40BM; W 851
A2　1842, Medium trees, Short nose beaver; Co 46BM; W 854
A3　1842, Short trees, Short nose beaver; Co 64 and 65BM; W 857

Variations: There are variations in this series due to the deterioration and reworking of the dies. Courteau gave numbers to die breaks as well as weak areas in the legend and design.

Note: For illustration of trees see page 186.

Cat.No.	Date	Description	VG	F	VF	EF	AU	UNC
PC-1A1	1842	Tall trees, Short nose			Rare			
PC-1A2	1842	Medium trees, Short nose	6.00	12.00	18.00	35.00	90.00	200.00
PC-1A3	1842	Short trees, Short nose	6.00	12.00	18.00	35.00	90.00	200.00

PC-1B   *HALFPENNY DATED 1844 BANK OF MONTREAL ON RIBBON*

Composition: Copper
Weight: 9.4 to 9.5 gms
Diameter: 28.2 to 28.7 mm
Die Axis: ↑↑
Edge: Plain
Ref.Nos.: Br 527; See below

Tall trees

Medium trees

Short trees

Varieties: Obverse and reverse
B1 Tall trees, Short nose beaver, Co 42 to 45BM; W 852
B2 Tall trees, Long nose beaver, Co 41BM; W 853
B3 Medium trees, Short nose beaver, Co 54 to 63BM; W 855
B4 Medium trees, Long nose beaver, Co 47 and 53BM; W 856
B5 Short trees, Short nose beaver, Co 69 and 70BM; W 858
B6 Short trees, Long nose beaver, Co 66 to 68BM; W 859

Note: For illustration of beavers see page 185. For medium trees, Courteau states "There is a short line from the base of the left fence running upwards."

Cat.No.	Date	Description	VG	F	VF	EF	AU	UNC
PC-1B1	1844	Tall trees, Short nose	4.00	7.00	12.00	30.00	75.00	150.00
PC-1B2	1844	Tall trees, Long nose	5.00	8.00	15.00	35.00	85.00	175.00
PC-1B3	1844	Medium trees, Short nose	2.00	5.00	10.00	25.00	65.00	125.00
PC-1B4	1844	Medium trees, Long nose	3.00	6.00	12.00	30.00	65.00	125.00
PC-1B5	1844	Short trees, Short nose	4.00	7.00	12.00	30.00	75.00	150.00
PC-1B6	1844	Short trees, Long nose	5.00	8.00	15.00	35.00	85.00	175.00

PC-1C **HALFPENNY DATED 1845 BANK OF MONTREAL ON RIBBON**

Composition: Copper
Weight: 9.5 gms
Diameter: 28.7 mm
Die Axis: ↑↑
Edge: Plain
Ref Nos.: Br 527; W 860

Cat.No.	Date	Description	VG	F	VF	EF	AU	UNC
PC-1C1	1845	Halfpenny			Only two known, Extremely Rare			

PC-2 BANK TOKEN ONE PENNY 1837 — PROVINCE OF CANADA BANK OF MONTREAL

PC-2A **ONE PENNY DATED 1837 CITY BANK ON RIBBON**

This token has long been considered a mule of the 1842 and the 1837 one penny tokens. The 1842 obverse of PC-2B (Br 526) and the reverse of LC-9A (Br 521). It was believed by Courteau that PC-2A1 was issued in early 1842, prior to the release of the 1842 (PC-2B) pennies. It is not a mule of the 1842/1837 penny as the obverse die is different from the 1842 obverse die used to mint PC-2B.

PC-2A1 is possibly the W. J. Taylor specimens from the Soho Mint dies.

Composition: Copper
Weight: See below
Diameter: 34.0 mm
Die Axis: See below
Edge: Plain
Ref.Nos.: Co 88 BM; W G13

Varieties: Composition
A1 Weight — 16.1 to 18.9 gms; Die axis — medal; Regular size flan
A2 Weight — 23.0 to 24.0 gms; Die axis — coinage; Thick flan

Variations: Specimens are known in nickel and brass. They are extremely rare.

Cat.No.	Date	Description	VG	F	VF	EF	AU	UNC
PC-2A1	(1842)	Medal	100.00	150.00	200.00	275.00	350.00	500.00
PC-2A2	(1870)	Coinage (Taylor)	-	-	-	-	-	400.00

PC-2B   *ONE PENNY DATED 1842 BANK OF MONTREAL ON RIBBON*

Composition: Copper
Weight: 17.7 to 18.9 gms
Diameter: 34.0 mm
Die Axis: ↑↑
Edge: Plain
Ref.Nos.: Br 526; Co 71 to 87BM; W 861 to 872

Variations: Extensive varieties exist due to the retouching of dies.
Proofs exist but are very rare.

Cat.No.	Date	Description	VG	F	VF	EF	AU	UNC
PC-2B	1842	Penny	5.00	8.00	18.00	45.00	125.00	250.00

QUEBEC BANK TOKENS

In 1851 the Quebec Bank asked for permission to import copper because of its shortage in Quebec. This and a further request were refused because the Bank of Upper Canada had already agreed to land some of its copper coinage of 1850 at Quebec. A third request was granted because the promised copper landed at Quebec late and in insufficient amounts.

The coins were struck by Ralph Heaton & Co. from designs probably suggested by the Quebec Bank but it is not known who cut the dies.

PC-3   *QUEBEC BANK TOKEN HALF PENNY 1852 —*
PROVINCE DU CANADA UN SOU

Composition: Copper
Weight: 9.5 to 9.8 gms
Diameter: 28.3 to 28.4 mm
Die Axis: ↑↑
Edge: Plain
Ref.Nos.: Br 529; Co 5 to 5hH
         W 873 to 876

Variations: Minor varieties exist due to retouching of the dies.
Proofs exist but are very rare.

Cat.No.	Date	Description	VG	F	VF	EF	AU	UNC
PC-3	1852	Half Penny	3.00	6.00	15.00	30.00	75.00	200.00

PC-4   *QUEBEC BANK TOKEN ONE PENNY 1852 —*
PROVINCE DU CANADA DEUX SOUS

Composition: Copper
Weight: 18.8 to 19.3 gms
Diameter: 34.1 to 34.2 mm
Die Axis: ↑↑
Edge: Plain
Ref.Nos.: Br 528; Co 15fH;
         W 877, 878

Variations· Minor variations exist due to the retouching of dies.
Proofs exist but are very rare.

Cat.No.	Date	Description	VG	F	VF	EF	AU	UNC
PC-4	1852	Penny	4.00	8.00	20.00	45.00	150.00	300.00

BANK OF UPPER CANADA TOKENS

The Bank of Upper Canada was organized at York in 1820, usurping the charter of a Kingston institution of the same name which never actually started up.

As the instrument of the Family Compact, the bank steadily opposed the chartering of other banks and dominated the government to the extent of effectively retarding the development of banking in Upper Canada. This situation abruptly changed after 1839 and with the union of Upper and Lower Canada in 1841 the monopoly was broken and the government deposits transferred to Montreal.

Toronto became the capital of Canada in 1849 when the government withdrew from Montreal after the serious riots when the "Rebellion Losses Bill" was passed. The Bank of Upper Canada received government deposits and the right to import copper.

The orders were placed through Rowe, Kentish & Co. of London whose initials appear on the token. The tokens of 1850 were struck at the Royal Mint but did not arrive in Canada until 1851. The Royal Mint also began the coinage of 1852 but was unable to complete the order and contracted the work to Ralph Heaton & Co. of Birmingham. The strikings of the Royal Mint have straight (medal) reverses, the Heaton strikings have upset reverses. The coinages of 1854 and 1857 are the work of the Heaton Mint. The design was suggested by the bank. The dies were cut by John Pinches. Courteau has listed over 300 minor varieties of this token.

PC-5   ***BANK TOKEN ONE HALF-PENNY 1850/1852/1854/1857—***
BANK OF UPPER CANADA

PC-5A   ***ONE HALF–PENNY DATED 1850***

Composition: Copper
Weight: 7.9 gms
Diameter: 27.6 to 27.9 mm
Die Axis: ↑↑
Edge: Plain
Ref.Nos.: Br 720; Co 1
     to 75UC; W 879

Note: Proofs exist but are very rare.

Cat.No.	Date	Description	VG	F	VF	EF	AU	UNC
PC-5A	1850	Half-penny	3.00	5.00	10.00	20.00	60.00	125.00

PC-5B   ✳   *ONE HALF–PENNY DATED 1852*

Composition: Copper
Weight: 7.9 to 8.3 gms
Diameter: 27.6 to 27.9 mm
Die Axis: ↑↑ ↑↓
Edge: Plain
Ref.Nos.: Br 720; See below

Varieties: Die Axis
  B1 Royal Mint, Medal; Co 89 to 110UC; W 879
  B2 Heaton Mint, Coinage; Co 76 to 88UC; W 879

Cat.No.	Date	Description	VG	F	VF	EF	AU	UNC
PC-5B1	1852	Royal Mint, Medal	3.00	5.00	10.00	20.00	60.00	125.00
PC-5B2	1852	Heaton Mint, Coinage	3.00	5.00	10.00	20.00	60.00	125.00

PC-5C   *ONE HALF–PENNY DATED 1854*

Composition: Copper
Weight: 7.9 to 8.4 gms
Diameter: 27.6 to 27.9 mm
Die Axis: ↑↓
Edge: Plain
Ref.Nos.: Br 720; See below

Plain "4"   Crosslet "4"

Varieties: Obverse
  C1 Plain "4"; Co 111 to 113, 115 to 158UC; W 879
  C2 Crosslet "4"; Co 114UC; W 879

Cat.No.	Date	Description	VG	F	VF	EF	AU	UNC
PC-5C1	1854	Plain "4"	3.00	5.00	10.00	20.00	60.00	125.00
PC-5C2	1854	Crosslet "4"	15.00	25.00	40.00	80.00	150.00	250.00

PC-5D   *ONE HALF–PENNY DATED 1857*

Composition: Copper
Weight: 7.9 to 8.5 gms
Diameter: 27.6 to 27.9 mm
Die Axis: ↑↓
Edge: Plain
Ref.Nos.: Br 720; Co 159
           to 207UC; W 879

Cat.No.	Date	Description	VG	F	VF	EF	AU	UNC
PC-5D	1857	Halfpenny	2.00	4.00	8.00	15.00	60.00	125.00

PC-6   *BANK TOKEN ONE PENNY 1850/1852/1854/1857—BANK OF UPPER CANADA*

PC-6A   *ONE PENNY DATED 1850*

Composition: Copper
Weight: 15.6 to 15.8 gms
Diameter: 33.0 to 33.3 mm
Die Axis: ↑↑
Edge: Plain
Ref.Nos.: Br 719; Co 208
          to 233UC; W 880

Without dot   With dot

Varieties: Reverse
    A1   Without dot between tips of cornucopia
    A2   With dot between tips of cornucopia

Cat.No.	Date	Description	VG	F	VF	EF	AU	UNC
PC-6A1	1850	Without dot	4.00	7.00	15.00	25.00	75.00	150.00
PC-6A2	1850	With dot	5.00	10.00	25.00	50.00	125.00	250.00

PC-6B   *ONE PENNY DATED 1852*

Composition: Copper
Weight: 15.5 to 15.8 gms
Diameter: 33.1 to 33.3 mm
Die Axis: ↑↑ ↑↓
Edge: Plain
Ref.Nos.: Br 719; W 880;
          See below

   Royal Mint   

Small "2"   Large "2"

   Heaton Mint   

Narrow "2"   Large "2"

Varieties: Obverse and die axis
     B1 Small "2", Royal Mint, Medal; Co 234 to 236UC
     B2 Large "2", Royal Mint, Medal; Co 242 to 246, 249 to 253UC
     B3 Wide "2", Royal Mint, Medal; Co 254 to 257UC
     B4 Narrow "2", Heaton Mint, Coinage; Co 237 to 241UC
     B5 Large "2", Heaton Mint, Coinage; Co 247, 248UC

Note: Proofs exist and are very rare.

Cat.No.	Date	Description	VG	F	VF	EF	AU	UNC
PC-6B1	1852	Small "2", Royal, Medal	4.00	6.00	12.00	30.00	75.00	150.00
PC-6B2	1852	Large "2", Royal, Medal	4.00	6.00	12.00	30.00	75.00	150.00
PC-6B3	1852	Wide "2", Royal, Medal	4.00	6.00	12.00	30.00	75.00	150.00
PC-6B4	1852	Narrow "2", Heaton, Coinage	3.00	5.00	10.00	25.00	60.00	125.00
PC-6B5	1852	Large "2", Heaton, Coinage	3.00	5.00	10.00	25.00	60.00	125.00

PC-6C
ONE PENNY DATED 1854

Composition: Copper
Weight: 15.8 to 16.0 gms
Diameter: 33.1 to 33.4 mm
Die Axis: ↑↓
Edge: Plain
Ref.Nos.: Br 719; W 880

Plain "4"   Crosslet "4"

Varieties: Obverse
C1 Plain "4"; Co 258 to 273UC
C2 Crosslet "4"; Co 274UC

Cat.No.	Date	Description	VG	F	VF	EF	AU	UNC
PC-6C1	1854	Plain "4"	3.00	5.00	10.00	30.00	75.00	150.00
PC-6C2	1854	Crosslet "4"	8.00	12.00	25.00	60.00	125.00	250.00

PC-6D
ONE PENNY DATED 1857

Composition: Copper
Weight: 15.8 to 16.0 gms
Diameter: 33.1 to 33.3 mm
Die Axis: ↑↓
Edge: Plain
Ref.Nos.: Br 719; Co 275
to 319UC; W 880

Cat.No.	Date	Description	VG	F	VF	EF	AU	UNC
PC-6D	1857	Penny	3.00	5.00	10.00	20.00	50.00	125.00

ANONYMOUS AND MISCELLANEOUS TOKENS

Most of the tokens listed by the early numismatists as anonymous or miscellaneous are now attributed to specific colonies, provinces or geographical regions. Only those yet to be assigned to some definite locale are listed here. Most are of English or Irish origin, having circulated elsewhere before being imported for use in Canada. Some may have been imported by collectors because their legends carried messages common to other issues.

BRETON CROSS REFERENCE TABLE FOR
ANONYMOUS AND MISCELLANEOUS TOKENS

Breton No.	Charlton Cat. No.	Page No.	Breton No.	Charlton Cat. No.	Page No.
966	AM-1	195	1009	AM-4	197
975	AM-2	196	1013	AM-5	197
983	AM-3	196			

AM-1   *PURE COPPER PREFERABLE TO PAPER HALF PENNY TOKEN— FOR GENERAL ACCOMMODATION*

This token was designed and engraved by Thomas Halliday with two of the popular slogans of the day. The obverse legend indicates that the reason for issuing this token was to supply small change for everyday business.

Composition: Copper
Weight: 7.4 to 8.6 gms
Diameter: 27.2 to 27.3 mm
Die Axis: ↑↑ ↑↓
Edge: Plain, engrailed
Ref.Nos.: Br 966; Co 18NL; W 152

Varieties: Edge
  A1 Plain, Medal
  A2 Plain, Coinage
  A3 Engrailed, Coinage
  A4 Engrailed, Medal

Cat.No	Date	Description	VG	F	VF	EF	AU	UNC
AM-1A1		Plain, Medal	15.00	30.00	60.00	150.00	300.00	-
AM-1A2		Plain, Coinage	5.00	10.00	20.00	65.00	150.00	-
AM-1A3		Engrailed, Coinage	5.00	10.00	20.00	65.00	150.00	-
AM-1A4		Engrailed, Medal	5.00	10.00	20.00	65.00	150.00	-

AM-2   *FOR PUBLIC ACCOMMODATION ONE PENNY—*
1805 HIBERNIA

This token is an anonymous Irish penny used in Dublin. It was designed by Peter Wyon and was antedated. Small quantities were found in Lower Canada.

Composition: Copper
Weight: 17.9 gms
Diameter: 34.7 to 34.8 mm
Die Axis: ↑↓
Edge: Engrailed
Ref.Nos.: Br 975; W C1

Cat.No.	Date	Description	VG	F	VF	EF	AU	UNC
AM-2	1805	One penny	25.00	50.00	100.00	225.00	400.00	-

AM-3 *COMMERCE RULES THE MAIN— 1812 SUCCESS TO TRADE*

This is an anonymous piece with altered legends. "Success to Trade" was punched over "George III Rules" and "Commerce" was punched over Britannia. This piece has been ascribed to Halliday, but the workmanship is inferior to Halliday's.

Composition: Copper
Weight: 6.9 to 7.6 gms
Diameter: 28.5 to 28.8 mm
Die Axis: ↑↓
Edge: Plain
Ref.Nos.: Br 983; Co 36NL;
         W C5

Cat.No.	Date	Description	VG	F	VF	EF	AU	UNC
AM-3	1812	Halfpenny	25.00	45.00	125.00	225.00	350.00	-

AM-4   *PURE COPPER PREFERABLE TO PAPER —*

Designed and engraved by Thomas Halliday, this token originally circulated in Ireland and later appeared in British North America. Lower Canada saw numerous pieces circulating and small quantities circulated in the United States.

Composition: Copper
Weight: 6.7 to 7.7 gms
Diameter: 27.7 to 28.0 mm
Die Axis: ↑↑
Edge: Reeded
Ref.Nos.: Br 1009; Co 4NL;
       W 153

Cat.No.	Date	Description	VG	F	VF	EF	AU	UNC
AM-4		Halfpenny	5.00	10.00	25.00	65.00	200.00	350.00

AM-5   *COMMERCE — 1781 NORTH AMERICAN TOKEN*

This North American token was struck in Dublin around 1825 and antedated to evade the importation laws. The token was struck without a collar to create the look of an earlier token. This piece saw limited circulation in the United States.

Composition: Copper, brass
Weight: 7.7 to 7.8 gms
Diameter: 27.6 to 27.8 mm
Die Axis: ↑↑
Edge: Plain
Ref.Nos.: Br 1013; See below

Varieties: Composition
     A1   Copper; Co 1NL; W 151
     A2   Brass; Co 2NL; W 151

Cat.No.	Date	Description	VG	F	VF	EF	AU	UNC
AM-5A1	1781	Copper	20.00	40.00	90.00	150.00	250.00	-
AM-5A2	1781	Brass	40.00	75.00	150.00	250.00	400.00	-

THE VEXATOR CANADIENSIS TOKENS

These crude pieces are among the world's most interesting coins. They are a threefold evasion, designed to prevent their issuers from prosecution for sedition, forgery and importing private tokens. Their types, a bust and a seated female figure, resembled those of the regal copper closely enough to insure ready acceptance. Their blundered legends were designed to protect the issuers from accusations of forgery and sedition. The obverse legend meant, to those who thought the pieces seditious, "The Tormentor of Canada." The issuers, on the other hand, said that it meant, "A Canadian Trapper." To create this double meaning they deliberately made the third letter vague in form, so it could be read as an X or an N. Combined with the shaggy bust, the inscription could be construed as identifying the pieces as medalets honouring the fur trade. The reverse inscription means, "Wouldn't you like to catch them?" and could allude to fur-bearing animals or to the issuers of the tokens. The inscription's original compositions in Latin testify that the issuers were educated men and probably numismatists well acquainted with the methods employed by the makers of the English Bungtowns to evade similar English laws against forgery. The "1811" is an antedate to evade regulations against the import of private tokens. The coins appeared after 1830 and possibly allude to King William IV as the Tormentor of Canada or to some local governor or obnoxious official whose identity is now forgotten.

BRETON CROSS REFERENCE TABLE FOR VEXATOR CANADIENSIS TOKENS

Breton NO.	Charlton Cat. No.	Page No.	Breton No.	Charlton Cat. No.	Page No.
558	VC-1, 2	199	559	VC-3	199

VC-1   *VEXATOR CANADINSIS 1811*

Composition: Copper
Weight: 2.9 to 6.5 gms
Diameter: 25.9 to 26.1 mm
Die Axis: Variable
Edge: Plain
Ref.Nos.: Br 558; W 676

Cat.No.	Date	Description	VG	F	VF	EF	AU	UNC
VC-1	1811	Copper			Extremely Rare			

VC-2   *VEXATOR (OR VENATOR) CANADINSIS 1811*

Composition: Copper, brass
Weight: 2.9 to 6.5 gms
Diameter: 25.9 to 26.7 mm
Die Axis: Variable
Edge: Plain
Ref.Nos.: Br 558; W 675

Varieties: Composition
A1 Copper
A2 Brass

Cat.No.	Date	Description	VG	F	VF	EF	AU	UNC
VC-2A1	1811	Copper	200.00	350.00	600.00	-	-	-
VC-2A2	1811	Brass	500.00	750.00	950.00	-	-	-

VC-3   *VEXATOR (OR VENATOR) CANADIENSIS ML 1811*

Composition: Copper, brass
Weight: 2.6 to 6.5 gms
Diameter: 25.6 to 26.1 mm
Die Axis: Variable
Edge: Plain
Ref.Nos.: Br 559; W 677

Varieties: Composition
A1 Copper
A2 Brass

Cat.No.	Date	Description	VG	F	VF	EF	AU	UNC
VC-3A1	1811	Copper	200.00	350.00	600.00	-	-	-
VC-3A2	1811	Brass			Very Rare			

BLACKSMITH TOKENS

About 1835, according to McLachlan, a dissolute blacksmith in Montreal began to make his own halfpennies to pay for liquor. He made counterfeits of the battered, worn-out, old English and Irish regal halfpennies of George III. His dies were purposely left unfinished in order to create the appearance of a badly worn coin. His halfpennies were then artifically darkened, probably by overheating, to create the illusion of age. Only a crude outline of the type was cut, without date or legend.

A peculiarity of these pieces is that the types are almost always reversed because the die-sinkers cut the types on the dies to face the same way as on the coins they used as models. These pieces were accepted in trade because of the almost insatiable demand for small change in Lower Canada at that time, particularly in Montreal.

CROSS REFERENCE FOR BLACKSMITH TOKENS

Charlton Cat. No.	Willey No.	Wood Number	Remarks (Others)	Page No.
BL-1	629	Wo 1		202
BL-2	630	Wo 2,3		202
BL-3	631	Wo 4		203
BL-4	632	Wo 5		203
BL-5	633	Wo 6		204
BL-6	634	Wo 7,8		204
BL-7	635	Wo 11		205
BL-8	636	Wo 12		205
BL-9	638	Wo 13		206
BL-10	637	Wo 14		206
BL-11	639	Wo 16		207
BL-12	640	Wo 17		207
BL-13	641	Wo 18		208
BL-14	642	Wo 38		208
BL-15	—	—		209
BL-16	643	Wo 39		209
BL-17	644	Wo 40		210
BL-18	645	—		210
BL-19	646	—		211
BL-20	647	Wo 41		211
BL-21A,B	648	Wo 43		212
BL-22	—	—		212
BL-23	—	—		213
BL-24A	655	—	Br 997, Lees 3	213
BL-24B	654	—	Br 997, Lees 4	214
BL-24C	657	—	Br 999, Lees 5a	214
BL-25	652	Wo 9		215
BL-26	653	Wo 9A	Br 997, Lees 5	215
BL-28	656	Wo 10	Br 998	216
BL-29	347	—	Co 361a NS	217

CROSS REFERENCE FOR BLACKSMITH TOKENS

Charlton Cat. No.	Willey No.	Wood Number	Remarks (Others)	Page Number
BL-30	345	—	Co 361 NS	217
BL-31	346	—	Co 360 NS	218
BL-32	649	Wo 19,20	Br 1008	218
BL-33	650	Wo 21		219
BL-34	651	Wo 22		219
BL-35	603	—	Br 1012, Co 25,26	220
BL-36	604	—	Br 1012, Co 20	220
BL-37	658	Wo 33		221
BL-38	659	Wo 34		221
BL-39	660	Wo 35		222
BL-40	661	Wo 23		222
BL-41	662	Wo 24		223
BL-42	665	Wo 25		223
BL-43	663	Wo 26		224
BL-44	666	Wo 27		224
BL-45	667	Wo 28		225
BL-46	669	—		225
BL-47	668	Wo 29		226
BL-48	664	Wo 30		226
BL-49	—	Wo 31		227
BL-50	—	Wo 45		227
BL-51	—	—		228
BL-52	—	—		228
BL-53	670	Wo 32		229
BL-54	671	Wo 44		229
BL-55	672	Wo 46		230
BL-56	673	Wo 36		230
BL-57	674	—		230

BLACKSMITH IMITATIONS OF REGAL COINAGE

BUST OF GEORGE III FACING LEFT

BL-1

OBVERSE: Laureate bust of George III facing left, the chaplet being tied in a double bow with loops of equal size. The ends of the ribbon are thin, the upper one curving upwards and the lower one being nearly straight.

REVERSE: A crude Britannia seated to the right with a spear and spray of leaves copied from the English regal halfpenny of 1770-1775. The bust and lap are prominent.

Composition: Copper
Weight: 6.8 to 7.8 gms
Diameter: 27.0 mm
Die Axis: ↑↓
Edge: Plain
Ref.Nos.: W 629; Wo 1

Cat.No.	Date	Description	VG	F	VF	EF	AU	UNC
BL-1			-	-	80.00	-	-	-

BL-2

OBVERSE: Laureate bust of George III. Similar to BL-1, but the mouth is slightly open, the Adams apple larger and the shoulder humped. The bow is double with the upper loop larger and both ribbon ends pointing upwards.

REVERSE: Britannia seated to the right, as BL-1, from a worn die.

Composition: Copper, brass
Weight: See below
Diameter: 26.3 to 26.7 mm
Die Axis: ↑↑ ↑↓
Edge: Plain
Ref.Nos.: W 630; See below

Varieties: Composition and weight
    A1 Copper, Thick flan, Early issue, Wt 6.5 to 9.5 gms; Wo 2
    A2 Copper, Thin flan, Late issue, Wt. 3.7 to 4.3 gms; Wo 2
    A3 Brass, Wt 4.2 to 5.7 gms; Wo 3

Variations: With and without rusted reverse dies.

Cat.No.	Date	Description	VG	F	VF	EF	AU	UNC
BL-2A1		Copper, Thick, Early	-	-	30.00	-	-	-
BL-2A2		Copper, Thin, Late	-	-	30.00	-	-	-
BL-2A3		Brass	-	-	350.00	-	-	-

BL-3

OBVERSE: Laureate bust of George III as BL-2.
REVERSE: Britannia seated right is poorly designed, with a small head and a long, thin neck. The bust is prominent and the shield is of a simpler design.

Composition: Copper
Weight: 4.2 to 6.7 gms
Diameter: 27.3 mm
Die Axis: ↑↓
Edge: Plain
Ref.Nos.: W 631; Wo 4

Cat.No.	Date	Description	VG	F	VF	EF	AU	UNC
BL-3		Copper, Coinage	-	-	50.00	-	-	-

BL-4

OBVERSE: Laureate bust of George III as BL-2.
REVERSE: A harp facing left with ten strings. The die is badly cracked, especially parallel to the body of the harp.

Composition: Copper
Weight: 3.6 to 4.5 gms
Diameter: 27.3 mm
Die Axis: ↑↓
Edge: Plain
Ref.Nos.: W 632; Wo 5

Cat.No.	Date	Description	VG	F	VF	EF	AU	UNC
BL-4		Copper, coinage	-	-	40.00	-	-	-

BL-5

OBVERSE: Laureate bust of George III as BL-2.
REVERSE: Similar to BL-4 but the angel has a larger breast. This die broke, producing several flaws.

Composition: Copper
Weight: 4.5 to 7.5 gms
Diameter: 26.6 to 26.8 mm
Die Axis: ↑↑ ↑↓
Edge: Plain
Ref.Nos.: W 633; Wo 6

Variation: A brass uniface example of the reverse weighing 3.2 gms sold as Lot 2437, Torex Auction, Fall 1989.

Cat.No.	Date	Description	VG	F	VF	EF	AU	UNC
BL-5			-	-	40.00	-	-	-

BL-6

OBVERSE: As BL-2 but from a rusted die.
REVERSE: Britannia seated right as on English regal copper of 1797-1807. Fine lines, resembling water, fill the exergue. The die is so badly cracked that the centre of the type is obliterated.

Composition: Copper, brass
Weight: 5.0 to 5.4 gms
Diameter: 26.7 mm
Die Axis: ↑↓
Edge: Plain
Ref.Nos.: W 634; Wo 7,8

Varieties: Composition
    A1 Copper; Wo 7
    A2 Brass; Wo 8

Variation: A brass uniface example of the reverse exists.

Cat.No.	Date	Description	VG	F	VF	EF	AU	UNC
BL-6A1		Copper	-	-	225.00	-	-	-
BL-6A2		Brass	J. Hoare Auction, October 1999, Lot 591, VF - $1,870.00					

BL-7

OBVERSE: Laureate bust of George III similar to BL-1 but the eyebrows are flush with the forehead, the neck merges into the chin and the mouth is more open. The back of the head is incomplete. The loops of the bow are small and the ribbons are of equal length.

REVERSE: A tall, thin Britannia seated right copied from the English regal copper of 1770-1775 with a small shield.

Composition: Copper
Weight: 5.0 to 5.4 gms
Diameter: 27.4 mm
Die Axis: ↑↓
Edge: Plain
Ref.Nos.: W 635; Wo 11

Cat.No.	Date	Description	VG	F	VF	EF	AU	UNC
BL-7			-	30.00	-	-	-	-

BL-8

OBVERSE: Laureate bust of George III as BL-7.
REVERSE: A harp facing left with seven strings. The die is badly cracked.

Composition: Copper
Weight: 4.6 gms
Diameter: 27.2 mm
Die Axis: ↑↓
Edge: Plain
Ref.Nos.: W 636; Wo 12

Cat.No.	Date	Description	VG	F	VF	EF	AU	UNC
BL-8			-	-	30.00	-	-	-

BL-9

OBVERSE: A large bust facing left with a long nose and pointed chin. The bow is plain. The cuirass has horizontal lines in front.

REVERSE: A large broad-shouldered Britannia seated right with a short left forearm.

Composition: Brass
Weight: 6.0 to 6.3 gms
Diameter: 27.3 mm
Die Axis: ↑↓
Edge: Plain
Ref.Nos.: W 638; Wo 13

Cat.No.	Date	Description	VG	F	VF	EF	AU	UNC
BL-9			-	-	40.00	-	-	-

BL-10

OBVERSE: A smaller bust facing left with a pointed chin. The lower loop of the bow is angular.

REVERSE: A headless Britannia seated right with a long, thin forearm. The exergue line runs to the shield.

The existence of the coin Wo 15, which Wood listed as having a composition of copper, cannot be confirmed. No example of BL-10 (W14 - Brass) has yet surfaced in copper. Courteau, Mabbott and Baker have not seen copper examples and the coins from Woods collection that are listed as copper upon closer examination were found to be brass.

Composition: Brass
Weight: 5.9 to 6.3 gms
Diameter: 27.0 to 27.2 mm
Die Axis: ↑↓
Edge: Plain
Ref.Nos.: W 637; Wo 14

Cat.No.	Date	Description	VG	F	VF	EF	AU	UNC
BL-10		Brass	-	30.00	50.00	-	-	-

BL-11

OBVERSE: Bust facing left with a low forehead, large nose and weak chin. The front of the bust has a double outline. The chaplet has short ribbons.

REVERSE: A small Britannia seated right with a small head and short, well-proportioned arms. The spear shows between the arm and the drapery. The exergue line reaches the shield.

Composition: Brass
Weight: 6.2 gms
Diameter: 27.2 mm
Die Axis: ↑↓
Edge: Plain
Ref.Nos.: W 639;Wo 16

Cat.No.	Date	Description	VG	F	VF	EF	AU	UNC
BL-11			-	-	30.00	-	-	-

BL-12

OBVERSE: Bust facing left with a long neck, strong chin, angular forehead and a thin, pointed nose. The ribbon of the chaplet is tied with a long, slender bow.

REVERSE: As BL-11.

Composition: Brass
Weight: 6.0 to 6.5 gms
Diameter: N/A
Die Axis: ↑↓
Ref.Nos.: W 640; Wo 17

Cat.No.	Date	Description	VG	F	VF	EF	AU	UNC
BL-12			-	-	400.00	-	-	-

BL-13

OBVERSE: Bust facing left as BL-12.
REVERSE: A headless Britannia seated right with thick right arm. The drapery under the right arm is large and angular. The exergue line does not reach the shield.

Composition: Brass
Weight: 6.3 to 6.5 gms
Diameter: 27.0 mm
Die Axis: ↑↓
Edge: Plain
Ref.Nos.: W 641; Wo 18

Cat.No.	Date	Description	VG	F	VF	EF	AU	UNC
BL-13			-	-	40.00	-	-	-

BUST OF GEORGE III FACING RIGHT

BL-14

OBVERSE: A small, faceless head facing right with a broad truncation.
REVERSE: A crowned harp facing left.

Photograph not available

Composition: Brass
Weight: N/A
Diameter: N/A
Die Axis: N/A
Edge: N/A
Ref.Nos.: W 642; Wo 38

Cat.No.	Date	Description	VG	F	VF	EF	AU	UNC
BL-14					Less than five known, Extremely Rare			

BL-15   *ONE PENNY*

OBVERSE: Crude bust facing right.
REVERSE: Britannia seated right, crude attempts at lettering.

Composition: Copper
Weight: 23.8 gms
Diameter: 34.4 mm
Die Axis: ↑↑
Edge: Plain
Ref.Nos.: Not previously
listed

Cat.No.	Date	Description	VG	F	VF	EF	AU	UNC
BL-15					Two known, Extremely Rare			

UNIFACE BLACKSMITH TOKENS

All the tokens in this series are extremely rare. They are uniface and variable in weight.

BL-16

OBVERSE: Head facing left with a protruding tongue and a small cross behind the head.
REVERSE: Blank.

Photograph not available

Composition: N/A
Weight: N/A
Diameter: N/A
Edge: Plain
Ref.Nos.: W 643; Wo 39

Cat.No.	Date	Description	VG	F	VF	EF	AU	UNC
BL-16					Less than five known, Extremely Rare			

BL-17

OBVERSE: Large head facing right with a broad truncation. The back of the head is unfinished.
REVERSE: Blank.

Composition: N/A
Weight: 3.2 gms
Diameter: N/A
Edge: Plain
Ref.Nos.: W 644; Wo 40

Cat.No.	Date	Description	VG	F	VF	EF	AU	UNC
BL-17				Probably unique. Baker Sale 1987, $4,000.00				

BL-18

OBVERSE: Large, incomplete head facing right with a broad truncation. There are two ribbons protruding from the back of the neck. A large dot appears below the head. Not listed by Wood.
REVERSE: Blank.

Composition: Copper
Weight: 3.5 gms
Diameter: 27.0 mm
Edge: Plain
Ref.Nos.: W 645; Not
            listed by Wood.

Cat.No.	Date	Description	VG	F	VF	EF	AU	UNC
BL-18				Probably unique. Baker Sale 1987, $1,900.00				

BL-19

OBVERSE: Crude laureate bust facing right with a long nose, a pointed chin and a flat truncation. The ribbon of the chaplet has short ends and no bow. Two marks, apparently intended to imitate a badly worn inscription, appear behind the head at the top.

REVERSE: Blank.

Composition: Copper
Weight: 5.9 gms
Diameter: 27.0 mm
Edge: Plain
Ref.Nos.: W 646; Not
       listed by Wood

Cat.No.	Date	Description	VG	F	VF	EF	AU	UNC
BL-19				Two known, Extremely Rare				

BL-20

OBVERSE: Poorly defined, faceless laureate bust facing left. Two marks which suggest a worn inscription show behind the head in the same relative position as those on BL-19, proving the former to be the prototype of this coin.

REVERSE: Blank.

Composition: Copper
Weight: 8.0 gms
Diameter: 27.0 mm
Edge: Plain
Ref.Nos.: W 647; Wo 41

Cat.No.	Date	Description	VG	F	VF	EF	AU	UNC
BL-20				Probably unique. Baker Sale 1987, $3,350.00.				

BL-21

BL-21A
OBVERSE: Crudely cut head facing right in a border of large dots.
REVERSE: Blank.

BL21-B
OBVERSE: Crudely cut head facing right in a border of large dots.
REVERSE: Same as obverse.

Composition: Copper
Weight: 5.7 gms
Diameter: 26.4 mm
Edge: Plain
Ref.Nos.: W 648; Wo 43

Note: Die axis of BL-21B is N.W.

Cat.No.	Date	Description	VG	F	VF	EF	AU	UNC
BL-21A					Rare			
BL-21B					Less than five known. Baker Sale 1987, $1,600.00			

BL-22

OBVERSE: Tall thin bust facing right.
REVERSE: Blank.

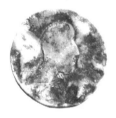 

Composition: Copper
Weight: 3.43 gms
Diameter: 27.0 mm
Edge: Plain
Ref.Nos.: Not previously listed.

Cat.No.	Date	Description	VG	F	VF	EF	AU	UNC
BL-22					Less then ten known. Baker Sale 1987, $750.00			

BL-23

OBVERSE: Horned bust facing left.
REVERSE: Blank.

Composition: Copper
Weight: 4.48 gms
Diameter: 27.0 mm
Edge: Plain
Ref.Nos.: Not previously listed.

Cat.No.	Date	Description	VG	F	VF	EF	AU	UNC
BL-23		Less than five known. Baker Sale 1987, $1,200.00						

BL-24   *BLACKSMITH IMITATIONS OF SHIPS COLONIES AND COMMERCE TOKENS*

This section of the Ships, Colonies and Commerce Tokens derives its title from the crude workmanship of this series. Because these tokens may vary in fabric and weight it is impossible to attribute them to any one minter.

Please refer to page 22 for cross listings of BL-24, 25 and 26.

BL-24A   *SHIPS COLONIES & COMMERCE — (SAILING SHIP DESIGN)*

OBVERSE: A frigate sailing to the right flying an ensign drooping almost to the deck.
REVERSE: SHIPS COLONIES & COMMERCE in four lines, but the first "S" in SHIPS is right over the first "O" in COLONIES.
Beading occurs on both the obverse and reverse rims.

Composition: Copper
Weight: See below
Diameter: 26.0 to 26.9 mm
Die Axis: ↑↑ ↑↓
Ref.Nos.: Br 997; W 655; Lees 3

Varieties: Weight and die axis
A1 Weight 6.9 to 7.9 gms, Medal
A2 Weight 4.2 to 4.7 gms, Medal and Coinage
A3 Weight 2.9 to 3.5 gms, Coinage
A4 Weight 2.9 to 3.2 gms, Medal

Cat.No.	Date	Description	G	VG	F	VF	EF	AU
BL-24A1		Thick, Medal	25.00	50.00	100.00	-	-	-
BL-24A2		Thin, Medal	40.00	70.00	150.00	-	-	-
BL-24A3		Thin, Medal, Coinage	40.00	70.00	150.00	-	-	-
BL-24A4		Thin, Medal			Rare			

BL-24B   *SHIPS COLONIES & COMMERCE — (SAILING SHIP DESIGN)*

OBVERSE: A frigate sailing to the right flying an ensign drooping almost to the deck.
Beading is found on the obverse rim only.

REVERSE: Similar to BL-24A but a flaw usually showing over the "P" of SHIPS.
No beading.

Composition: Copper
Weight: 2.4 gms
Die Axis: ↑↓
Edge: Plain
Ref.Nos.: Br 997; W 654; Lees 4

Cat.No.	Date	Description	VG	F	VF	EF	AU	UNC
BL-24B		J. Hoare Auction, October 1995, Lot 1942, F - $715.00						

BL-24C *SHIPS COLONIES & COMMERCE — (SAILING SHIP DESIGN)*

Composition: Copper
Weight: 5.0 to 7.0 gms
Diameter: 26.5 mm
Die Axis: Variable
Edge: Plain
Ref.Nos.: Br 999; W 657; Lees 5A

OBVERSE: A frigate sailing right with a short hull curving up to the top of a very high
poopdeck. The prow joins the deckrail and the lower part of the open spritsail
joins the hull. The mainmast has no staysail. The ensign is wide with three
hollows at the top and flies from a flagstaff set well forward of the stern. The
flagstaff is double-cut near the deck and extends high above the ensign. The
exergue is small with pointed lines. The border is of straight, square-ended teeth.

REVERSE: SHIPS COLONIES & COMMERCE in four lines of crude lettering, unevenly
spaced and misaligned, and varying in size. The ampersand has a thick, blunt
upper end. The border is finely saw-toothed. Issued on thin and thick flans.
There is no obverse or reverse beading.

Note: For Lees No. 5 see BL-26 page 215.

Cat.No.	Date	Description	VG	F	VF	EF	AU	UNC
BL-24C		J. Hoare Auction, February 1995, Lot 1858, VF - $4,800.00						

BL-25 *(SAILING SHIP DESIGN) — (LAUREATE BUST DESIGN)*

OBVERSE: Laureate bust of George III, as BL-1.
REVERSE: A frigate flying a straight, rectangular pennant from the mainmast, with no square hollow next to the mast. There are no balls where the guys join the mainmast and the balls of the other masts are small. A short spike projects from the stern and the afterbrace of the mizzenmast joins the flagstaff. The ensign droops slightly. Similar to BL-24A, B.

Photograph not available

Composition: Copper
Weight: 3.6 to 3.9 gms
Diameter: N/A
Die Axis: ↑↓
Edge: Plain
Ref.Nos.: W 652; Wo 9

Cat.No.	Date	Description	VG	F	VF	EF	AU	UNC
BL-25				Less than five known, Extremely Rare				

BL-26 **SHIPS COLONIES & COMMERCE — (SHIP DESIGN)**

OBVERSE: A frigate flying a straight, rectangular pennant from the mainmast, with no square hollow next to the mast. There are no balls where the guys join the mainmast and the balls of the other masts are small. A short spike projects from the stern and the afterbrace of the mizzenmast joins the flagstaff. The ensign droops slightly. As BL-25.
REVERSE: SHIPS COLONIES & COMMERCE in four lines with the first "S" in SHIPS a little to the right of the first "O" in COLONIES.

Composition: Copper
Weight: 3.6 to 3.9 gms
Diameter: N/A
Die Axis: ↑↓
Edge: Plain
Ref.Nos.: Br 997; W 653;
　　　　　 Wo 9a; Lees 5

Cat.No.	Date	Description	VG	F	VF	EF	AU	UNC
BL-26			1,000.00	1,250.00	1,500.00	-	-	-

BL-27   *NO LISTING*

BL-28   *SHIPS COLONIES & COMMERCE — (HARP DESIGN)*

OBVERSE: Similar to the reverse of BL-4, a harp facing left. From a badly cracked die.
REVERSE: Similar BL-24B. Issued on thin and thick flans.

Composition: Copper
Weight: 3.3 to 6.5 gms
Diameter: 26.4 mm
Die Axis: ↑↑
Edge: Plain
Ref.Nos.: Br 998; W 656;
                 Wo 10

Varieties: Thick and thin flans
  A1 Thick flan, wt. 6.5 gms
  A2 Thin flan, wt. 3.3 to 3.7 gms

Cat.No.	Date	Description	VG	F	VF	EF	AU	UNC
BL-28A1		Thick flan	-	300.00	-	-	-	-
BL-28A2		Thin flan	-	300.00	-	-	-	-

BLACKSMITH IMITATIONS OF NOVA SCOTIA TOKENS

Towards the end of the period of private tokens in Nova Scotia, John Brown, and possibly others, had recource to an anonymous manufacturer and issued halfpenny tokens of crude fabric on thin flans.

BL-29   *(HARP DESIGN)—*
HALF PENNY TOKEN (BUST OF GEORGE III)

OBVERSE: Laureate bust of George III facing right. Crudely fashioned.
REVERSE: Crowned harp within a wreath facing left.

Composition: Copper
Weight: 3.7 gms
Diameter: 24.5 mm
Die Axis: ↑↓
Edge: Plain
Ref.Nos.: Co 361aNS; W 347

Cat.No.	Date	Description	VG	F	VF	EF	AU	UNC
BL-29					Only four known, Extremely Rare			

BL-30   *(HARP DESIGN)— HALFPENNY (WAREHOUSE DESIGN)*

OBVERSE: Warehouse building.
REVERSE: Crowned harp within a wreath facing left, as BL-29.

Photograph not available

Composition: Copper
Weight: 5.2 gms
Diameter: N/A
Die Axis: N/A
Edge: Plain
Ref.Nos.: Co 361NS; W 346

Cat.No.	Date	Description	VG	F	VF	EF	AU	UNC
BL-30					Extremely Rare			

BL-31
JB (SCRIPT INITIALS)—
HALFPENNY (WAREHOUSE DESIGN)

OBVERSE: Warehouse building, as BL-30.
REVERSE: Script letters "JB."

Composition: Copper
Weight: 4.1 to 4.2 gms
Diameter: 28.5 mm
Die Axis: ↑→
Edge: Plain
Ref.Nos.: Co 360NS; W 345

Cat.No.	Date	Description	VG	F	VF	EF	AU	UNC
BL-31					J. Hoare Auction, February 1995, Lot 1786, AU - $1,350.00			

BLACKSMITH IMITATIONS OF "TIFFIN" TOKENS

BL-32
(COMMERCE SEATED) 1820 — (BUST DESIGN)

OBVERSE: Laureate bust facing right, with an aquiline nose, a long, pointed chin and a broad truncation. Three tufts of hair stand on the head. The ends of the ribbon curve outward.
REVERSE: Commerce seated left on a bale, with cornucopia and balances. Dated 1820.

Composition: Copper, brass
Weight: 4.3 to 5.5 gms
Diameter: 26.7 to 27.6 mm
Die Axis: ↑↑ ↑↓
Edge: Plain
Ref.Nos.: Br 1008; W 649;
      See below

Varieties: Composition
    A1 Copper, Medal; Wo 19
    A2 Brass, Coinage; Wo 20

Cat.No.	Date	Description	VG	F	VF	EF	AU	UNC
BL-32A1	1820	Copper, Medal, Coinage	-	1,000.00	-	-	-	-
BL-32A2	1820	Brass, Coinage		Less than ten known, Very Rare				

BL-33

OBVERSE: Bust facing right with a small nose and weak chin. The ends of the ribbon point inward.
REVERSE: As BL-32.

Composition: Copper
Weight: 4.2 gms
Diameter: 26.0 mm
Die Axis: ↑→
Edge: Plain
Ref.Nos.: W 650; Wo 21

Cat.No.	Date	Description	VG	F	VF	EF	AU	UNC
BL-33	1820				Unique. Baker Sale 1987, $6,850.00			

BLACKSMITH IMITATIONS OF "BUST AND HARP" TOKENS

BL-34

OBVERSE: As BL-33.
REVERSE: A harp facing left.

Composition: Copper
Weight: 3.8 to 4.4 gms
Diameter: 25.8 to 26.2 mm
Die Axis: ↑→
Edge: Plain
Ref.Nos.: W 651; Wo 22

Cat.No.	Date	Description	VG	F	VF	EF	AU	UNC
BL-34					Approximately six known.			
					J. Hoare Auction, Fall 1989, Lot 2455, F-VF - $2,500.00			

BL-35

OBVERSE: Bust facing left. Very crude with poorly cut side curls, the cuirass has six flaps and the shirt frill has four ruffles.

REVERSE: Harp facing left. The harp has eight strings with the first attached to the wing. The foot of the harp points between "I" and "8" of the date, if the date is present. A large, centrally positioned dot appears among the strings.

Composition: Copper, brass
Weight: 4.9 to 5.5 gms
Diameter: 27.4 to 27.5 mm
Die Axis: ↑↑ ↑→
Edge: Plain
Ref.Nos.: Br 1012; Co 25,26
            W 603

Varieties: Reverse and composition
     A1 Copper; Co 25; W 603
     A2 Brass; Co 26; W 603

Cat.No.	Date	Description	VG	F	VF	EF	AU	UNC
BL-35A1	1820	Copper	175.00	250.00	500.00	1,200.00	-	-
BL-35A2	1820	Brass	50.00	100.00	225.00	-	-	-

BL-36

OBVERSE: Laureate bust facing right with nine leaves in the chaplet. A meaningless legend sometimes appears as CHCOBRDGES III RUBUS.

REVERSE: Harp facing right with nine strings and an ornamental top. The foot of the harp points to the "2" in the date. The legend may read RUMG EBUCAO BOUGO SO.

Composition: Copper
Weight: 7.1 to 7.8 gms
Diameter: 25.9 to 27.5 mm
Die Axis: ↑→
Edge: Plain
Ref.Nos.: Br 1012, Co 20;
            W 604

Cat.No.	Date	Description	VG	F	VF	EF	AU	UNC
BL-36	1820		-	500.00	800.00	-	-	-

THE BITIT TOKENS

This series of tokens, of which the most common has legends, has been considered by some as an English Bungtown token or coinage for the state of Vermont.

BL-37

OBVERSE: Large laureate head facing right with a pug nose. Legend reads: GLORIOVS III. VIS.
REVERSE: Crude seated figure of Hibernia seated left, holding a shamrock. Legend: BITIT; blank exergue.

Composition: Copper
Weight: 5.6 to 6.1 gms
Diameter: 26.5 to 26.8 mm
Die Axis: ↑↓
Edge: Plain
Ref.Nos.: W 658; Wo 33

Cat.No.	Date	Description	VG	F	VF	EF	AU	UNC
BL-37			5.00	15.00	25.00	-	-	-

BL-38

OBVERSE: Crude laureate bust facing left with a long nose. The legend is illegible.
REVERSE: Crude Britannia seated left holding a shamrock. An oval shield rests at her side. Legend: IIII; this is an imitation of BL-37.

Composition: Copper
Weight: 4.9 to 5.2 gms
Diameter: 25.7 mm
Die Axis: ↑↑ ↑↓
Edge: Plain
Ref.Nos.: W 659; Wo 34

Varieties: Die Axis
A1 Medal
A2 Coinage

Cat.No.	Date	Description	VG	F	VF	EF	AU	UNC
BL-38A1		Medal	-	550.00	-	-	-	-
BL-38A2		Coinage	-	-	-	-	-	-

BL-39

OBVERSE: Similar to BL-38 but cruder with a turned-up nose.
REVERSE: A crude harp facing left.

Photograph not available

Composition: Copper
Weight: N/A
Diameter: N/A
Die Axis: N/A
Edge: N/A
Ref.Nos.: W 660; Wo 35

Cat.No.	Date	Description	VG	F	VF	EF	AU	UNC
BL-39				Less than five known, Extremely Rare				

DANIEL AND BENJAMIN TRUE TOKENS

A number of American Hard Times tokens were struck by Daniel and Benjamin True of Troy, New York, after 1830. About 1835 they began to produce lightweight tokens for export to Canada, including one of the more common "Blacksmith" pieces. The dies of this piece they later muled with badly dilapidated dies of American store cards to produce some extremely rare pieces.

BL-40

The heaviest specimens are the earliest and the best while the lightest are struck from the worst of the dies. It is possible to arrange specimens to show the progressive deterioration of the dies. The reverse die was often touched up, producing many variations.

OBVERSE: Laureate bust facing right with a double chin and a prominent lower jaw. The ribbons are tied with a single bow. A large die crack runs through the shoulder to the border behind the head.
REVERSE: Seated Britannia facing right, as on the English regal copper of the period. Coarsely toothed borders.

Composition: Copper
Weight: 3.6 to 5.8 gms
Diameter: 26.5 to 28.1 mm
Die Axis: ↑↓
Edge: Plain
Ref.Nos.: W 661; Wo 23

Cat.No.	Date	Description	VG	F	VF	EF	AU	UNC
BL-40			-	15.00	-	-	-	-

BL-41

The reverse of this coin is so poor that only the examination of more than one specimen simultaneously could result in its proper identification. There were in this period many "Riseing Sun" taverns in Upper and Lower Canada. Ferguson considered it to have been issued by James Watson, the owner of a tavern of this name in Toronto between 1833 and 1837. Troy had almost no business dealings with Upper Canada, but had plenty with Lower Canada through Montreal. For this reason it is generally believed that the token is for a Lower Canadian tavern of this name.

OBVERSE: As BL-40. The die is badly cracked.
REVERSE: RISEING SUN TAVERN in large letters is close to and parallel to a coarsely toothed border.

Composition: Copper
Weight: 3.8 to 4.8 gms
Diameter: 26.6 to 27.0 mm
Die Axis: ↑→
Edge: Plain
Ref.Nos.: W 662; Wo 24

Cat.No.	Date	Description	VG	F	VF	EF	AU	UNC
BL-41			-	300.00	-	-	-	-

BL-42

OBVERSE: As BL-40.
REVERSE: A screw. Legend: MACHINE SHOP, SCREEN FOR PAPER, OIL AND CIDER MILLS, TURNING AND BORING.

Compositon: Copper
Weight: 3.2 to 3.4 gms
Diameter: 25.8 mm
Die Axis: ↑↓
Edge: Plain
Ref.Nos.: W 665; Wo 25

Cat.No.	Date	Description	VG	F	VF	EF	AU	UNC
BL-42			-	500.00	-	-	-	-

BL-43

OBVERSE: As BL-40, from a very badly worn and cracked die.
REVERSE: An eagle with a thin neck and clear wing feathers. Toothed borders.

Composition: Copper
Weight: 3.2 to 3.4 gms
Diameter: 25.9 mm
Die Axis: ↑→
Edge: Plain
Ref.Nos.: W 663; Wo 26

Cat.No.	Date	Description	VG	F	VF	EF	AU	UNC
BL-43			-	775.00	-	-	-	-

BL-44

OBVERSE: As the reverse of BL-43.
REVERSE: As the reverse of BL-42.

Photograph not available

Composition: Copper
Weight: 3.2 gms
Diameter: 25.7 mm
Die Axis: N/A
Edge: Plain
Ref.Nos.: W 666; Wo 27

Cat.No.	Date	Description	VG	F	VF	EF	AU	UNC
BL-44								

Four known, two of which are in public collections.
J. Hoare Auction, Fall 1989, Lot 2467, F-VF - $3,300.00

BL-45

OBVERSE: As the reverse of BL-43.
REVERSE: Legend: PECK'S PATENT TIN MACHINES enclosing the words INCOMPLETE SETS MADE AT TROY N.Y., with a spindle or windlass.

Composition: Copper
Weight: 5.0 to 5.2 gms
Diameter: 26.7 mm
Die Axis: ↑→
Edge: Plain
Ref.Nos.: W 667; Wo 28

Cat.No.	Date	Description	VG	F	VF	EF	AU	UNC
BL-45			-	700.00	-	-	-	-

BL-46

OBVERSE: LEGEND: PECK'S PATENT TIN MACHINES, INCOMPLETE SETS MADE AT TROY, N.Y., with a spindle or windlass. As BL-45.
REVERSE: Seated Britannia facing right as on the reverse of BL-40.

Composition: Copper
Weight: 3.3 to 3.4 gms
Diameter: 25.9 mm
Die Axis: ↑↑
Edge: Plain
Ref.Nos.: W 669

Cat.No.	Date	Description	VG	F	VF	EF	AU	UNC
BL-46					Four known.			

J. Hoare Auction, Fall 1989, Lot 2469, VF - $1,900.00

BL-47

OBVERSE: LEGEND: PECK'S PATENT TIN MACHINES, INCOMPLETE SETS MADE AT TROY, N.Y., with a spindle or windlass. As BL-45.
REVERSE: As BL-42.

Composition: Copper
Weight: See below
Diameter: 25.6 to 27.1 mm
Die Axis: ↑↓ ↑←
Edge: Plain
Ref.Nos.: W 668; Wo 29

Varieties: Thin and thick flans
A1 Thick flan, wt. 6.7 to 6.8 gms
A2 Thin flan, wt. 3.4 gms

Cat.No.	Date	Description	VG	F	VF	EF	AU	UNC
BL-47A1		Thick flan	-	125.00	-	-	-	-
BL-47A2		Thin flan	-	125.00	-	-	-	-

BL-48

OBVERSE: An eagle with a thick neck.
REVERSE: Same as obverse.

Composition: Copper
Weight: 5.2 gms
Diameter: N/A
Die Axis: ↑↓
Edge: Plain
Ref.Nos.: W 664; Wo 30

Cat.No.	Date	Description	VG	F	VF	EF	AU	UNC
BL-48		Less than five known. Baker Sale 1987, $300.00						

BLACKSMITH IMITATIONS OF UPPER CANADA TOKENS

BL-49

OBVERSE: Sloop.
REVERSE: Crossed shovels.

Photograph not available

Composition: N/A
Weight: N/A
Diameter: N/A
Die Axis: N/A
Edge: N/A
Ref.Nos.: Wo 31

Cat.No.	Date	Description	VG	F	VF	EF	AU	UNC
BL-49					Unique			

BL-50

OBVERSE: Bust facing right.
REVERSE: Legend: TO FACILITATE TRADE

Composition: Brass
Weight: 6.1 gms
Diameter: 28.2 mm
Die Axis: ↑↓
Edge: Plain
Ref.Nos.: Wo 45

Cat.No.	Date	Description	VG	F	VF	EF	AU	UNC
BL-50					Extremely Rare			

BLACKSMITH IMITATION OF LOWER CANADA TOKENS

BL-51

OBVERSE: Mexican-Bouquet.
REVERSE: Standing Indian (Copy of 1850, Copper Mexican coin, State of Chihuahua).

Composition: Copper
Weight: 7.1 gms
Diameter: 28.0 mm
Die Axis: ↑↑
Edge: Plain
Ref.Nos.: Not previously listed

Cat.No.	Date	Description	VG	F	VF	EF	AU	UNC
BL-51		J. Hoare Auction, October 1999, Lot 595, AVE - $3,520.00						

BL-52

OBVERSE: Bust similar to LC-51.
REVERSE: U.S. Hard Times token, similar to Wood 25, 27, 28 and 29 which are the Starbuck and U & C Peck reverse.

Photograph not available

Composition: N/A
Weight: N/A
Diameter: N/A
Die Axis: N/A
Edge: N/A
Ref.Nos Not previously listed

Cat.No.	Date	Description	VG	F	VF	EF	AU	UNC
BL-52					Extremely Rare			

MISCELLANEOUS BLACKSMITH TOKENS

BL-53

OBVERSE: A Union Jack in an oval shield and a partial wreath. The border is large dots.
REVERSE: A fouled anchor between two branches in a border of large dots.

Composition: Copper, brass
Weight: 3.1 to 5.8 gms
Diameter: 26.0 to 28.0 mm
Die Axis: ↑→ ↑←
Edge: Plain
Ref.Nos.: W 670; Wo 32

Varieties: Composition
A1 Copper, Thick flan, wt. 5.7 gms
A2 Copper, Thin flan, wt. 3.2 gms
A3 Brass

Cat.No.	Date	Description	VG	F	VF	EF	AU	UNC
BL-53A1		Copper, Thick flan	J. Hoare Auction, October 1997, Lot 1142, EF - $1,265.00					
BL-53A2		Copper, Thin flan	-	-	-	-	-	-
BL-53A2		Brass	J. Hoare Auction, Fall 1989, Lot 2475, $1,500.00					

BL-54

OBVERSE: A crude, dog-like head.
REVERSE: Same as above.

Photograph not available

Composition: Copper
Weight: 4.7 gms
Diameter: 27.3 mm
Die Axis: N/A
Edge: Plain
Ref.Nos.: W 671; Wo 44

Cat.No.	Date	Description	VG	F	VF	EF	AU	UNC
BL-54			Four known of which three are in Public Institutions. J. Hoare Auction, Fall 1989, Lot 2479, F - $2,000.00					

BL-55

OBVERSE: Part of a head facing right.
REVERSE: A safe on the back of a tortoise with a partial legend.

Photograph not available

Composition: N/A
Weight: N/A
Diameter: N/A
Die Axis: N/A
Edge: N/A
Ref.Nos.: W 672; Wo 46

Cat.No.	Date	Description	VG	F	VF	EF	AU	UNC
BL-55				Less than five known, Extremely Rare				

BL-56

OBVERSE: A very large laureate bust facing left. Crudely rendered numerals 1417 below.
REVERSE: Uniface.

Photograph not available

Composition: N/A
Weight: N/A
Diameter: N/A
Die Axis: N/A
Edge: N/A
Ref.Nos.: W 673; Wo 36

Cat.No.	Date	Description	VG	F	VF	EF	AU	UNC
BL-56	1417			Less than five known, Extremely Rare				

BL-57

OBVERSE: A windmill between two vines.
REVERSE: A horse tied in front of a tavern. Legend: NO CREDIT.

Composition: Copper
Weight: 9.1 gms
Diameter: 28.0 mm
Die Axis: ↑←
Edge: Plain
Ref.Nos.: W 674

Cat.No.	Date	Description	VG	F	VF	EF	AU	UNC
BL-57	1810			Less than ten known. Baker Sale 1987, $950.00				

CANADIAN COLONIAL TOKENS CROSS REFERENCED BY BRETON, COURTEAU AND WILLEY NUMBERS TO CHARLTON CATALOGUE NUMBERS

Breton Number	Courteau Number	Willey Number	Charlton Cat.No.	Breton Number	Courteau Number	Willey Number	Charlton Cat.No.
520	-	500	LC-1	688	41B	709	LC-31A
521	8-11H	745-748	LC-9A	689	24B	733	LC-43
521	12-14bH	757-759	LC-9B	690	40B	G2	LC-44
521	16-17dH	764-765	LC-9C	691	43-44B	710	LC-27
521	24-29BM	772-775	LC-9D	692	39B	711	LC-32B
522	1-2lH	736-744	LC-8A	693	37B	712	LC-31B
522	3-4iH	749-756	LC-8B	694	38B	713	LC-31C
522	6-7bH	760-763	LC-8C	695	46B	714	LC-29A
522	14-22BM	766-771	LC-8D	696	45B	715	LC-29B
523	36-37BM	779-780	LC11A	697	33-34B	716	LC-29E
523	38BM	784	LC-11B	698	36B	717	LC-30A
524	30-32BM	776-778	LC-10A	699	35B	718	LC-30B
524	33-35BM	781-783	LC10B	700	32B	719	LC-29C
525	39BM	785	LC-11C	701	31B	720	LC-29D
526	71-87BM	861-872	PC-2B	702	29B	721	LC-28
527	41-45	852-853	PC-1B	703	30B	722	LC-30F
	47, 53-63	855-856		704	27-28B	723	LC-33A
	66-70BM	858-859		705	25B	725	LC-33C
527	40,46	851,854	PC-1A	706	23B	726	LC-34
	64-65BM	857		707	22B	727	LC-35
527	-	860	PC-1C	708	20B	728	LC-36
528	15fH	877-878	PC-4	709	21B	729	LC-37
529	5-5hH	873-876	PC-3	710	19B	730	LC-38
531	47W	541	LC-12	711	18B	731	LC-39
532	-	575	LC-13A,B	712	-	G3	LC-38
533	-	574	LC-14	713	8-13B	678-683	LC-2
558	-	675-676	VC-1-2	714	3-7B	684-688	LC-3
559	-	677	VC-3	715	15-17B	690-691	LC-5
561	-	576-577	LC-15	716	14B	689	LC-4
562	-	579	LC-16	717	-	823	UC-3
563	-	573	LC-17	718	-	824-828	UC-2
564	-	572	LC-18	719	208-319UC	880	PC-6A-D
565	-	578	LC-19	720	1-207UC	879	PC-5A-D
670	71B	C28	LC-45	721	-	A2	UC-1
671	72B	580	LC-20	723	-	801	UC-5
672	1B	692	LC-6	724	-	802-808	UC-6
673	2B	693	LC-7	725	-	809	UC-7
674	63-70B	734	LC-40	726	-	819,822	UC-8
675	61B	694	LC-23A	727	-	810-814	UC-9
676	57B	695	LC-22A	728	-	815	UC-10
677	58B	696	LC-23B	729	-	816	UC-11
678	56B	697	LC-23C	730	-	817-818	UC-12A
679	54-55B	699	LC-24	730	-	821	UC-12B
680	53B	700	LC-21	731	-	-	UC-13
681	60B	701	LC-22C	732	-	831	UC-14
682	59B	702	LC-22B	867	251-257NS	351-358	NS-1A-B
683	51-52B	703	LC-25	868	260-264NS	361-365	NS-2A
684	49-50B	732	LC-41	869	258-259NS	359-360	NS-1C
685	48B	705	LC-30C	870	284-285aNS	381-383	NS2B
686	47B	706	LC-30D	870	286-289aNS	391-393	NS-4
687	42B	707	LC-32A				

Breton Number	Courteau Number	Willey Number	Charlton Cat.No.
871	265-267NS	366-380	NS-1D
871	277-279NS	384,386	NS-3A
871	281NS	388	NS-3C
871	282-283NS	389-390	NS-3D
872	280NS	385	NS-3B
873	309-314NS	415-420	NS-2C-D
874	290-308NS	394-413	NS-1E-F
875	318NS	423	NS-6
876	315-316NS	421	NS-5
879	325-329NS	313-317	NS-7A-B
880	333-334NS	318	NS-8
881	331NS	319	NS-9
882	335NS	321	NS-10A
883	336-337NS	322-323	NS-10B
884	338-339NS	340	NS-11
885	340NS	341	NS-12
886	347-350NS	333-336	NS-25
887	346NS	337	NS-26
888	353-356NS	329-332	NS-23
889	351-352NS	324-325	NS-27
890	341NS	342	NS-13
891	342-345NS	326-328	NS-14
892	358NS	343	NS-15A
893	357NS	344	NS-15B
894	3NL	348	NS-24
895	330NS	339	NS-28
896	359NS	338	NS-16
899	362-363NS	349-350	NS-17
909	21-29NB	465-468	NB-2A
910	3-20NB	453-464	NB-1A
911	42-52NB	474-475	NB-2B
912	30-41NB	469-473	NB-1B
913	1NB	451	NB-4
914	2NB	-	NB-3
916	3PEI	238	PE-4
917	4-12PEI	239-246	PE-5A-B
918	13-15PEI	251-253	PE-7A
919	16-23, 25-26,28 33-40PEI	254-269	PE-7B-C
920	41-44PEI	247-250	PE-6
921	45PEI	272	PE-8
952	1-2NF	180,182	NF-1A-B
953	3,5,7, 8NF	183-186	NF-1C
954	9NF	187-188	NF-3
955	10NF	189	NF-4
956	-	-	NF-2
957	39-40T	C26-27	LC-47A
958	34-35, 37-38T	C22-25	LC-47B-C
959	28-33T	C17-21	LC-47D
960	9-24T	606-620	LC-48A-B
960	25-27T	C14-16	LC-46
961	1-8T	621-628	LC-48C
962	8-13NL	304-309	NS-20A-B
963	6-7NL	302	NS-19A-B
964	5NL	301	NS-18
965	15-17NL	310-312	NS-21
966	18NL	152	AM-1
967	14NL	B8	NS-22
969	26W	522	WE-1
970	31W	527	WE-4A
971	30W	526	WE-2A
972	27-28W	523-524	WE-2B
973	-	528	WE-2C
974	29W	521	WE-3
975	-	C1	AM-2
976	1-2W	C7-8	WE-5
977	43W	C9	WE-6
978	44W	C10	WE-7
979	33-38W	529-534	WE-8
980	39W	535	WE-9
981	40-42W	538-540	WE-10
982	40NL	542	LC-49
983	36NL	C5	AM-3
984	23W	520	WE-12
985	24W	C11	WE-13
986	12-21W	509-518	WE-11B-C
987	4-11W	502-508	WE-11A
988	22W	519	WE-11D
989	34NL	C4	LC-52
990	33NL	C3, 571	LC-51
991	32NL	C2	LC-50
992	47-48NL	561-562	LC-53A
994	25-31NL	543-548	LC-54A-D
995	1PEI	206	PE-9A
996	2PEI	207	PE-9B
997	-	208-234, 555-557, 559-560	PE-10-1 to PE-10-44
998	-	656	BL-28
999	-	657	BL-24C
1000	-	558	PE-10-5B
1001	-	567	LC-55
1002	41-43NL	549-551	LC-58A
1002	44NL	552	LC-58B
1003	46W	537	WE-14
1004	20-24NL	569-570	LC-56A-B
1005	19NL	568	LC-56C
1006	45W	536	WE-15
1007	45-46NL	553-554	LC-59A-B
1008	-	-	BL-32
1009	4NL	153	AM-4
1010	-	829-830	UC-4
1011	37-39NL	564-565	LC-57
1012	1-26H	581-595, 596-604	LC-60A-F BL-35-36
1013	1-2NL	151	AM-5

CANADIAN COLONIAL TOKENS CROSS REFERENCED BY CHARLTON CATALOGUE NUMBERS TO BRETON, COURTEAU AND WILLEY

Charlton Cat.No.	Breton Number	Courteau Number	Willey Number	Charlton Cat.No.	Breton Number	Courteau Number	Willey Number
NF-1A	952	1NF	180	NS-12	885	340NS	341
NF-1B	952	2NF	182	NS-13	890	341NS	342
NF-1C	953	3,5,7,8NF	183-186	NS-14	891	342-345NL	326-328
NF-2	956	-	-	NS-15A	892	358NS	343
NF-3	954	9NF	187-188	NS-15B	893	357NS	344
NF-4	955	10NF	189	NS-16	896	359NS	338
PE-1	-	-	201-202	NS-17	899	362-363NS	349-350
PE-2	-	-	236	NS-18	964	5NL	301
PE-3	-	-	237-237a	NS-19A	963	6NL	302
PE-4	916	3PEI	238	NS-19B	963	7NL	302
PE-5A	917	4-8PEI	239-243	NS-20A	962	8-11NL	304-307
PE-5B	917	9-12PEI	244-246	NS-20B	962	12-13NL	308-309
PE-6	920	41-44PEI	247-250	NS-21	965	15-17NL	310-312
PE-7A	918	13-15PEI	251-253	NS-22	967	14NL	B8
PE-7B	919	16-18PEI	254-256	NS-23	888	353-356NS	329-332
PE-7C	919	19-23, 25-28 33-40PEI	257-269	NS-24	894	3NL	348
PE-8	921	45PEI	272	NS-25	886	347-350NS	333-336
PE-9A	995	1PEI	206	NS-26	887	346NS	337
PE-9B	996	2PEI	207	NS-27	889	351-352NS	324-325
PE-10A	997	-	208-211 555, 559-560	NS-28	895	330NS	339
				NS-29	-	-	-
				NS-30		35NL	154
PE-10B	997	-	212-213	NB-1A	910	3-20NB	453-464
PE-10C	997	-	214-222	NB-1B	912	30-41NB	469-473
PE-10D	997	-	223-234	NB-2A	909	21-29NB	465-468
PE-10E	997	-	556-557	NB-2B	911	42-52NB	474-475
PE-10F	1000	-	558	NB-3	914	2NB	-
NS-1A	867	251-253NS 256-257NS	351-354 357-358	NB-4	913	1NB	451
				NB-5	-	-	452
NS-1B	867	254-255NS	355-356	LC-1	520	-	500
NS-1C	869	258-259NS	359-360	LC-2	713	8-13B	678-683
NS-1D	871	265-276NS	366-380	LC-3	714	3-7B	684-688
NS-1E	874	290-298NS	394-402	LC-4	716	14B	689
NS-1F	874	299-308NS	403-413	LC-5	715	15-17B	690-691
NS-2A	868	260-264NS	361-365	LC-6	672	1B	692
NS-2B	870	284-285aNS	NS381-383	LC-7	673	2B	693
NS-2C	873	309-311NS	415-417	LC-8A	522	1-2IH	736-744
NS-2D	873	312-314NS	418-420	LC-8B	522	3-4iH	749-756
NS-3A	871	277-279NS	384, 386	LC-8C	522	6-7bH	760-763
NS-3B	872	280NS	385	LC-8D	522	14-22BM	766-771
NS-3C	871	281NS	388	LC-9A	521	8-11H	745-748
NS-3D	871	282-283NS	389-390	LC-9B	521	12-14bH	757-759
NS-4	870	286-289aNS	391-393	LC-9C	521	16-17dH	764-765
NS-5	876	315-316NS	421	LC-9D	521	24-29BM	772-775
NS-6	875	318NS	423	LC-10A	524	30-32BM	776-778
NS-7A	879	325NS	313	LC-10B	524	33-35BM	781-783
NS-7B	879	326-329NS	314-317	LC-11A	523	36-37BM	779-780
NS-8	880	333-334NS	318	LC-11B	523	38BM	784
NS-9	881	331NS	319	LC-11C	525	39BM	785
NS-10A	882	335NS	321	LC-12	531	47W	541
NS-10B	883	336-337NS	322-323	LC-13	532	-	575
NS-11	884	338-339NS	340	LC-14	533	-	574

CANADIAN COLONIAL TOKENS CROSS REFERENCED BY CHARLTON
CATALOGUE NUMBERS TO BRETON, COURTEAU AND WILLEY

Charlton Cat.No.	Breton Number	Courteau Number	Willey Number	Charlton Cat.No.	Breton Number	Courteau Number	Willey Number
LC-15	561	-	576-577	LC-47A	957	39-40T	C26-27
LC-16	562	-	579	LC-47B	958	34-35T	C22-23
LC-17	563	-	573	LC-47C	958	37-38T	C24-25
LC-18	564	-	572	LC-47D	959	28-33T	C17-21
LC-19	565	-	578	LC-47E	-	36T	A1
LC-20	671	72B	580	LC-47F	-	30T	C12
LC-21	680	53B	700	LC-47G	-	41T	C13
LC-22A	676	57B	695	LC-48A	960	21-24T	606-608
LC-22B	682	59B	702	LC-48B	960	9-20T	609-620
LC-22C	681	60B	701	LC-48C	961	1-8T	622-628
LC-23A	675	61B	694	LC-49	982	40NL	542
LC-23B	677	58B	696	LC-50	991	32NL	C2
LC-23C	678	56B	697	LC-51	990	33NL	C3, 571
LC-23D	-	62B	698	LC-52	989	34NL	C4
LC-24	679	54-55B	699	LC-53A	992	47-48NL	561-562
LC-25	683	51-52B	703	LC-53B	-	49NL	563
LC-26	-	-	704	LC-54A	994	25NL	543
LC-27	691	43-44B	710	LC-54B	994	26-27NL	544
LC-28	702	29B	721	LC-54C	994	28-29NL	545-546
LC-29A	695	46B	714	LC-54D	994	30-31NL	547-548
LC-29B	696	45B	715	LC-55	1001	-	567
LC-29C	700	32B	719	LC-56A	1004	20-22NL	569-570
LC-29D	701	31B	720	LC-56B	1004	23-24NL	570
LC-29E	697	33-34B	716	LC-56C	1005	19NL	568
LC-30A	698	36B	717	LC-57	1011	37-39NL	564-565
LC-30B	699	35B	718	LC-58A	1002	41-43NL	549-551
LC-30C	685	48B	705	LC-58B	1002	44NL	552
LC-30D	686	47B	706	LC-59A	1007	45NL	554
LC-30E	-	-	708	LC-59B	1007	46NL	553
LC-30F	703	30B	722	LC-60A	1012	21-22H	581-582
LC-31A	688	41B	709	LC-60B	1012	23H	583
LC-31B	693	37B	712	LC-60C	1012	9-13, 24H	584-589
LC-31C	694	38B	713	LC-60D	1012	4-8, 18H	590-594
LC-32A	687	42B	707	LC-60E	1012	1, 3, 14-17, 19H	595-601
LC-32B	692	39B	711				
LC-33A	704	27-28B	723	LC-60F	1012	2H	602
LC-33B	-	-	724	LC-61	-	-	605
LC-33C	705	25B	725	WE-1	969	26W	522
LC-34	706	23B	726	WE-2A	971	30W	526
LC-35	707	22B	727	WE-2B	972	27-28W	523-524
LC-36	708	20B	728	WE-2C	973	-	528
LC-37	709	21B	729	WE-3	974	29W	521
LC-38A	710	19B	730,	WE-4A	970	31W	527
LC-38B	712	-	G3	WE-4B	-	32W	525
LC-39	711	18B	731	WE-5	976	1-2W	C7-8
LC-40	674	63-70B	734	WE-6	977	43W	C9
LC-41	684	49-50B	732	WE-7	978	44W	C10
LC-42	-	-	735	WE-8	979	33-38W	529-534
LC-43	689	24B	733	WE-9	980	39W	535
LC-44	690	40B	G2	WE-10	981	40-42W	538-540
LC-45	670	71B	C28	WE-11A	987	4-11W	502-508
LC-46	960	25-27T	C14-16	WE-11B	986	12-19W	509-516

CANADIAN COLONIAL TOKENS CROSS REFERENCED BY CHARLTON
CATALOGUE NUMBERS TO BRETON, COURTEAU AND WILLEY

Charlton Cat.No.	Breton Number	Courteau Number	Willey Number	Charlton Cat.No.	Breton Number	Courteau Number	Willey Number
WE-11C	986	12-19W	509-516			47,53-63,	855-856,
WE-11D	988	22W	519			66-70BM	858-859
WE-12	984	23W	520	PC-1C	527	-	860
WE-13	985	24W	C11	PC-2A	-	88BM	G13
WE-14	1003	46W	537	PC-2B	526	71-87BM	861-872
WE-15	1006	45W	536	PC-3	529	5-5hH	873-876
UC-1	721	-	A2	PC-4	528	15fH	877-878
UC-2	718	-	824-828	PC-5A	720	1-75UC	879
UC-3	717	-	823	PC-5B	720	76-110UC	879
UC-4	1010	-	829-830	PC-5C	720	111-158UC	879
UC-5	723	-	801	PC-5D	720	159-207UC	879
UC-6	724	-	802-808	PC-6A	719	208-233UC	880
UC-7	725	-	809	PC-6B	719	234-257UC	880
UC-8	726	-	819, 822	PC-6C	719	258-274UC	880
UC-9	727	-	810-814	PC-6D	719	275-319UC	880
UC-10	728	-	815	AM-1	966	18NL	152
UC-11	729	-	816	AM-2	975	-	C1
UC-12A	730	-	817-818	AM-3	983	36NL	C5
UC-12B	730	-	821	AM-4	1009	4NL	153
UC-13	731	-	-	AM-5	1013	1-2NL	151
UC-14	732	-	831	VC-1	558	-	676
PC-1A	527	40, 46,	851, 854,	VC-2	558	-	675
		64-65BM	857	VC-3	559	-	677
PC-1B	527	41-45	852-853				

Application for Membership/Subscription

Applications for membership/subscription in the Canadian Numismatic Association may be made by any reputable party upon payment of the required dues.

(check one of each group)

❑ New   ❑ Renewal ___(member number)___   ❑ Reinstatement

❑Regular   ❑Junior   ❑Family

❑Corporate   ❑Life Membership

❑Mr.   ❑Mrs.   ❑Ms.   ❑Club

Name:

Street: Address may be published in the Journal ❑ yes ❑ no

City: Province/State   Postal Code/Zip

Country   Birthdate

Signature of applicant   Signature of Sponsor

Signature of guardian (if under 18 years of age)

Dues

Dues shown are in Canadian dollars to Canadian addresses and in U.S. dollars to all other addresses. Payment may be made by money order, bank draft or personal cheque. We regret that we are unable to offer credit card services. Postage stamps are not acceptable. Currency (U.S. or Canadian only) is acceptable and should be sent by security registered mail only. Membership is not Goods and Services taxable.

REGULAR* - Applicants 18 years of age or over......................**$33.00**

JUNIOR - Applicants under 18 years of age **$16.50**
     Persons under 18 must be sponsored by a parent or guardian

FAMILY - Husband, wife and children at home, under 18 years of age
     One Journal only **$44.00**

CORPORATE - Clubs, Societies, Libraries and other non-profit
     organizations..**$33.00**

LIFE MEMBERSHIP **$495.00**
(After one year of regular membership. Details on payment plan available on request.)

First class mailing of the Journal is available on remittance of $9.00 (Cdn.) to Canadian addresses, $7.50 (U.S.$) to U.S.A. addresses and $15.00 (U.S.$) to all other addresses. Addresses of all new members are published in the Journal.

Please mail application and payment to the Canadian Numismatic Association, P.O. Box 226, Barrie, Ontario, Canada, L4M 4T2.
Application must be complete and accompanied by full dues to be accepted.